D0936519

Pancho Villa's
Revolution by Headlines

Pancho Villa's Revolution by Headlines

Mark Cronlund Anderson

University of Oklahoma Press : Norman

This book is published with the generous assistance of The McCasland Foundation, Duncan, Oklahoma.

Library of Congress Cataloging-in-Publication Data

Anderson, Mark Cronlund, 1960–
    Pancho Villa's revolution by headlines / Mark Cronlund Anderson.
        p.   cm.
    Includes bibliographical references (p.   ) and index.
    ISBN 0-8061-3172-1 (cloth : alk. paper)
    1. Mexico—History—Revolution, 1910–1920—Mass media and the revolution.   2. Mexico—History—Revolution, 1910–1920—Public opinion—History.   3. Villa, Pancho, 1878–1923—In mass media.
    4. Villa, Pancho, 1878–1923—Public opinion—History.   5. Mass media—Political aspects.   6. Press and propaganda—Mexico—History.
    7. Press and propaganda—United States—History.   8. Public opinion—United States—History.   9. Public opinion—Mexico—History.
    10. United States—Foreign relations—1913–1921.   I. Title.
    F1234.A547   1997
    972.08'16—dc21   99-14135
                                                                               CIP

Text design by Gail Carter.

The paper in this book meets the guidelines for permanence and durability of the Committee on Production Guidelines for Book Longevity of the Council on Library Resources, Inc. ∞

For the boolee girls, Dagmar and Madelaine

CHAPTER ONE

A MAN ON HORSEBACK, A REVOLUTION, AND THE MASS MEDIA

In the fiercest hours of the Mexican Revolution, 1913–1915, General Francisco "Pancho" Villa sought to market his two-track rhetorical foreign policy in and through the mass media. Villa's primary foreign policy goal consisted of nurturing cordial relations with the United States in an effort to gain American support and, ultimately, United States diplomatic recognition. Secondarily, and partially to deflect hostile Mexican responses to his pro–United States actions and rhetoric, Villa also promoted himself in American and Mexican media as a Mexican nationalist. To accomplish these aims, Villa and his lieutenants implemented a comprehensive and nuanced propaganda effort to promote Villa's image in positive ways both in the United States and in Mexico. With customary bombast, he announced to a reporter for the *Chicago Tribune* in 1915, "I don't care what they write about me as long as it is the truth."[1]

Villa galloped onto the international diplomatic stage in 1913 and remained there for two years. He rose from international obscurity to become a media sensation—from one revolutionist among many in early 1913 to Mexican revolutionary without equal eighteen months later. So remarkable was his sudden visibility that in late 1914 he began to jockey for American diplomatic recognition of his movement. In early 1915 he attempted to seize the political reins of the land by declaring himself "in charge" of the Mexican presidency, although he did not claim the presidency itself. Then, suddenly, in the spring of 1915, his fortunes plummeted, perhaps even faster than they had soared. A series of stunning military setbacks delivered by Villa's military nemesis, the Carrancista general Alvaro Obregón, signified the end for Villa. By the summer of 1915 his tenure as a viable national contender approached an unhappy conclusion. On October 19, 1915, Venustiano Carranza, Villa's erstwhile colleague and bitter rival, gained de facto American diplomatic recognition, effectively ending Villa's political struggle, though he continued to vie with the national authority for several more years.

In this book I examine the ways in which Villa and his two chief rivals in the Mexican Revolution, Carranza and the dictator Victoriano Huerta, each tried to sway the mass media's depiction of himself and his opponents, especially in the United States, and how those depictions were colored by Americans' long-held, belittling stereotypes of Mexicans. I begin in chapter 2 by examining Villa's two-track foreign policy of plying friendly relations with the United States while publicly championing Mexican nationalism. The evidence shows that Villa conducted a rhetorically pro-American policy all the way—but he couched it in Mexican-nationalistic terms. The overall pitch amounted to this: Villa's foreign policy was good for the United States and good for Mexico, too. Generally, Villa's policy actions reveal a cautiously choreographed sensitivity to American concerns, as Villa interpreted them, as well as to a domestic constituency that Villa feared might be alienated by over-obsequious, too-friendly relations with the United States.

In chapter 3 I turn to Villa's efforts to manage the terms in which his image was "framed," or placed within a model of interpretation, by the mass media in both Mexico and the United States. Villa explored a number of avenues to generate favorable coverage, including employing press agents in the United States, bribing reporters and editors, funding his own propaganda organ in Mexico (and providing support to others), selling his story to motion pictures, and charming, bullying, lying to, and cajoling foreign news reporters. Throughout the book, I attribute propaganda efforts to "Villa" alone in cases where sources speak of no clear distinction between what Villa himself did and what his subordinates—Villistas—did to promote his image.

Chapter 4 investigates Huerta's and Carranza's responses to Villa's media efforts and image-building. Huertista reaction to Villa's media posturing was highly charged, as Huertista officials expressed exasperation over their inability to have Huerta cast in a favorable light by American newspapers, despite energetic propaganda undertakings. Carrancistas, too, expressed consternation over an early lack of success in having Carranza portrayed favorably. Unlike the Huertistas' media campaign, however, the Carrancistas' propaganda efforts ultimately earned the desired rewards.

In chapter 5 I trace the historical evolution of American images of Mexico and Mexicans, as well as images cast of Mexico and Mexicans in the American press from 1913 to 1915. The United States media during the Revolution often employed models consistent with long-standing American tendencies to portray Mexicans as culturally, racially, and morally inferior.

Chapter 6 assesses the American media's images of Huerta and Carranza. Both leaders were tainted and condemned by and for their Mexicanness, but for different reasons. The press framed Huerta as the archetypal Mexican Savage and Carranza as the archetypal Mexican Sneak.

The American press's treatment of Villa is surveyed in chapter 7. The press depicted him as the archetypal Mexican Warrior in two basic guises—villain and hero. As warrior-villain, he was portrayed as less barbaric and depraved and more civilized than Huerta. As warrior-hero, the dominant framing, Villa very nearly emerged as fully Americanized—framed in a manner contrary to that of both Carranza and Huerta.

Finally, in chapter 8 I assess how United States diplomatic correspondence treated Mexico and Mexicans, how it portrayed Villa, and how the press influenced the diplomatic record. Depictions of Mexico and Mexicans similar to those in the American press emerge in the diplomatic files. Villa was portrayed both favorably (as a Mexican warrior-hero) and unfavorably (as a warrior-savage) by representatives of the Woodrow Wilson administration.

BANDIT CUM REVOLUTIONARY

The Mexican Revolution, by the hand of Chihuahua's governor, Abraham González, adopted Villa in early October 1910. Villa had been a notorious bandit who first gained public prominence and sanction among the masses of north-central Mexico's poor through a long series of violent crimes committed against northern Mexico's *hacendado* class. At González's urging, Villa embraced the cause of Francisco I. Madero, the Coahuila *hacendado* challenging the thirty-five-year presidency of strongman Porfirio Díaz.

Villa rose to the rank of colonel in the insurgent army and played an active role in defeating federal forces at Ciudad Juárez in 1911. Not long after, the revolutionary front prevailed, forcing Díaz to resign and withdraw from Mexico, and Madero assumed the presidency. Meanwhile, in mid-May 1911, after quarreling with Madero, Villa retired to private life, operating a butcher shop in Chihuahua City.

He rejoined the fray in the spring of 1912 after the revolutionary general Pascual Orozco rose against Madero, with whom Villa had reconciled. Villa was assigned to federal forces led by General Victoriano Huerta, who would later rebel successfully against Madero. As Orozco's rebellion was put down, Villa almost lost his life in a confrontation with Huerta, who leveled charges against him for insubordination. Only a last-minute intervention by Madero's brother, Raúl, saved Villa from death by firing squad.

Villa was incarcerated, however, in early June in Mexico City, where he awaited trial on the charges Huerta had brought against him. He took advantage of his time behind bars to become literate. "I studied day and night there, and when I was given my freedom I could read and write well enough for ordinary purposes. . . . A rifle sight was the only spelling book I knew until I was grown man," he told the *Los Angeles Times*.[2] But he was never "given" his freedom; he escaped the day after Christmas, 1912, and made his way north again. After crossing the international border on January 28, 1913, he quietly took up exile in El Paso, Texas.

Yet again Villa rejoined the Revolution when Huerta overthrew Madero and had both Madero and his vice president, José María Pino Suárez, killed on February 21, 1913. "The common people of our country are the people who should reap the benefits" of revolutionary change, Villa argued, outlining his philosophical opposition to the conservative Huerta. "The grandees have enjoyed what prosperity there has been. The government's new land laws must allow them to own their own lands, and, above all else, own the profits. Agriculture, mining, and cattle raising must be encouraged instead of the make-believe variety which has been forced upon them for so many years."[3] Within two weeks of Madero's death, Villa and a small band of followers crossed the Rio Grande and took up arms against Huerta, who had proclaimed himself president. So began Villa's involvement in the next military phase of the Mexican Revolution.

FROM BANDIT TO MEDIA STAR TO BANDIT

Villa's first foreign policy campaign to the mass media developed over the autumn of 1913 and early winter of 1914 in conjunction with several military victories—the beginning of a series of highly charged events that marked turning points in Villa's revolutionary career and around which I have organized much of this book.

During this period Villa emerged as Mexico's most important revolutionary military commander. The cornerstone of his success was laid with the first taking of Torreón (it was subsequently abandoned and recaptured) on October 1, 1913, after an intense three-day battle. By late autumn he had captured the important centers of San Andrés, Ciudad Juárez, and Chihuahua City in addition to Torreón. By late January 1914 he had gained the whole state of Chihuahua, following through on his confident assertion, "We will strike a blow which the Huerta government will be unable to withstand."[4] At the same time, with blossoming intensity and to increasing interest, his story spilled across the front pages of the American popular press and even reached newsreel audiences at movie houses in the United States.

The development of Villa's foreign policy paralleled his career as military commander and media darling. The political implications of his military emergence and the commensurate media presence he gained were intimately conjoined. His sudden—and growing—popularity in American mass media accounts should be seen first as a function of his burgeoning military prowess, second as a signature of his efforts to generate propaganda politically favorable to himself, and third as the reflection of American media notions about what constituted "good copy."

A second charged episode occurred in late February 1914, coincidentally at about the time Villa's media popularity veritably exploded in the United States. On February 17, 1914, a British national and long-time resident of Mexico, William S. Benton, stormed into Villa's headquarters in Ciudad Juárez charging that Villistas had appropriated his livestock without providing due compensation. Benton was never seen alive again. In the ensuing weeks his fate became a diplomatic cause célèbre.

Benton had been killed, it became apparent, either by Villa's order or by Villa's own hand. Because it supported Huerta, Great Britain demanded satisfaction both from Villa and, to a lesser extent, from the Wilson administration. The British correctly saw the Wilson regime as endorsing the rebels and sought to pressure the administration to drop such support. Villa, meanwhile, and ultimately to the Wilson administration's satisfaction, justified Benton's demise by claiming that Benton had drawn a pistol and attempted to fire on him. The issue was defused further in three steps: Carranza established an official tribunal to investigate the case; Villa's continued military triumphs drew attention away from the imbroglio; and the simple passage of time muted interest in the affair.

A third incident occurred in late April 1914, after the Wilson administration dispatched United States marines to occupy the important port city of Veracruz to avenge a trumped-up diplomatic slight committed by representatives of Huerta's government. Huerta had refused to bend to U.S. demands for a salute of the American flag, and on this pretext Wilson, aiming to force Huerta from power, sent in the troops. Carranza, still nominally Villa's ally among the Constitutionalist revolutionaries, so strongly denounced Wilson's actions that Mexico and the United States edged briefly toward war—until Villa cannily announced his ringing public endorsement of the occupation and Carranza toned down his inflammatory rhetoric.

A fourth turning point came after relations between Villa and Carranza fell apart in September 1914. Villa renounced Carranza and redoubled his efforts to promote his own cause. At the same time, he contributed to a pan-revolutionary conference in October— the Convention of Aguascalientes—designed to patch up his differences with Carranza. It failed, and in late January 1915 Villa declared himself "in charge" of the presidency, though not presi-dent. At no point did Villa more energetically cultivate his friendship with the United States than during this period. His administration became increasingly sensitive to and adept at identifying American concerns.

A fifth and final charged event occurred as Villa's military and diplomatic fortunes waned in 1915. The official United States recognition of Carranza's government in October 1915 confirmed the drawn-out eclipse of Villa as a key player in the national theater of operations. His decline began in April 1915 when he suffered two debilitating losses at Celaya, just north of Mexico City, from which he was never able to recover fully. In the following months his fortunes dwindled until by summer he was a spent force.

When Villa queried a reporter from the *San Francisco Examiner* in 1914, "Tell me about the United States. . . . What do they think of me?" his question derived not from simple vanity but also from larger policy concerns.[5] From the autumn of 1913 through the late summer of 1915, when Carranza gained de facto United States recognition, Villa energetically sought to promote friendship between himself and Americans and with the United States government. Speaking candidly to the *San Francisco Examiner*, he noted, "There are two reasons why we should be friendly to the United States: One is that Americans have helped us greatly; the other is that they are immeasurably stronger than we." Additionally, though to a lesser extent, Villa's policies promoted Mexican nationalism, as an oft-repeated sentiment printed in the *Chicago Tribune* illustrates: "All of us [competing revolutionary factions] would fight united against a common enemy."[6] His manipulation of the American press to achieve these policy ends was highly effective and won him continued official American support even months after he had been eliminated as a viable contender for the Mexican presidency.

SETTING MEDIA AGENDAS

I focus in this book on three basic issues relating to the press in the Mexican Revolution: first, Villa's (as well as Carranza's and Huerta's) efforts to use the mass media as a foreign policy weapon to generate American support for himself and to blunt support for his rivals; second, the depth and durability of American cultural visions of Mexican inferiority, which surfaced repeatedly in the American press and diplomatic correspondence; and, third, Villa's successes and failures in surmounting these stereotyped American visions through the manufacture of effective propaganda. I approach these three issues by examining Mexican archives to uncover the workings of Villa's (and Carranza's and Huerta's) propaganda systems and by assessing representations of these key players in the United States media and diplomatic correspondence.

I attempt to tackle the historical Francisco Villa head-on, while avoiding the traditional scholarly partisanship that has tended to paint him as an avenging angel, a violent devil, or both. The overwhelming bulk of the Villa literature falls into the Great-Men-of-History camp, so that whether he is loved, hated, or both, Villa has emerged from the literature as a mythical figure rather than as the complex historical actor I have tried to engage.

The historical sources that I employ both embody and demonstrate the process of the creation of the Villa myth. Yet if employed carefully, they unveil a historical reality confounding the myth. Much of this source material—mass media reports and diplomatic correspondence—perpetuates the myth of Villa along lines similar to those sketched by the Villa literature (and in some cases the same hands were responsible for both). In the United States press, for example, Villa was cast as the warrior-hero or the warrior-villain, and in the diplomatic record he appears as the warrior-friend or the warrior-savage. These renderings parallel, and probably have influenced, the historiography's tendency to treat Villa as angel or devil.

From the press and the diplomatic record, however, a historical Villa can be discovered who rises above simplistic images. These sources reveal him as, among other things, a canny propagandist. Yet this historical reading of Villa has gone largely unnoted by Villa authors, sometimes because of partisanship and at other times because of an inclination to uncritically conflate isolated media and diplomatic facts as "proof" of historical trends. For example, some authors cite single excerpts from the *New York Times* as indicative of American press or—even worse—American popular opinion.

A close examination demonstrates that the historical Villa was a calculating and effective manipulator of the United States press, an assessment based on careful dissection of a variety of sources: Mexican correspondence and other papers, United States diplomatic reports, and Mexican and United States media sources. The analysis reveals that many of the commendatory renderings of Villa in the media and in American diplomacy reflected Villa's intentions to elicit such coverage. In other words, through carefully designed and effectively executed propaganda, Villa contributed mightily to the approbatory construction of his own myth both in Mexico and in the United States. Moreover, the mythologization of Villa occurred within the elastic constraints of long-standing, persistent American cultural visions of Mexico.

Ironically, Villa's propaganda success suggests that Americans' stereotypes of "Mexicanness," which reflected their perceptions of Mexican racial, cultural, and moral inferiority, although pernicious, were neither rigid nor inflexible. As Villa manipulated the United States media and American diplomats, he employed, in the way he promoted himself and disparaged Huerta and Carranza, many of the same representations used by the media and by diplomats in their portrayals of Villa, his rivals, and other Mexicans of the revolutionary era. And when the press and the diplomats took those pro-Villa and anti-Carranza or anti-Huerta themes and framed them in widespread American perceptions of Mexicanness, they did little more than Villa's own propaganda sought to do.

While this study details the powerful endurance of American visions of Mexico—and, indeed, of Latin America more generally—it also demonstrates that these common stereotypes were flexible, porous, and even manipulable. In his shrewd attempts to handle the U.S. press and American diplomats, Villa, for example, achieved for a time a framing draped in the language of heartfelt Americana, an imagery that reached all the way to the White

House. In short, Villa as Mexican hero for a time became Villa the Americanized hero.

A second irony echoes the Carrancista complaint that Villa was more a media creation than a bona fide historical contender for the Mexican presidency. To what extent was this criticism valid? At what point do the Villa-encouraged (sometimes Villa-created) media and propaganda images leave off and the contours of the historical fighting man begin? On the eve of his rupture with Carranza, Villa told the *New York Times*, "I consider myself the moral and physical champion of the Mexican people, especially here in the North."[7] What did he mean by this? In part, the answer awaits a definitive Villa biography. Yet clearly, Villa's image-making machinery influenced both the press and the literature.

Villa's successful propaganda campaign well exemplifies the phenomenon of media agenda-setting, wherein the media tell an audience not only what to think about but even what to think. Villa's successful attempts to manipulate public and political opinion in the United States earned him diplomatic and press goodwill. Such efforts clearly worked to Villa's favor on President Woodrow Wilson and Secretaries of State William Jennings Bryan and Robert Lansing, on countless diplomatic agents, and on an unknown number of newspaper and news magazine readers. In short, agenda-setting works and can be observed, as it is in Villa's case, outside the experimental fishbowl of controlled social-science research.

On another level, this study contributes to the ongoing debate about the role of cross-cultural perceptions in inter-American relations. It illustrates the persistence of American cultural visions of Mexico during the Revolution and the influence of these visions on press and diplomatic treatment of Villa. In other words, in the North American tendency to dismiss Villa, Huerta, and Carranza— indeed, all Mexicans—as Other, a larger American cultural project can be discerned: cultural imperialism.[8] This in itself is hardly remarkable. American culture stereotypes; all cultures are so inclined. What is striking in terms of this study is the Mexican revolutionaries' understanding of the cultural process at work north of the Rio Grande—and their clever, if ironic, responses to it.

In particular, Villa ably cast himself as an exception to deeply seated American assumptions about Mexicanness, and indeed he briefly became the embodiment of U.S. Americanness. The role and the impact of such intercultural perceptions in inter-American relations have yet to receive the airing they deserve, but at the least I try to show that cross-border intercultural perceptions can influence and shape governmental policy.

I hope, then, to accomplish two things in this study. The first is to add a new dimension—and depth—to the exploration of Villa's foreign policy. This entails examining it not simply from a single perspective such as his policy of friendship, his alliance with or dependence on the United States, or his Mexican nationalism (as the historians Clarence Clendenen, Friedrich Katz, and Nancy Furman, respectively, have done). Instead, I seek to integrate these three perspectives into an overarching analysis that engages an important element missing in previous studies of the Mexican Revolution as well as in work on Mexico–United States relations.

Second, by exploring Villa's complex relationship with the media, I hope to fashion an audience-reception tool—that is, a practical means by which to assess propaganda influence. This raises several crucial issues. For one, how is it possible to weigh the success or failure of propaganda? One avenue of communications research that I employ is agenda-setting theory.[9] Its conclusions have been tested by a generation's worth of empirical study that relies on extensive public-opinion polling; it assumes that if nonmedia influences can be factored out and if public opinion can be shown to have changed over time, then it has changed as a result of exposure to mass media.[10]

Studying Villa's relationship with the press helps to confirm the premises of agenda-setting theory in a way that opens fresh possibilities for historical research. I analyze the contents of selected newspapers and magazines, but how might I show that this media content influenced anybody? Obviously, I had no way to conduct an opinion poll, the standard method in traditional agenda-setting research. Instead, the answer lay in the American diplomatic record. By analyzing the contents of diplomatic dispatches, I was able to witness and assess the direct effects of media agenda-setting on a particular reading audience, U.S. diplomats.

A diplomatic paper trail loaded with media references and extracts and leading all the way to the White House confirmed that the United States media influenced American diplomatic opinion up to the highest levels of government. By helping to shape American media content, Villa's propaganda therefore also influenced American policymakers. In addition to using this media-conveyed influence, Villa also sought to manipulate American diplomatic agents directly, through personal contact.

From this starting point I raise other queries. How did Villa and his rivals, Carranza and Huerta, attempt to use the press as a foreign policy weapon? To what extent were their efforts successful? Further, what sorts of images of each leader emerged in the press? And what were some of the influences, apart from propaganda, that shaped those images? Finally, how was Villa portrayed in United States diplomatic correspondence, and in what respects were such depictions similar to or different from press portrayals? The answers to these questions shed light not only on Mexico–United States relations but also on relations between the United States and Latin America more generally, and on the nature, practice, and limits of political propaganda.

Villa's impressive propaganda operations compare favorably to the public relations efforts of other noted twentieth-century political figures such as the American president Franklin Roosevelt,[11] the Argentine *político* Eva Perón,[12] and the Brazilian head of state Getúlio Vargas.[13] With Roosevelt, Villa shared a calculated personal charm, and both men worked energetically and successfully to establish media agendas based in part on man-of-the-people themes. Neither leader was above deluding the press or planting stories. Like Eva Perón, Villa operated his own propaganda organ (she had many) and bribed other media outlets to gain favorable coverage. Because of her government resources, Perón could wield a heavier hand than Villa, yet both were successful in agenda-setting largely because of the persuasiveness of the images they cast. With an even heavier censoring hand than Perón's, Vargas, too, cast himself favorably in the mass media to generate political support. In light of Vargas's and Perón's greater power to censor and close opposition papers, Villa's propaganda operations seem all the more effective. With far fewer tools at his command, Villa shrewdly manipulated both the American press and the U.S. State Department.

In short, Villa deserves to be recognized as a master propagandist. He cleverly and often successfully managed to influence the content of American press reports and diplomatic communications, despite the historical depth and durability of the anti-Mexican ethnocentrism and racism that permeated American thinking during the Mexican Revolution.

CHAPTER TWO

VILLA'S FOREIGN POLICY

The Buddy System

"Where is Villa?" I enquired.
"Who knows?" replied [Major Jesús] Aguilar.
"Villa is everywhere. Sometimes he is here. Sometimes he is there. Great Men multiply themselves. No one knows but Villa."

—*CHICAGO TRIBUNE*[1]

Once the immediate goal of ridding Mexico of Victoriano Huerta had been achieved in July 1914, Mexico's leading revolutionaries turned their sights toward earning another victory—diplomatic recognition from the United States. Victory ultimately went to Venustiano Carranza, who received official American recognition on October 19, 1915. Yet only months before, Francisco "Pancho" Villa had attained the clearly preeminent military position in Mexico. He easily cast the longest shadow along the Mexican-American border.

When Villa proclaimed himself "in charge" of Mexico in late January 1915, a very real chance existed that his energetic cultivation of friendly relations with the United States might earn him diplomatic recognition. Since the autumn of 1913 Villa's foreign policy had seemed purposefully tailored for this end: his primary foreign policy aim was to maintain an open and friendly relationship with the United States. Simultaneously, he espoused a virile Mexican nationalism, which served the dual purpose of promoting his cause in Mexico and deflecting criticism that his primary policy represented a sell-out to American interests.

On the primary foreign policy side, Villa quite literally had everything to gain—and everything to lose. Early on he needed a weapons supply, access to credit, and occasional safe haven over the U.S. border.[2] The loss of any one of these might spell the end of his struggle. Later, to effectively challenge Carranza's political position—especially after Villa and Carranza officially split in September 1914—Villa would require American diplomatic recognition.

The necessity of United States recognition seemed clear. Without it Huerta had been unable to survive.[3] And once Carranza had won it, the United States lent him material support that enhanced his military position relative to Villa's. Finally, American policy toward Mexico, like a spreading dye, colored the Mexican policies of European nations.[4]

The outline of Villa's foreign policy took shape after he rejoined the Revolution in March 1913, following Francisco Madero's death. Within months Villa's policy became clearly established: to develop and nurture a cordial relationship with the United States. So important did Villa consider American friendship that in order to achieve or maintain it, he frequently altered his plans—in part to promote goodwill and in part to avoid censure.

In this chapter I explore the contours of Villa's foreign policy by examining policy actions taken during the charged events outlined in chapter 1—decisive victories in the fall of 1913 and early winter of 1914, the Benton affair in late February 1914, the occupation of Veracruz in April–November 1914, the Villa-Carranza rupture in September 1914 and the subsequent declaration of Villa's government on January 31, 1915, and American recognition of Carranza's regime.

After hearing of Francisco Madero's murder in late February 1913, Villa redonned his revolutionary garb.[5] He remained less than prominent, though not quite anonymous, until autumn.[6] Then his story began to garner a media prominence paralleling his emerging military presence. Villa's foreign policy story can be teased out of two sources—reports by the mass media and discussion in official government documents.

American print media publications serve as key primary-source documents for charting Villa's policy. It is critical to keep in mind that Villa sought to manipulate the press into portraying him in lights of his own choosing. Therefore, these publications provide information and American perspectives simultaneously with evidence of Villa's press campaign. Official government sources are best represented by correspondence, usually diplomatic, both American and Mexican. Unfortunately, although Carrancista, Huertista, and American diplomatic communication is available, there is no Villa archive.

ON BECOMING FRIENDS

Villa's willingness to acquiesce to American concerns, particularly demands that the lives and property of all foreigners be respected, became apparent from the start. For as long as Villa remained a player in Mexican affairs, this theme never abated. Beginning with Villa's first taking of Torreón in the fall of 1913, the United States, through its diplomatic channels, stressed its concerns about the welfare of foreign interests in Mexico, and Villa, usually vigorously, complied.

His first capture of Torreón serves as a good starting point because with it Villa assumed enhanced stature as a rebel leader. Only days before, on September 23, he had assumed the role of commander of the Division of the North (División del Norte). Moreover, at Torreón, immediate American calls for protection of the rights and prerogatives of all foreigners were met promptly on Villa's part.

Within days of Villa's October 1 capture of the city, the Wilson administration asserted that all foreign lives and property—not just American—should be respected. In an October 18 note to American secretary of state William Jennings Bryan, the United States chargé d'affaires in Mexico, Nelson O'Shaughnessy, voiced concerns about the fate of German, English, French, Spanish, and Italian "hostages" whom Villa allegedly held in order to forestall a counterattack by federal forces.[7] Bryan responded with directions "to unofficially request Carranza to order that all foreigners in Torreón be given immediately absolute liberty to depart from Torreón at will, and that ample protection be afforded by authorities over whom he is to exercise control."[8]

But even as these communications were filed, Villa had taken steps to protect foreigners. Despite early fears "that rebels intended to massacre" Torreón's Spanish colonists, Villa offered to ensure their protection after U.S. State Department special agent George C. Carothers made representations to him.[9]

Carothers toured American businesses damaged during the three-day battle. "I visited these places personally," he reported, "and traces of the rebels were everywhere—old hats, shoes and clothing left on the floor . . . [for which] new clothing had been substituted."[10] Carothers claimed to have taken immediate action to forestall further depredations against foreign lives and property: "At six a.m. on the morning of the 2nd, I wrote to General Villa demanding protection for the American colony and for other foreigners. At eight forty-five I received a reply from him stating that it was his intention to give absolute protection to the American colony and their interests, as well as to other foreigners and their properties, and that he was sending an officer with 25 men to me to act under my orders in protecting American property."[11] Villa's hospitality also included the offer of a special train that would take any Americans who wanted to leave to Saltillo.[12]

Additionally, Carothers reported that Villa had informed him "that it was his intention to favor Americans in every way possible, in as much as the United States had never recognized the Huerta government, and for that reason we deserved more consideration than any other nationality."[13] Villa's good intentions seemed to be compromised, however, when news surfaced that he planned to exact forced loans from all merchants and that he had issued a proclamation requiring all merchants to accept his fiat money at face value. Carothers again took action—and again Villa proved amenable to American persuasion.

Villa left enforcement of the loan extraction in the hands of one of his lieutenants, Lázaro de la Garza. And de la Garza, Carothers noted, had already been made aware that Americans "had been advised not to pay it." Carothers considered any Villista reaction to nonpayment "most improbable."[14] The imposition of Villa's currency, meanwhile, proved not to be an issue of contention, because most companies agreed to accept it.[15]

In short, from a Villista perspective, Villa's foreign policy actions at Torreón had succeeded fully. He not only placated United States interests but also positioned himself as being sensitive to them. Clearly, this served Villa's self-interest inasmuch as, first, he might hope to gain political mileage from his friendliness at a later date and, second, he had identified and was fulfilling a sort of quid pro quo for the earlier American refusal to recognize Huerta's government.

Yet Villa's protections at Torreón did not inspire across-the-board confidence on the part of American diplomatic agents in Mexico, nor did Villa offer blanket protection to all foreigners at all times. Whereas some diplomatic reports expressed mild pleasure at Villa's concern with restoring order quickly,[16] Bryan also received from consular officials accusations about wanton, Villa-sanctioned executions committed in Ciudad Juárez in late November, after Villa had added that conquered city to his growing list of accomplishments.

Further, the United States consul at Ciudad Juárez, Thomas Edwards, voiced the concerns of Secretary of War Lindsey M. Garrison that "Villa is becoming very independent in his attitude toward the United States." The implication drawn by Edwards was that should the United States intervene in Mexico, it might expect "active measures" from Villa.[17]

More damning were notes sent by Marion Letcher, the American consul at Chihuahua. A dogged Villa opponent, Letcher espied hypocrisy in Villa's professions of goodwill toward American interests. He questioned the advisability of Americans' continuing to do business in northern Mexico and blasted Villa's decrees as "harsh, unjust and barbarous."[18] In December he accused Villa of breaking an agreement to protect noncombatants.[19]

Letcher's allegations generated concern in Washington. Undersecretary of State John Bassett Moore stressed in a note to Carothers that Villa should be pressed on the points raised by Letcher. He added that "such action cannot fail to place the constitutionalist cause in a bad light before the eyes of the world."[20]

At the same time, Washington recognized that the chaotic conditions generated by the Revolution were sometimes impossible to control. For example, Theodore Hamm, the American consul in Durango, noted to Bryan: "Robbery, expropriation and violence are the offspring of conditions of absolute anarchy prevailing."[21] Disagreements among consular agents aside, the point remains that Villa exhibited a general willingness to protect American interests and to abide by U.S. requests to afford similar protection to other foreigners.[22]

On the other hand, Villa made it clear that he offered no guaranteed protection to non-neutral foreigners. Edwards reported to Bryan that at the very least, Villa "will confiscate their property."[23] Bryan ultimately accepted Villa's position on non-neutrals but vowed that he would excuse no violence against them. "Villa may have a right to insist that foreigners should not interfere in local politics," he said in a February 1914 cable to Carothers, but "cause him to realize that it will greatly hamper this Government in its dealings with other nations if he uses personal violence against any foreigners."[24] In marked contrast to Villa, his Constitutionalist colleague, General Alvaro Obregón, commander of forces in the northeast, hinted that death might fairly befall any non-neutrals.[25]

Yet even Obregón's threats must have seemed mild compared with proclamations Bryan received in a dispatch from Carothers in early 1914, to the effect that in the event of revolutionary forces capturing Mexico City, all foreign residents found to be affording protection to the Huerta regime would be summarily executed. Bryan expressed alarm in a note to Carothers and asked him to continue to gain assurances from Villa that life and property would be respected.[26] Both Carothers and Villa complied. Villa believed, said Carothers, that Huertistas had penned the statement and that it aimed to elicit fear and distrust between the United States and the Constitutionalists.[27]

Still, doubts lingered in Washington about Villa's willingness to protect all foreigners—especially Spaniards, whom he despised. Spaniards, one of his supporters alleged in epithetic terms, "are commercially in Mexico what the Jews are in Russia."[28] And while Villa had heeded American demands to respect Spanish rights, as he prepared for a second time to move on Torreón in February 1914 he also continued to receive reports from his own sources that Spaniards there were actively assisting in federal efforts to defend the city.[29] Nevertheless, Villa respected United States wishes and provided protection to the Spaniards at Torreón, despite the frustration expressed by Carothers that the Spaniards remained ungrateful for the help.[30]

In early February, Villa also pounced on an opportunity to showcase his "friendship" after the bandit Máximo Castillo was charged with blowing up a passenger train bound for Tampico on February 5, an act of sabotage that killed nine Americans. Villa promised to capture and personally execute Castillo.[31] Villa's zeal to demonstrate comity extended to inviting every available

American to witness the execution. "I feel a great responsibility in this awful disaster," he said. "I want to vindicate myself."[32]

Conveniently for Villa, Castillo's demise would also settle an old score. Castillo had been assessing export duties on cattle shipped from Mexico through border crossings at Palomas, Chihuahua, and Columbus, New Mexico, without sharing the revenue with the Constitutionalists.[33] Further, Villa had already placed three hundred men in the field in pursuit of Castillo after Castillo's gang, on January 29, robbed a Ciudad Juárez–bound passenger train carrying twenty-five Americans.[34]

But Villa never captured Castillo. Indeed, on February 16, 1914, Castillo landed in an American jail, where he spent many months. In October 1914, the American acting secretary of state, Robert Lansing, who officially replaced Bryan on June 18, 1915, observed that while Castillo was "apparently responsible" for the train disaster, the United States could do little because the alleged crime had taken place on Mexican soil.[35]

In the year after Madero's death, a Villa policy of nurturing friendship with the United States had definitely taken shape. As Villa stressed somewhat lavishly in an interview with a correspondent from the *New York Times*, he sought close relations with the United States, and he hinted that such a relationship would satisfy the needs of both parties. "We wish our friends in the United States would help us," he said, "because we are your friends." He continued, with one of his typical rhetorical flourishes, "You have the greatest government on earth and your president [Wilson] is the best."[36]

From the beginning, Villa had conducted his affairs in a way designed to win him favor in Washington. He could justify these efforts, he said, because he so appreciated Wilson's nonrecognition of Huerta. As a consequence, he bent to Bryan's demands of protection for all foreigners—even Spaniards.

While the United States gained satisfaction from Villa's willingness to abide by the promotion of its interests, Villa, too, reaped rewards from the "friendship." The best example came on February 3, 1914, when Wilson lifted the cross-border embargo against shipments of arms to Mexico. Villa reacted happily and praised Wilson for this "act of justice."[37]

On the eve of the first anniversary of Madero's death, then, Villa's foreign policy had proved successful. Indeed, by February, President Wilson concluded at a news conference: "I understand his [Villa's] attitude is becoming a very correct one." Moreover, in a private conversation with Henry Lane Wilson, the American ambassador to Mexico, the president, over Ambassador Wilson's objections, lauded Villa as a "patriot and an honorable gentleman."[38]

From where Villa stood, satisfying the United States had cost little—except perhaps the opportunity to wreak vengeance upon the scorned Spaniards.[39] Villa's policy had apparently won him new access to arms, credit, and goodwill north of the border. Further, he could reasonably expect the United States to maintain pressure on Huerta to resign.

THE BENTON COMPLICATION

Although many foreign nationals were killed during the Revolution,[40] the death of British subject William S. Benton while in Villa's care led to a full-blown international incident.[41] A twenty-year resident of Mexico, Benton stormed into Villa's headquarters in Ciudad Juárez on February 19, 1914, to confront the general about cattle losses on Benton's ranch. A heated argument ensued; Benton—with whom Villa had quarreled a year earlier[42]—was never seen alive again.

Carothers's initial report to Washington said Benton would be released unharmed. Having investigated the incident before receiving instructions from Washington, Carothers had taken Villa at his word, he said, when the general reported that "Benton was alright, that nothing had happened to him." At the same time, however, Edwards, the Ciudad Juárez consul, dispatched a note to Washington noting Benton's death at the hand of Rodolfo Fierro, Villa's bodyguard. The Edwards cable explained that Benton had drawn on Villa and consequently had been executed on the spot. Edwards's report, like Carothers's, was based on information gained from Villa.[43]

The clouded circumstances surrounding Benton's death opened the door for Great Britain to try to drive a wedge between Washington and the rebels.[44] Although England had long recognized the Huerta regime, it had been unsuccessful in persuading the United States to follow suit. Then, suddenly, the Benton case erupted; it appeared to provide the impetus England needed to discredit Huerta's enemies, the Constitutionalists headed by generals Carranza and Villa.[45]

Not surprisingly, England demanded that the United States take appropriate action against the party England held responsible for Benton's alleged murder—Villa. But the U.S. government refused, in part because, as the *New York Times* noted, "[in] the absence of any satisfactory evidence to the contrary, it will be difficult for this government to reject Villa's version."[46] According to the historian Clarence Clendenen, the Wilson regime exerted no greater effort on behalf of Benton than it had in "previous and less well-publicized cases." Clendenen and his fellow historian Friedrich Katz also discern American domestic political pressures that forced Wilson to rebuff perceived British meddling in inter-American affairs. The Wilson regime could not afford politically to appear to wilt under such pressure—especially, these writers argue, to a European country that strongly supported Huerta.[47]

Secretary of State Bryan also evinced reluctance to let Huerta gain politically by the killing. In a note to Woodrow Wilson's special emissary to Mexico, former Minnesota governor John Lind, he observed, "Huerta has taken advantage of the . . . Benton killing but it will avail him to nothing."[48] Bryan's comments came days after Lind, echoing the tone of Carothers's statements, had informed the secretary that "Benton was a quarrelsome domineering Englishman, very abusive at times. A man who knew him well . . . said he had abandoned his wife in England and lived with a Mexican woman."[49]

From Chihuahua, Marion Letcher put a similar spin on events, writing that "the Englishman addressed Villa menacingly and abusively and the latter stepped behind him on the pretext of opening a door, felt for and discovered [a] pistol on Benton and then sprang upon him."[50] Then Villa had Benton shot without trial, the cable continued. Letcher concluded that Villa simply did not understand the seriousness of the case.[51]

In subsequent cables, Carothers claimed that Benton went to visit Villa "seeking trouble,"[52] and he stressed that Villa had witnesses to support his story.[53] Carothers also opined that while "[s]uch incidents as the Benton execution are lamentable . . . we may expect others to happen before the end of the struggle."[54]

Villa, meanwhile, engaged in damage control. His final position—and the one he communicated to Carranza—claimed that Benton had been shot after a court-martial had found the Briton guilty of attempting to assassinate the general.[55] Villa explained that during the argument Benton had drawn a revolver and menaced him. But Villa was quick and summarily disarmed the Briton. Then Villa convened a military tribunal, which heard the case and sentenced Benton to death.[56] In keeping with this new story, one of Villa's publicly released statements read: "A court-martial sentenced Benton to death with complete justification, due to his crimes in having made an attempt on my life, as I am able to prove."[57]

In short, according to Villa, Benton had threatened his life, and so killing him was only appropriate—and entirely legal.[58] Cleverly, in a press release, Villa sought to justify the event by citing American army regulations that would have pardoned a killing under similar circumstances in the United States.[59]

In both the United States and England, the killing generated intense publicity, to which the Constitutionalists reacted keenly.[60]

And the issue refused to die, in part because Villa's changing story suggested unreliability on his part.[61] After all, he had told several versions of it—that Benton was about to be released, that Benton had been gunned down by Fierro on the spot, and that Benton had been tried and executed for making an attempt on Villa's life. A final complication derived from Villa's initial reluctance to release the corpse, though he noted shortly, "When the time comes to do it, I will comply with my obligations."[62]

Bryan believed that an autopsy by American experts would, at the least, have absolved Villa from charges that Benton had died under circumstances other than those Villa claimed. One theory holds that Villa had the body dug up, reshot (from the front), and then reburied.[63] Bullets fired into a rotting corpse would have been easily distinguishable from those of an earlier fusillade.[64]

Carranza stepped into the scene following calls in Washington for President Wilson to launch an official American inquiry into Benton's death. Carranza expressed unconditional support for Villa and rejected the idea that any foreign board of inquiry had the right to meddle in what Carranza considered to be solely a Mexican matter.[65] Further, in a bold move aimed at forcing Great Britain either to back off or to grant the Constitutionalists de facto recognition, he issued instructions that forthwith his office alone would deal with foreign officials.[66]

Under pressure, however, Carranza partially relented to bipartisan American calls for a commission to investigate the case by appointing his own board of inquiry.[67] But he made it clear that he considered the issue to be a matter for Mexico alone to judge. Bryan expressed relief at Carranza's apparent willingness to compromise, albeit slightly, and claimed that it would "assist the constitutional cause."[68]

By early March the issue began to fade under the glare of more pressing revolutionary concerns. Villa's preparatory moves for a second campaign against Torreón drew media attention away from the Benton affair. Similarly, Carranza had dampened interest in the incident by ordering an inquiry.

Both available evidence and recent scholarship point to two explanations for Benton's death—neither of which supports Villa's official story. The first holds that Benton met his end at the edge of a shallow pit intended to be his grave. After the initial argument with Villa, according to this version, Fierro led Benton away and forced him to watch soldiers dig his grave. Then Fierro smashed Benton's skull with a shovel. Any release of Benton's body in such a condition would surely have worked against Villa's pro-American policy because it would have suggested, first, that Villa did not seek to protect foreigners as he professed and, second, that Villa had lied about the circumstances of Benton's death.[69]

Another report comes from Villa's widow, Luz Corral de Villa, who claimed, according to one of Villa's many biographers, that "she was bringing in a tray of lunch 'for the general' just as Benton and Fierro both drew."[70] Death by pistol at point-blank range would again have been detectable by autopsy and thus might have controverted Villa's version had he released the body. This story was seconded by British consul Cunard Cummins and has been accepted by Katz.[71]

Throughout the Benton incident, Villa continued to ply the same foreign policy rhetoric he had established in the preceding months—friendship toward American interests. He might well have concluded that his policy was succeeding, despite the heat generated by Benton's death. After all, the United States had rebuffed the British government over the affair, in favor of Villa. Further to Villa's good fortune, as alluded to by the *Los Angeles Times*, media interest in the Benton affair had all but disappeared by early March.[72]

Villa had reentered the revolutionary struggle a year earlier as a bandit and had fought his way to a measure of political and military respectability (and the leadership of a sizable army) through a series of convincing military engagements. Even if his policy reputation had been tarred slightly by the Benton killing, the setback had been momentary. Now, with the Benton killing behind him, in April 1914 Villa's foreign policy became more sensitive to the detection of American concerns and correspondingly quicker to react to them.

In March and April, as he led his forces successfully against the strategic center of Torreón and, later, unsuccessfully against Tampico, Villa pledged to maintain his practice of providing protection to foreign interests.[73] Bryan responded gratefully.[74] There was a catch in Villa's pledge, however—his animosity toward Spanish colonists seemed to remain undiminished. From Torreón, Consul Hamm identified a three-step Villa approach to dealing with foreign interests. First, Americans remained "the most favored with absolutely no restrictions placed upon their business transaction." Next, foreigners other than Spaniards or Americans "must pay moderately for the privilege of transacting their own business." Finally, Spanish property would be seized and considered "booty of war." Hamm stressed that Villa very much wanted Bryan to be informed that "he was scrupulously complying with all the usages of civilized warfare in regard to his treatment of prisoners and the wounded of the enemy, his treatment of neutrals and their interests, with the single exception of the Spaniards, who he claims have forfeited all rights to protection on account of their avowedly hostile attitude towards the [Constitutionalist] cause."[75]

Villa's military actions at Torreón and Tampico also signaled his ascent to the last few rungs of the Mexican military ladder. His foreign policy, too, would gain new stature in Wilsonian eyes—especially with the American occupation of the Mexican port of Veracruz in late April.

The historian Alan Knight has argued that until the Benton imbroglio, Villa's "main concerns were domestic and parochial," and only through the furor caused by the Briton's death did Villa come "to appreciate the value of American goodwill."[76] Yet the evidence suggests that Villa both understood and sought American goodwill as early as the first taking of Torreón in October 1913. That he clearly understood the value of American favor well before the Benton affair was also evidenced by his expressions of thanks when President Wilson lifted the arms embargo early in 1914.

More importantly, from the beginning Villa's policy actions vis-à-vis the United States were premised upon the expectation that his foreign policy would be favorably received there and so might elicit support from the American government. Villa learned at least two important diplomatic lessons from the Benton affair. First, and most obviously, he learned not to kill foreigners openly. Second, the way the case turned out proved the value of the very policy he had championed for months—friendship with the United States.

THE VILLA COROLLARY:
AMERICAN OCCUPATION OF VERACRUZ

At Tampico on April 9, 1914, a handful of American sailors in search of gasoline were arrested by Huertista soldiers for trespassing in a restricted area. The party was released almost immediately and received an apology—but not to the satisfaction of Rear Admiral Henry T. Mayo, commander of American naval forces off Tampico. Among other things, he demanded a twenty-one-gun salute of the United States flag.[77] From the White House, Wilson backed the demand. Huerta demurred. Then Washington learned that the German ship *Ypiranga* would shortly deliver a sizable shipment of arms to Huerta. Wilson ordered the immediate occupation of Veracruz by the United States Navy.[78]

Carothers detected a "very strong undercurrent of resentment" in northern Mexico when it was learned that American marines had landed at Veracruz.[79] O'Shaughnessy, the U.S. chargé d'affairs, voiced similar concern about the feeling in Mexico City.[80] Indeed, Carranza reacted angrily to Wilson's decision.[81] So insistent was he that the forces be withdrawn that for a moment the threat of war loomed between the two countries,[82] as Carranza threatened in a note to Wilson.[83]

Thomas Edwards, the American consul at Ciudad Juárez, voiced a theory that Carranza had little choice in the matter, because to have protested in milder form would have jeopardized his hold on the loyalty of Constitutionalist generals.[84] The Wilson administration, however, chose to accept Carranza's statements at face value, and Bryan took pains to convey to Carranza that the United States did not want war.[85]

But then, in a brilliant foreign policy move, Villa helped save the day. In strong terms, he publicly approved of the occupation. The United States was his friend, he said, and in his capacity as leader of the Division of the North he would countenance nothing that might upset such a friend. Villa's statements contributed to dissipating the war scare.[86] Carothers reported: "I dined with [Villa]. He was very cordial. We discussed situation at length. He said there would be no war . . . that he is too good a friend of ours . . . [and] that as far as he was concerned we could keep Vera Cruz and hold it so tight that not even water could get in to Huerta and that he [Villa] could not feel any resentment."[87]

Bryan responded happily to Carothers' note, commenting, "It shows a largeness of view on [Villa's] part and a comprehension of the whole situation which is greatly to his credit. . . . We are earnestly desirous that the most friendly relationships should exist."[88]

If the Benton killing had in any way tarnished Villa's foreign policy in official American eyes, his decision to back Wilson over Veracruz achieved the opposite effect. From El Paso, United States customs inspector Zach Lamar Cobb noted, "Villa's attitude [has] relieved tension here. Everything becoming normal."[89] The *Independent*, an American weekly news magazine, agreed, noting that Wilson and Bryan "were reassured by the attitudes and declarations of Villa."[90]

Villa then slightly—yet importantly—modified his public position on Veracruz. He did so by incorporating his pro-occupation stance into a larger picture championing Mexican nationalism. In an appeal to his domestic constituency, he said the following in an interview with the *New York Times*:

> After all, . . . our interests are mutual. A boundary is only an imaginary political line. Socially and economically the Rio Grande has never proven a stiff barrier to the nations separated by it. I believe that all enlightened Americans take this stand. I know I do. However, there is much in society. The Mexicans would remain Mexicans just as the Americans prefer to remain Americans. For that reason we Mexicans would defend our country to the last. I take the liberty to say that before a war between the United States and Mexico would be terminated, few Mexicans would be left alive. . . . But I am now and always have been for peace.[91]

Recasting his policy as nationalistic probably stemmed from the domestic pressures Villa felt.[92]

The impetus behind Villa's exclamation of nationalism may have come from an appeal by federal general Joaquín Maas, the commander Villa had defeated at Torreón. Maas had written to Villa days earlier in May to invite him to join a coalition to fight the "grave offense" of the American landing at Veracruz. Villa thundered in response that Maas, along with Huerta and his adherents, had sold out to "Científico" elements (Mexican Positivists who were responsible for modernizing the country after 1876 and for the further impoverishment of its masses) and had actually invited the "foreign invaders" as a ploy to deflect criticism away from Huerta's murder of Francisco Madero. Copies of the two letters were released to the American press. Villa's reply read in part:

> Now you desire to provoke a foreign war to save yourselves from the disaster coming from the civil conflict. You show even

less wisdom when you pile up mountains of machinations and lies, which will crumble about your ears. . . . It will soon be proven that the satanic declaration which you traitors to the fatherland have made in stating that we have formed a union with the North Americans is a stupid assertion. . . . The Constitutionalists have the desire to do all possible to avoid a foreign war, but if we are not able to avoid it we will face the two enemies, the powerful stranger and the depraved compatriot.[93]

The Veracruz occupation, which lasted into November, gave Villa's primary foreign policy the opportunity to shine. This policy—to placate American interests—blended with Wilson's own policy hand-in-glove at Veracruz. In short order Villa had taken advantage of an opportunity to express his friendship tangibly and to outmaneuver Carranza politically on the foreign policy front.

Villa also wrote to Wilson, downplaying the "worthy pride" of Carranza as "quite excusable," albeit misguided. Carranza did not really intend to convey hostility toward the United States, he stressed.[94] But Villa's unmistakable point was that Carranza *had* expressed hostility, whereas Villa had voiced just the opposite. Wilson seemed satisfied, too. Only days before, he had written to the American general Hugh Scott that "Villa certainly seems capable of some good things and often shows susceptibilities of the best influences."[95] The *Saturday Evening Post* reported that Wilson looked favorably on Villa's improving treatment of prisoners of war.[96] Villa remained "hard to understand, however."[97]

As Villa worked to defuse the Veracruz situation, his military reputation prospered, fueling the growing official interest in him in the United States. For Villa, the picture appeared rosy: his foreign policy had generated expressions of friendship from the United States, whereas Carranza's policy, which championed nationalism first, earned a contrary reaction from Washington. At least for an instant, Villa's foreign policy had achieved its ultimate expression—perfect harmony with American policy. At that point, he could scarcely have expected more.

By late September 1914, on the eve of the formal rupture in Villa-Carranza relations, the public contours of Villa's foreign policy had experienced a necessary tightening of focus. Although the policy continued to rest firmly on the promotion of friendship with the United States, in a pronounced way its success had become more directly tied to Villa's own military fortunes. In the past, he had fought the rhetorical component of the battle against Huerta alongside other Constitutionalists. But by November 1914, after the Convention of Aguascalientes had failed to bridge the differences between Villa and Carranza, he was on his own. Lack of success on the battlefield might now be translated in Washington as failed policy. Villa had to win militarily, on his own, to remain politically viable both in the United States and in Mexico—because without political viability in Mexico he would not be taken seriously by the United States.

OVER THE TOP

The outbreak of World War I in Europe in August 1914 drew American interests across the Atlantic Ocean, far from Mexico's shores. Meanwhile, the Mexican civil war raged on. During the months following the Veracruz landing, the Villa-Carranza association collapsed. Huerta resigned and fled in mid-July, and by late September Villa had disavowed Carranza's constitutional authority.

The conference held in October at Aguascalientes failed to patch up their differences, and by December Villa and Carranza were on a collision course.[98] By Christmas 1914, not only had Villa taken Mexico City but his armies stood poised to strike a final and crushing blow at Carranza's forces. But Villa hesitated, giving Carranza's army time to regroup.

Clearly favored over Carranza in Washington after his Veracruz stand, Villa continued to work hard to promote his friendship with the United States.[99] His efforts paid dividends. In a June letter to President Wilson, for example, Bryan noted, "The Associated press reports that Villa . . . was ready to do anything the U.S. wanted. . . . This is encouraging."[100] Villa rejoined, "I am fighting for the good of my country and am now and always shall be disposed to bow to the popular will."[101]

Glimmers of a nationalistic side to Villa's policy continued to peek through his otherwise emphatically pro-American stance. A September 1914 dispatch from the American consul at Saltillo, John R. Silliman, noted that Obregón had made anti-American remarks to Villa regarding American troops remaining in Mexico after Huerta's departure.[102] Villa, according to Silliman, had concurred and replied to Obregón, "I accept with enthusiasm your patriotic idea . . . for really it is humiliating and shameful for our beloved country for invading forces to remain still in Veracruz when there exists no reason for it."[103] Yet the principal thrust of Villa's policy remained courting and touting American friendship. Just days after his reply to Obregón, Villa penned a friendly note to Wilson to congratulate him on the decision to withdraw American forces.[104] Wilson responded in kind, writing to "express sincere appreciation" for Villa's warm note.[105]

Villa also sought to use his favored position with the Wilson administration to exact assistance in the United States against counterrevolutionaries. In October, via the customs agent Cobb, he wired Bryan to request help in "dissolving" reactionary juntas in New Orleans, San Antonio, and El Paso.[106] Bryan agreed to aid him, provided that Villa supply appropriate evidence.[107]

Meanwhile, the United States continued to press Villa to afford protection for foreign interests. The American diplomatic correspondence teems with reports of deplorable conditions for aliens in Mexico. Although many reports to Washington cite Villa's friendly rhetoric, others stress the State Department's desire that

Villa adhere to his policy of friendliness. Three examples illustrate American concerns and Villa's responses to them.

First, the "anti-American attitude" taken by Sonora governor José M. Maytorena, a Villa partisan, generated mild alarm in Washington.[108] Bryan made representation to Villa via Frederick Simpich, the Nogales consul, about curbing the anti-American and anti-Carrancista content of Maytorena's controlled press, because it threatened to spoil the harmony that Bryan desired among the revolutionaries. Further, Bryan expressed concern about the random public violence committed by some of Maytorena's adherents, which, again, imperiled Bryan's hope for a peaceful settlement of Villa-Carranza differences. A week later, Simpich reported that Villa had moved to fix the problems.[109] When they again flared up, Carothers noted, Villa continued to take action to address American worries and reapplied pressure on Maytorena—but Carothers also pointed out that the anti-Carrancista propaganda reflected a joint Maytorena-Villa endeavor.[110]

Second, on September 24, 1914, just one day after disavowing Carranza's leadership, Villa reiterated his pro-American rhetoric to Wilson's special agent Leon Canova.[111] And Acting Secretary of State Lansing, ever pressing the American case for protection of foreign interests, wrote to Cobb in El Paso on October 16 instructing him to "urge" upon Villa the "importance" of providing protection.[112]

Third, Lansing cautioned Villa about "the extreme importance" of taking steps to prevent looting and general disorder as Villa stood poised to capture Mexico City in late November.[113] Carothers answered: "There will be no disorders. General orders have been issued to execute anyone caught stealing or molesting women. Excellent order reigns in all cities that have been occupied by Villa's troops and citizens appear content."[114] Lansing was "much disappointed and distressed" to be informed that Villa was executing political prisoners in Mexico City.[115] The executions continued—but so did Villa's pro-American rhetoric.

In January 1915, months after the rupture with Carranza, Villa declared: "To president Wilson, the greatest American, I stand pledged to do what I can to keep the faith which he has in my people, and if there is anything he may wish I will gladly do it, for I know it will be for the good of my country."[116] Villa often punctuated his public pronouncements with puffery designed merely to flatter.

But the pressures of unremitting warfare in the winter of 1915 suggested that a new and possibly hostile reality for foreigners, including Americans, was on the horizon. Villa's easily gained war booty had been spent, and he increasingly found it necessary to tax foreign elements forcibly. Yet messages received in Washington did not paint a clear picture of his actions.

In early February Cobb reported, "I am confident there will be no further exactions."[117] Yet one day earlier State Department confidant José Manuel Cardoso de Oliveira, Brazil's minister to Mexico, suggested just the opposite—that exactions would continue and, because of the economic ravages of war, would probably increase in frequency.[118] Within eight weeks Cobb fell in line with Oliveira's assessment, noting a "tendency to confiscate any kind of property which might be readily turned into cash."[119]

The public gloss on Villa's policy of rhetorical friendship did not tarnish in 1914, despite a pronounced second current to his policy—Mexican nationalism—that partially belied his publicly trumpeted adulation of the United States. Yet on at least two occasions—in a pronouncement to the *New York Times* and in a note to Obregón—Villa expressed support for a Mexican nationalism that resented the Veracruz occupation. He suggested, moreover, that he would have little hesitation in fighting the United States in a war if conditions (unspecified) warranted.

Villa's nationalistic policy current, which in the United States was publicly subordinated to his pro-American rhetoric, would continue well into 1915. Even during the early winter of 1915, when cracks in the foundations of his economic support made it difficult for him to continue the policy without modification, Villa maintained his policy of friendship. Time and again he professed friendship to American diplomatic agents.

ON BECOMING DICTATOR

Villa's fortunes endured sweeping change over the late winter and spring of 1915. Despite oft-repeated claims that he would never do so, on January 31, 1915, he declared himself "in charge" of the presidency.[120] He claimed to rule on behalf of the democratic—as it declared itself to be—Convention of Aguascalientes.[121] In fact, he ruled as dictator, by decree. Further, because of the critical state of his pecuniary affairs, his decrees often generated tension with the letter and spirit of his pro-American policy.

In early March, Villa's nationalism again poked through the veneer of his carefully scripted pro-American rhetoric. Asked by the Associated Press about reports that he would support American intervention "provided he would be made commander of such a move," Villa hotly denied the charge: "There is nothing more grotesque and absurd than such an assertion, since I, as a true Mexican, have always insisted that all our troubles be settled solely among ourselves. Should, unfortunately, some nation invade our territory, I would be ready to fight against it without measuring the danger or the number of invaders. . . . All of us would unite against the common enemy."[122]

A final decisive turn of events began in April after Obregón's forces soundly drubbed Villa's—losses from which Villa would not recover. In a series of battles lasting through June, Obregón drove the final nails into Villa's military and political coffin.[123] But although financial and strategic considerations forced Villa to test the mettle of his pro-American policy rhetoric, during this period he plied his foreign policy more pointedly and sensitively than ever before.

A March 1915 report issued to Woodrow Wilson by Duval West, another of Wilson's special agents to Mexico,[124] typified the official assessment of Villa by American agents in the field. It stressed Villa's interest in receiving formal American diplomatic recognition.[125] At the same time, West outlined for Wilson his best estimation of Villa's main achievement—success in restoring and maintaining order—while also pointing out his limitations: failure in the rule of fair and just law, and a tendency toward failure on moral grounds because of unsubstantiated rumors that he had "forcibly taken" several women.[126]

Two early measures decreed by Villa in his capacity as dictator drew the ire of influential American interests in Mexico, to which Villa responded quickly. The first decree largely sought to return mining properties, mainly unutilized or underutilized, to the public domain. It allowed for forfeiture of properties in cases of voluntary cessation of work for ninety days or more, insufficient development of the property, or neglect to meet prescribed construction requirements. The State Department viewed it as harmful to American interests.[127] Rumors also circulated that Villa intended to proclaim a similar law for ranch properties.[128]

Bryan complained to Carothers about the mining decree on April 7.[129] Carothers came to Villa's defense on April 12, arguing that the mining law sought only to proscribe undue profit-taking by speculators.[130] Still, on April 15 Bryan instructed Carothers to seek a suspension of the decree, pending the presentation of further objections.[131] Just one day later Villa informed Carothers, who wired Bryan, that the decree would be modified to suit American concerns.[132] Then, three days later, on April 19, Villa's Washington agent, Enrique C. Llorente, wired Bryan to ensure him that the decree would be altered to reflect American wishes.[133]

In a second decree, Villa declared a one-million-dollar tax on the Monterrey Chamber of Commerce, which drew immediate

American opposition. Phillip C. Hanna, United States consular official at Torreón, notified Bryan, and Bryan responded with instructions to attempt to have the tax waived for Americans.[134] After Hanna made Washington's representations, and after a discussion with Villa, he reported that the tax levied on American firms would be negligible or nothing.[135] Again, Villa had moved swiftly to adjust his legislation to suit U.S. concerns.

Still, these decrees signaled that Villa's untenable financial situation was encroaching on his ability to cater to American demands. On one level Villa acted to continue protecting American interests, but two factors worked against him. First, because the countryside had been ravaged by war, traditional sources of revenue (that is, forced exactions of liquid property such as cattle and cotton) could no longer support him as they once had.[136] Second, his declining military fortunes made it ever more imperative that he raise new monies for battle.[137] The most obvious untapped source was taxation of foreign—including American—interests. In mid-July Cobb noted, "Villa's economic support has already collapsed, there being little left to it except such tribute [as] may be forced from Americans and other foreigners."[138]

Although Cobb's dispatches generally exhibited no fondness for Villa, even correspondents more sympathetic to him tended to agree with Cobb's findings, especially as the summer wore on. In June, meanwhile, the Villista Roque González Garza recorded: "All the day of the twelfth General Villa was thinking worriedly . . . all the time very sad and in great desperation because he was anxious to find a solution to the approaching conflict."[139] The United States vice-consul at Durango, Homer C. Coen, reported to Lansing that Villa's troops were "baffled, demoralized."[140] To forestall his military and political collapse, in mid-July Villa reexpressed the desperate willingness he had displayed in early June to arrange a compromise with Carranza—which might have effected a harmony among revolutionary factions that the United States had sought since the autumn of 1914.[141] As Carothers put it, Villa "will accept any reasonable proposition" to come to terms.[142] Cobb saw things differently, labeling Villa "beyond reason" and opining that "radical methods only can afford foreigners adequate relief."[143]

Still, with prodding, Villa continued to espouse pro-American-ism. After meeting with Villa and the American general Hugh Scott, Carothers reported that Villa "offered absolute protection." At the same time, Carothers and Scott thought it expedient to suggest that Lansing resist making further representations to Villa "for several days so as not to tire him."[144] Later, in early August, Villa offered to "make all kinds of efforts and all kinds of sacrifices" to make peace with Carranza.[145]

Lansing, meanwhile, because of his dissatisfaction with Carranza's attitude toward the United States, in early August suggested to President Wilson that the United States provide opportunities to support Villa against the "First Chief," as Carranza was known.[146] But Wilson waffled and said he was "puzzled" by Lansing's sug-gestion. "What will be gained?" he asked. Then, in an apparent concession to Villa, he queried, "Are you sure that he has in fact been doing all the lawless things he has been accused of doing?"[147]

Wilson's latter question was well placed, because days later General Scott convinced Villa to back away from plans to heavily tax American mining firms.[148] And even as late as September, according to Carothers, Villa took steps to protect American cattle interests from depredations.[149]

As Cobb correctly had it, however, Villa was effectively a spent force. By September 8, 1915, Villa's chief strategist, Felipe Angeles, reported to Carothers that Villa "realizes that he is lost and must subordinate himself to some one."[150] Villa's army and the armies of his allies had been reduced to marauding gangs. By early October, many of Villa's officers had fled and taken refuge in the United States.[151] Conditions in Sonora, a state nominally under the control of Villa's colleague Governor José M. Maytorena, were described as "atrocious and unbelievable."[152]

RECOGNITION AND RECKONING

By the eve of the October 19, 1915, U.S. recognition of Carranza's government, Villa had been wiped out. Yet even at this late hour, he appeared "cheerful" and "optimistic" to Carothers, and he expressed confidence that Carranza would not be recognized. If recognition did occur, he vowed to continue his fight to the death.[153] But it did, and he did not.

Recognition had clearly generated bitterness—and a reaction. The "love affair" had drawn to an unhappy conclusion for Villa.[154] The American general Frederick Funston cited a report that Villa, on learning of Carranza's recognition, "became angry and declared he was through with them [Americans] all and that was how he was to be repaid for the protection he has given to Americans and other foreigners . . . [and he] launched into a tirade against the United States."[155]

Upon United States recognition of Carranza, Villa's foreign policy underwent radical change. It took on, as Consul Edwards had predicted from Veracruz a month earlier, an anti-American flavor.[156] By the end of the month Cobb was reporting thefts of American cattle.[157] American miners also suffered at Villa's hands.[158] Carothers noted a report from an unidentified "newspaper man" that Villa would "attack" Americans "if necessary."[159] In early November Villa demanded a forced loan totaling one hundred thousand dollars from four American-owned companies. Moreover, he threatened to seize stock from an American cattle firm.[160]

With U.S. recognition of Carranza, then, Villa's pro-American policy abruptly ended. Culminating with an attack on Columbus, New Mexico, in March 1916, his post-recognition actions manifested his bitterness toward and sense of betrayal by the United States.[161]

For more than two years he had advocated and exhibited friendliness toward the United States. He had attempted to mold a policy rhetorically congruent with and amenable to American interests. His actions occasionally belied his words, as Villa's devolving story during the Benton affair illustrated. But he had learned from this imbroglio, as shown by the quickness he displayed in modifying his mining decrees in 1915. And when a misstep was made in predicting U.S. concerns, Villa showed no compunction about changing stories to meet perceived foreign policy needs—sounding and acting pro-American—as, again, the Benton affair showed.

Villa's two-track foreign policy in itself never failed him. Indeed, Lansing's support for Villa in the late summer of 1915 suggests the contrary. That is, by being friendly to the United States Villa gained American goodwill, as was demonstrated particularly by the mileage he gained from his Veracruz position. His friendliness probably contributed to his holding on longer as a political force in Mexico than his military position warranted, strictly speaking.

Villa's ability to maintain American support months after his military power had been spent also reflected the success of his propaganda. At every step of his rise to power Villa energetically promoted a public image designed to win him favor in the United States and to promote his foreign policy. So successful was Villa's propaganda that it prompted Carrancistas to complain bitterly that Villa was more a creation of the mass media than he was a substantial revolutionary force.

In any case, Villa's dual foreign policy of placating American interests while firmly espousing Mexican nationalism can be judged a ringing success. In its pro-American incarnation Villa's policy promoted and gained what it sought—American goodwill and official United States government support. In its Mexican-nationalist guise the policy kept Villa's enemies in Mexico at bay, lest his effusions of friendship toward the United States engender bitterness, alienation, and loss of support for his movement.

CHAPTER THREE

CUT-AND-PASTE REVOLUTIONARY

*There is something fine for you to write your papers
about . . .*

—VILLA TO JOHN REED[1]

A central pillar of Villa's attempt to ply his two-track foreign policy
in and through the mass media was orchestrated self-promotion.
To that end, he employed publicists in the United States, bribed
reporters and editors there, funded his own propaganda organ in
Mexico, provided financial support to other publications in both
Mexico and the United States, sold his story to the motion pictures,
and charmed, bullied, deceived, censored, and cajoled foreign
news reporters into casting him in a favorable light.[2]

Villa's propaganda strategies aimed to provide mass media
consumers with ready-made perceptions of him and his struggle
in terms of three fundamental issues—his morality, his and the
United States' mutual self-interest, and American pragmatism. In
the first case, Villa labored to project an image of robust morality
typified by honesty, altruism, and social justice for the downtrodden. Second, he attempted to project images in the media of a
self-interest consonant with and closely allied to the interests of the

United States. Finally, Villa promoted an image of himself as a winner, with the implication that by supporting him, the United States would pragmatically end up on the winning team.

Although Villa's propaganda machine served him well, the historical evidence necessary to reconstruct its workings remains scattered. There exists no Villa archive—for good reason. When Villa lost his share of the Revolution in the autumn of 1915, the victors had no compelling reason to preserve the sort of documentation, if it ever existed, that would enable a reconstruction of his propaganda structure and organization.[3] Still, evidence of the workings of Villa's propaganda can be found in a variety of locations: Constitutionalist correspondence in the Carranza archive (VC); revolutionary correspondence preserved in other Mexican archives, such as the Foreign Relations archive (AHSRE) and the Roque González Garza archive (ARGG); personal memoirs or reminiscences, either published or in archives such as the Terrazas Collection (STC); American diplomatic correspondence files (RDS); and media publications.

From these sources, the content and shape of Villa's propaganda operation emerge. The content—that is, the Villa message—championed democracy, anti-authoritarianism, formal education, self-reliance, egalitarianism, and social justice for the poor. It decried dictatorship (which, in time, Villa sought to identify with Carranza), lauded Woodrow Wilson as the world's greatest leader, and repeatedly expressed warmth and friendship for Americans doing business in Mexico and for the American people and government more generally.

Villa also sought to personify through his public statements (press releases, proclamations, and interviews) the ideals of rugged individuality, energetic organization, humble honesty, personal bravery, perseverance, and, in apparent contradiction to his expressed feelings for Wilson, antipathy for positions of authority.

In sum, Villa's propaganda draped his rhetorical primary foreign policy aim—to nurture cordial relations with the United States—

in tropes that might generate positive images and elicit favorable responses in the United States. Over time, Villa "changed his positions" to meet propaganda ends, "to project a more favorable image in the United States."[4] In this chapter I offer a chronological analysis of the rise and fall of Villa's propaganda machine.

THE COMET IS SIGHTED

Villa leapt onto America's front pages in the fall of 1913. His daring victories alone earned him the fascination of the American media.[5] But Villa also had agents in the field actively promoting his foreign policy. Consequently, the flood of American journalists southward in the fall of 1913 and winter of 1914 reflected a response both to Villa's bona fide military achievements and to the ability of Villa and his agents to package him and his foreign policy in alluring ways.[6]

In the fall of 1913, the *New York Times*, the Hearst news syndicate (for example, the *San Francisco Examiner*), the *Los Angeles Times*, and the *Washington Times* already had reporters stationed in Mexico. Villa's sudden public emergence had other newspapers and magazines clamoring to send reporters to the scene.[7] In time, publications such as the *Chicago Tribune, Collier's, Everybody's, Fortnightly Review, Forum, Harper's*, the *Independent, McClure's, The Nation*, the *North American Review*, the *Saturday Evening Post*, and *World's Work* also dispatched correspondents to a nerve-center of media attention—Villa's camp. Some publications relied on the wire services for revolutionary news, and almost all American news publications relied on wire reports to some extent.[8]

Villa treated his press entourage well, affording those he liked best accommodations in his private train, which included a "rich" drawing room, a salon car, "luxurious" sleepers, and a car housing a barbershop and a bathroom.[9] "The private boxcar fitted up for the correspondents, photographers, and moving picture men" came third in the train, along with "our bunks, our blankets, and Fong, our beloved Chinese cook," reported American journalist John Reed.[10] The sides of the car had the names of American news publications and news associations "plastered over its sides."[11]

Like Reed, journalist Timothy Turner recalled the car fondly: "It . . . was a work of art. It had been a grain car. After Villa gave it to the press, Mexican carpenters were employed and . . . transformed it into a side-door Pullman deluxe. Rough bunks were built, there was a toilet, and a kitchen with a stove and smoke stack through the roof; there was a long built-in table of planks on which we ate and on which the pride of the car, an old battered but faithful non-visible Remington typewriter sat."[12]

Villa enjoyed being interviewed,[13] especially in group settings, where he tended to deliver his statements "bombastically."[14] "Villa liked newspapermen, though it took him a while to 'warm up' to those he had met only once or twice," one author has noted.[15] Reed perceived a different source for Villa's conduct toward the pressmen: "The sight of us amused him profoundly; he could never take the correspondents seriously, anyway, and it seemed to him very droll that an American periodical would be willing to spend so much money just to get the news."[16]

According to the Villa chronicler Louis Stevens, Villa "realized, of course, that he must act 'generously' with them [foreign reporters]: for they helped form, by the articles they wrote, American public sentiment."[17] Echoing the conclusions of a number of other investigators, one of Villa's many biographers has noted that Villa "knew well the uses of publicity and propaganda and played to effective coverage of his campaigns."[18] Similarly, the historian Clarence Clendenen remarked that Villa "understood well the part that newspapers could play in forming public opinion in the United States favorable to himself and his cause."[19] In early February 1914, the *New York Times* put it this way: "No great man in the public eye at present understands the value of publicity to greatness better than FRANCISCO VILLA."[20]

The contours of Villista propaganda operations were established by the autumn of 1913 and underwent little modification after American troops landed at Veracruz in the spring of 1914. During the first year of renewed fighting, 1913, Villa honed his ability to promote a public message of friendship to the United States. He also warmly received—and coddled—a bevy of American journalists drawn south by tales of his battlefield exploits. All the while, Villa's agents in the field promoted their *jefe* and his foreign policy.

In the summer of 1913, Villa began bribing reporters and editors to plant false stories (something Huerta also allegedly engaged in, at the rate of four thousand dollars per week in 1914).[21] Carrancista author and propagandist Carlo de Fornaro claimed Villa paid off an El Paso reporter (probably from the Villista-sympathetic *El Paso Times*) in the summer of 1913. That same summer, according to Fornaro, Villa reportedly spent two hundred dollars bribing "a writer to get a story on Villa into a New York Sunday newspaper."[22] In 1915 Villa again bribed the *El Paso Times,* according to the Carrancista consul in El Paso, Andrés G. García,[23] and he bribed unidentified publications in southern California, according to Carranza's Los Angeles consular official E. González.[24]

As early as the month before Villa's formal rupture in relations with Carranza in August 1914, Villa provided funds for seven anti-Constitutionalist publications in Mexico and the United States—papers that attacked Carranza with "furious tenacity," claimed the Carrancista E. Mende Fierro.[25] In at least one case, that of the *San Antonio Express,* the Carrancistas banned a Villa-funded organ from their territory.[26] Villa's practice of paying for good press continued throughout 1915.[27]

AGENTS AND PROPAGANDISTS

Prior to the Benton imbroglio of late February 1914, the Villa propaganda machine was organized loosely. Villista agents in the United

States often doubled as arms purchasers and publicists—of the Constitutionalist Revolution, but especially of Villismo. Felix Sommerfeld, a former Associated Press reporter,[28] served the Revolution principally by expediting arms shipments out of El Paso, but he also sometimes promoted Villa in New York, the hub of American press activity.[29] Similarly, Sherburne Hopkins, an American lawyer and, like Sommerfeld, a former influential Madero adviser,[30] championed the Constitutionalist cause in Washington as early as May 1913, before taking up the reins of promoting Villa exclusively in the autumn of 1914.[31] At one point, for unspecified services, Hopkins received fifty thousand dollars.[32]

Concern was expressed on the floor of the United States Senate. Senator Morris Sheppard of Texas claimed that the two men, Hopkins and Sommerfeld, "are here [in Washington] now, carrying on this work and they are undertaking to influence, not corruptly, the course of public opinion and the actions of officials of this government."[33] Senator William Alden Smith of Michigan took Sheppard's charges one step further:

> The president of the United States in the crisis may be misled as are others. He may have misinformation. . . . [T]here is at the present moment in this capital a thorough, practical, systematic lobby, putting forth their revolutionary propaganda with a serious and definite object of affecting the American attitude toward the government of Mexico which Senators ought to fully understand. A man who stood at the elbow of the late President Madero, a witness before the committee of which I had the honor to be chairman, is now in this capital, as he has been for two years on our border, directing a war junta.[34]

Silvestre Terrazas, editor of the Constitutionalist organ *El Correo de Chihuahua*,[35] purchased arms in addition to promoting Villa in El Paso publications.[36] Huerta had *El Correo* shut down in the spring of 1913, but Carranza provided the support necessary to reestablish it after Terrazas appealed for help.[37] Villa lawyer Federico González Garza, too, promoted Villa in the American press, as did Enrique Llorente, a former Díaz agent in the United States whom Villa ultimately dispatched to Washington.[38]

Mexican lawyer and Villa confidante Roque González Garza penned Villista news releases from Mexico.[39] John W. Roberts, a former reporter for the pro-Villa *El Paso Times* and for the Hearst syndicate,[40] also served as Villa media intimate and press agent, "giving him as much publicity as possible."[41] Other arms purchasers moonlighting as press agents included Alberto Madero, brother of the slain president, and a certain Julio Muller.[42]

Despite nominal Constitutionalist ties, Sommerfeld, Hopkins, the two González Garzas, and Llorente had primarily Villista sympathies. In their roles as publicists, the five later opted in favor of Villa months before his break with Carranza. For instance—to jump ahead in the story slightly—by the time Villa's relations with the First Chief began to sour during the summer of 1914, Hopkins allegedly had already championed Villismo in the press at the expense of Carrancismo.[43] Indeed, by the summer of 1914 a prominent Carrancista, Rafael Zubarán Capmany, charged that a mechanism (which remained unexplained) to promote Villismo at the expense of Constitutionalism linked operatives in San Francisco, Chicago, and border cities such as El Paso, even though Villa did not formally establish consuls in the United States until October 1914, when offices were opened in New York and New Orleans.[44] Hopkins and Llorente served as the key New York operatives, E. A. Navarro ran the Chicago office, and Santiago S. Winfield operated out of New Orleans.[45]

Still, in January and February 1914, Villa remained nominally allied to Carranza. Moreover, the Benton case appeared to strengthen that tie when Villa took refuge behind Carranza's public support for him and declarations that all foreign representations be made to Carranza's offices. If the heat generated by Benton's death singed Villa politically, then his propaganda machine, working with Carrancistas Luis Cabrera, Eliseo Arredondo, and Robert V. Pesqueira, energetically sought to cool the fire.

MAKING THE NEWS

In its early stages, Villa's media campaign focused on promoting Villa as an American friend, as a heroic character, and as someone who could deliver on his promises. For example, citing rebel couriers in late October 1913, the *New York Times* reported Villa's plan to "move on" Chihuahua.[46] In reality, the "couriers," unidentified by name, were Villa's first press agents, albeit unpolished ones. And such announcements, usually hyperbolic and frequently delivered boastfully, increasingly tended to help frame Villa as friend (to friendly Americans) and formidable adversary (to hostile Mexican elements).

By the end of November 1913, Villa had begun routinely to deliver two types of written statements to the American press about his plans or most recent accomplishments—news releases and direct cables to magazines and newspapers.[47] News releases were printed and distributed to reporters by Villa's agents at any number of locations (for example, New York, El Paso, and wherever Villa happened to be fighting). Cables were wired to media outlets either from Villa or in his name (usually from agents in El Paso or New York).

News releases can be distinguished from cables in press reports because they attribute a given piece of information by applying commonly understood markers, such as "Villa said," "said Villa," "Villa claimed," "Villa said in a statement released," or "Villa told reporters." A press release was sometimes referred to as a "proclamation" or "announcement." Direct cables were referred to as such; they were typically boxed and frequently printed on the front page. Publications routinely edited both types of statements.

During the Revolution, the practice of cabling public statements directly to the press began prior to Villa's use of this public relations weapon. Huerta, for example, telegraphed the *Denver Post* just days after Madero's death to assure the publication that all was well in Mexico and that "through moderate councils" peace would shortly prevail.[48] Villa's press release "news," meanwhile, had been reported by large American daily newspapers since as early as late July 1913.[49]

Villista press releases tended to be boastful and to highlight elements of excitement and daring. With time, these elements would become more pronounced. The *New York Times* provides two good examples of the use of Villa press releases. One report noted: "Two Federal troop trains, en route from Chihuahua to Juarez, were blown up at Rancheria, sixty-six miles south of Juarez, this afternoon by dynamite mines placed along the railroad track by the rebels. This was the statement given out tonight by Gen. Francisco Villa."[50] The second example observed: "Gen. Francisco Villa, the commander of the rebel forces, to-night [*sic*] sent the following telegram to Col. Juan N. Medina, his chief of staff in Juarez: 'I communicate with satisfaction that we have completely routed the enemy. We took all his artillery and three trains. The Federals are in full and disgraceful retreat.'"[51] From November 1913 on, press releases became standard issue to reporters.

Villistas who were not necessarily press agents as such also sometimes promoted the general and his policies. A good early example can be found in the *New York Times*. In late November 1913 it quoted at length an American officer in Villa's army who had formerly been city chemist and bacteriologist in El Paso. The passage condenses Villa's deferential, pro–United States foreign policy stance into one short, compelling narrative:

> It was about 7:30 o'clock when I crossed the bridge [from El Paso to Ciudad Juárez]. Villa was then about to move against the 120 federal volunteers who had taken a position back of the concrete grand stand at the race track. I thought he might

shell the place, and this would have ruined a lot of American property, have killed the 300 horses stabled there, and undoubtedly would have been pretty serious for the Americans who were looking after them. I sent a friend to interview Villa, and the latter said that the only way to get the Federals out was to shell the grandstand. When it was pointed out what might be the other results, he decided to enfilade both sides of the track with machine guns. In the fight that ensued, Villa lost fourteen men. Had he shelled the place as he originally intended, he would have got off without the loss of a man. . . . The one American killed in Juarez during the fight was the driver of a public automobile. . . . Villa sent $500 to the widow and gave his guarantee that when the Constitutionalists got in she would get damages.[52]

Probably the most effective propaganda tool Villa had at his disposal was the personal interview, which he enjoyed. He liked reporters, and without exception he made strong (though not always favorable) impressions on those who sought to capture his image in print.[53] He radiated charisma.[54] Frequently, the results of an interview appeared as direct, hyperbolic quotations.

And Villa's quoted utterings, if limited somewhat by editor and reporter selectivity, tended to be loosely framed and presented as strictly factual. The *New York Times* inserted the following direct quotation into the middle of a story headlined "Villa to Attack Chihuahua": "'I will leave to attack Chihuahua just as soon as I can get my trains loaded with provisions and my troops, which will probably be tomorrow night.'"[55] This passage suggests that Villa was, one, organized, two, well-equipped, three, forthright, and four, confident. Over time, quoting Villa—with his charged, dramatic, and sometimes stentorian voice—became increasingly common in the press, although it remains unclear whether the increased frequency reflected Villa's becoming more quotable, his increased popularity, or both.

Even publications bitterly opposed to Villa cited him at length, often in ways that controverted their positi‿n(s) on him. For example, the *Los Angeles Times* quoted Villa in late November 1913:

> "I have left my army twelve miles outside the city [Juárez] so that I can give protection to families living here and across the river [in the United States]. After a battle fought along these lines only the victor will enter Juarez. . . . On the result of the battle that may be fought soon below here rests, to a great extent, the fate of the revolution in Chihuahua. If the Federals win they will have to fight us again, but if we win," and here Villa's eyes sparkled, "we will leave them in such shape that they will not be able to recuperate."[56]

Curiously, the *San Francisco Examiner*, another publication hostile to the Revolution, reported almost verbatim the same tale—with an interesting addition. After the second sentence the *Examiner* inserted the words, "If the Federals enter Juarez it will only be over my dead body."[57] It is unclear from the two reports which quotation is the more accurate. But it is worth noting that although both papers expressed strong misgivings about the Revolution, in time they also lauded Villa's forceful style of leadership.

In either version, the propagandistic value of the passage is subtle but pronounced. Villa is in charge ("I have left my army . . . so that I can give . . . "), optimistic ("but if we win, we will leave them in such shape . . . "), organized ("I have left my army twelve miles outside . . . After a battle fought along these lines . . . "), charming (his eyes "sparkled"), and indefatigable ("If the Federals win they will have to fight us again"). The *Examiner*'s version throws a measure of bravura into the mix ("over my dead body"). In any event, the key features of the personal interview—intimacy and the general's charisma—again afforded Villa the opportunity to speak directly to a reading public (if under the restraints of editorial selectivity and alteration) and the opportunity to charm favorable coverage from even a hostile publication.

Villa's propaganda to the American press climbed a notch in sophistication in early 1914. Although an initial pattern had been established—the charged news release, the hyperbolic public pronouncement, the dramatic personal interview—Villa's primary foreign policy message of friendship blossomed in the new year. Villa proclaimed friendship with the United States seemingly at every turn. To prove it, he expressed a willingness to do whatever he could to protect American interests, including adherence to an American code of conduct for warfare. Further, he decried dictatorship, championed democracy, and discounted any personal ambition for political office.

A *New York Times* report quoted from a press release in late January 1914:

> "I never will be President of Mexico," said Gen. Villa. "I never went to school a day in my life, and I am not educated enough for the post. My alphabet has been the sight and trigger of a rifle; my books have been the movements of the enemy. . . . We wish our friends in the United States would help us, because we are your friends," said Gen. Villa. "You have the greatest Government on earth and your President is the best. . . . Please tell your countrymen I know I am not competent to hold high office because of my lack of education, and that I can fight only for the liberation of my people."[58]

This passage, which also appeared in the *Los Angeles Times*,[59] touches on many of the features of Villa's effort to promote himself. He is alternately humble and friendly ("I am not competent . . . We wish our friends in the United States would help us"), humble and honest ("I will never be president . . . I am not educated enough"), flattering and hyperbolic ("You have the greatest Government on earth and your President is the best"), and noble and hardworking ("I can fight only for the liberation of my people").

The same *New York Times* article also noted an announcement by Villa that he intended to adopt the rules of a booklet supplied to him by the American general Hugh Scott titled "The Ethics of International Warfare." Villa took this step to counter repeated criticisms in the press that his treatment of prisoners of war violated international standards of conduct.[60]

Ideologically, Villa's statements frequently cast him as an altruistic republican. He told a *Chicago Tribune* reporter: "'I wish all the nations of the world to know that I am not fighting to make myself president'—and here Gen. Villa clenched his fists by way of emphasis. 'We are not fighting to make any man president, but we hope once and for all to save our country from spoliation and the ambitions of individuals. We are spreading the ideal of a republic.'"[61] A "republic," yes—but one draped in modesty ("I am not fighting to make myself president"), determination ("here Gen. Villa clenched his fists"), and social justice ("to save our country from . . . ").

Villa's expressed friendship toward the United States extended so far as his publicly inviting any interested American to witness the execution of the bandit Máximo Castillo, who had been charged with responsibility for a train explosion that killed a score of Americans. The *Los Angeles Times* recorded Villa's statement: "'Every American and every Mexican will be invited to attend the execution,' said he. 'I feel a great responsibility in this awful disaster because I had given the Americans my promise that they would be protected.'"[62] If the invitation was slightly macabre, Villa's self-portrayal nevertheless clearly highlights friendship, vengeful justice, and sense of responsibility. Citing the same report, the *Chicago Tribune* quoted Villa as wanting to "vindicate" himself.[63]

Villa's public statements often expressed outrage when he felt American interests had been violated or maligned. For example, he thundered to the *San Francisco Examiner* about the Huerta-

backed Científico "yellow" press in Mexico, which routinely and
unfairly attacked Americans:

> They referred to Americans in the vilest of terms, said the
> most loathsome and disgusting things about American
> women, and through their lying sheets blamed the American
> people and the American Government for all the misery and
> suffering in Mexico. I look upon the American people as the
> most civilized in the world. I have always found them just
> and fair in their dealings. . . . The nearest thing to my heart is
> schools. I want to see that every child of the coming genera-
> tion gets an education.[64]

The common theme again is friendship, animated by the spirit of
vengeance and candied in the humble desire to uplift the downtrodden by educating "every child."

In early 1914 Villa began liberally to employ the direct cable as
well as the news release. For example, after Wilson lifted the arms
embargo in early February, Villa wired the *New York Times* in a
message reeking of friendliness: "Raising the embargo on arms is
an act of justice on the part of the American government toward
the people of Mexico, and signifies the prompt pacification of the
Republic. Within three months the war will have ended."[65] Here
Villa again engages in the language of friendship—flattery ("an act
of justice . . . ") and personal modesty ("toward the people of
Mexico . . . ")—and he garnishes it all with a boast ("Within three
months the war will have ended").[66]

Villa elaborated on these comments in a cable to Hearst's
International News Service. The *San Francisco Examiner* quoted
him: "I fully appreciate what the American Government has done
for my country by President Wilson's action of to-day and that
action has done much to establish friendship between the Mexican
people and the people of the United States, which on my part I
appreciate to the fullest and hope to be able to give abundant

evidence of my appreciation in a material way in the very near future."[67] Again, the theme is friendship. And Villa promises to deliver a "material" quid pro quo for the action taken to lift the arms embargo.

On the same day, the *Chicago Tribune* added to the *Examiner's* report. It observed: "'In this connection,' Gen. Villa said, 'let me say that Americans may have no fear. I regard the high dignity with which Americans have conducted themselves during the revolution as a friendly act toward our cause. I feel the deepest friendship toward the United States. All American property will be protected.'"[68] Clearly, by the winter of 1914, Villa had made a case through the media for his "friendship" with the United States.

IN THE MOVIES

Over the winter of 1914, prior to the Benton affair, Villa pulled one more propaganda ace from his sleeve. He signed on, as the *New York Times* put it, "To War for 'Movies.'" For twenty-five thousand dollars,[69] Villa, through his lawyer Gunther Lessing, struck a deal with the Mutual Film Corporation of New York to cooperate in the filming of scenes depicting his efforts to rid Mexico of Huerta.[70] Mutual shot film during the fighting at Ojinaga (early January 1914), Gómez Palacio (early March 1914), and Torreón (late March 1914).[71]

Mutual's plans called for newsreel footage of the fighting to be released in Mexico, the United States, and Canada on a weekly basis until Huerta fell.[72] Mutual also sold still frames taken from its film to newspapers for reproduction. The stills showed up in the *New York World*, the *New York Sun, Metropolitan* magazine, the *San Antonio Express,* and other publications.[73] Additionally, Mutual Film planned to shoot a feature-length film about Villa, with Villa playing himself. Profits were to be divided evenly.[74]

Villa reportedly went so far as to delay an attack on Ojinaga in order for cameramen to arrive and film the assault, and he agreed to fight during daylight hours—a practice he had formerly eschewed for tactical reasons.[75] Further, if the photographers proved unable to capture good footage, Villa reportedly agreed to stage a mock battle for the benefit of Mutual Film cameras.[76]

A first screening of uncut footage took place on January 22, 1914, before a private New York audience that included Francisco Madero's father and son.[77] Using this and other footage, much of it shot by Mutual's chief cameraman, Herbert Dean,[78] the American director William Christy Cabanne produced a film titled "The Life of Villa," which aired publicly on May 9, 1914, at New York's Lyric Theater.[79]

Mutual Film additionally contributed to Villa's propaganda by advertising the film in newspapers. A flyer proclaimed: "Newspapers throughout the world are printing pages of matter about this war—and the amazing contract of the Mutual Film Corporation with Gen. Villa. The public is clamoring for a sight of the pictures—which are far more exciting and sensational than any pictures of actual happenings that have ever been shown before."[80] In a sort of back-handed publicity promotion, Harry Aitken, president of Mutual Film, also reported in the press: "I found him [Villa] a very different man from the uncouth bandit he has been painted in this country. He is a serious dignified man who conducts the affairs of his army in a systematic and orderly manner, which would do credit to a much older and experienced military man."[81]

Villa never fully gained the expected propaganda rewards from his association with Mutual Film. The films were not widely distributed. Much of the problem stemmed from the unworkable premise of the venture: Mutual claimed exclusive filmic rights, but the cameras of other newsreel enterprises went right on filming the revolutionaries in action and distributing the product to movie houses around the world.[82] Newsreel footage of the Revolution abounded in the United States, and some of it included scenes with Villa from as early as 1913.[83] On the other hand, to the extent that the films received even limited screening, they served a useful propaganda end. Further, the Villa-Mutual relationship itself became a newsworthy topic, as the *New York Times*'s coverage of the story exemplified.

In mid-July, Villa declined an offer from A. E. Wallace, a newsreel director for Hearst's International News Service,[84] to film Villa and his forces in battle. Villa's refusal may have been wise, because, as a State Department official not improbably alleged, "Hearst's intention was to get the most sensational pictures possible in order to use them to influence public opinion in the [United] [S]tates to further the Hearst anti-administration [Wilson] and [pro-]intervention campaign."[85]

Villa's association with Mutual Film, meanwhile, proved to be a turning point in the evolution of his promotion of a media image. At Mutual's insistence, after the filming at Ojinaga in early January 1914, Villa shed everyday clothing—to which he never returned as a soldier—in favor of military-style uniforms, in an effort to appear more professional. The historian Aurelio de los Reyes claims that the first Mutual films represented a propagandistic miscarriage for Villa because the lack of uniformed soldiery suggested an ad hoc, unprofessional approach to fighting that made a poor impression on American viewers.[86] The *New York Times* reported that Villa had been reluctant to change his wardrobe but became convinced when a Mutual executive explained "that moving picture lovers would think it strange and suspicious if they saw none of the trappings of glorious war on the man who purported to be the leader of a revolution."[87]

This sartorial transformation represented one of the final maneuvers in consolidating the Villa-propagandized media image. The construction he now presented to the public had become more fully a conscious production that included a package (self-reliant, rugged, uniformed warrior), a content (friendship at any cost), and a pitch (honesty, virtue, courage, love of democracy, and fatuous praise of the United States and Wilson). To the day of Wilson's recognition of Carranza in October 1915, Villa promoted this depiction. Indeed, with time, the Villa public-relations rhetoric became increasingly obsequious toward American interests.

By early 1914, on the eve of Benton's death, Villa's propaganda machine had proved successful at promoting his foreign policy friendship message in American publications, and his propaganda efforts with Mutual Film appeared poised to strike the same message on American cinema screens. The messages, often presented in Villa's own voice, clearly addressed the building blocks of his foreign policy image. They stressed the ideals of friendship and social justice, and they depicted the protection of American interests as vital, all of which served to champion Villa's self-interest as congruent with that of the United States. They also stressed modesty, personal courage, humility, honesty, and sense of responsibility—all of which served to promote Villa's self-styled morality in an alluring way. In short, Villa, through press releases, direct cables, personal interviews, and the assistance of the Mutual Film Corporation, portrayed the elements of his foreign policy in a light warmly favorable to himself, and in shades of his own coloring.

ASSASSINATING BENTON'S CORPSE

American newspapers splashed the news of Benton's death all over the front pages. The papers framed Villa as menacing, hyper-aggressive, bloodlusting, and out of control. Villa responded quickly to control the propaganda damage that such negative casting of the affair threatened. He also received help from Carranza's camp. The effective Constitutionalist propaganda strategy was threefold: to defend Villa's actions as just and reasonable, to so thoroughly discredit Benton that his death might seem to have been a good thing, and to defuse international concern by appointing an official board of inquiry to investigate the killing.

A Villa wire to the *New York Times*, printed in both Spanish and English, captured the basic Villa defense. In it Villa noted: "A court-martial sentenced Benton to death with complete justification, due to his crimes in having made an attempt on my life, as I am able to prove."[88] In other words, Villa had killed Benton in self-defense.

Carranza's Washington agent, Robert V. Pesqueira, argued that international codes on the conduct of war exonerated Villa. He also embellished the claim, as quoted by the *San Francisco Examiner* and the *Los Angeles Times:* "There is absolutely no doubt that Benton, a Huertista sympathizer and murderer of Mexican citizens, deliberately attempted an act of violence against the person and life of the commanding general, and for that reason, in accordance with laws and usages of war, he was tried by a military tribunal, constituted for that purpose, and executed pursuant to its sentence, a proceeding sustained by European and American precedents."[89]

The assertion of a military trial was bold but impossible to disprove. In a statement reported by the *San Francisco Examiner*, Villa agent and lawyer Federico González Garza reiterated the point: "Benton's case was tried before a military court . . . and he was found guilty of drawing a pistol, provoking the general and insulting him."[90]

Carranza's propagandists, motivated by the First Chief's jealous insistence that no foreign interference in Mexican affairs would be allowed on his watch,[91] sought to assist Villa and to defuse the issue by assassinating Benton's character. Pesqueira fired off a news release that claimed Benton was generally "bad," that he was not in fact a British subject, that his behavior had always been reprehensible, and that he had "mistreated peons on his ranch even to the point of taking their lives."[92] A copy of Villa's cable to Pesqueira was released to the press, too, in which Villa noted that "in addition to the many crimes committed by this man . . . he tried to assassinate me. . . . I managed to disarm him, and I still have the loaded revolver in my possession."[93]

Another cable, from Carrancista agent Luis Cabrera to Pesqueira, circulated in the press. It condemned the Briton: "Benton had nothing in his own right. He managed to marry into a well-known Mexican family, and in this way acquired an interest in the Rosaria ranch, the title to which has long been a matter of dispute. . . . Benton's record throughout Chihuahua is very bad, and his disposition was quarrelsome and offensive to a degree. He was a loud partisan of Porfirio Diaz and openly boasted of his approval of Huerta."[94] In short, not only was Villa justified, according to Cabrera, but Benton's death—under nearly any circumstances, he implied—might have been well deserved.

The establishment of Carranza's official board of inquiry to examine and assess the circumstances leading up to Benton's death also served to defuse the furor generated by the killing. As Cabrera noted to Pesqueira, "we need to convince the press and Washington that the commission appointed is quite reliable and means serious investigation not merely working proper shielding [sic] such appointment was made to avoid irregular intrusive investigation contemplated by foreign commission."[95] Not surprisingly, the commission issued a lengthy report completely exonerating Villa of any wrongdoing.[96]

Still, the Benton case raised questions in the American press about Villa's conduct. Villa responded energetically. For example, in another cable to the *New York Times* he found it necessary to deny that he had killed other foreigners: "It is absolutely false that any foreigner has been put to death except Benton, who was tried and sentenced to death because he made an attempt on my life."[97] Isidro Fabela, Carranza's secretary of foreign relations, also wired the *Times* in defense of Villa. In part his cable noted: "Benton tried to assassinate Gen. Francisco Villa at Ciudad Juarez, but, owing to the energy with which Gen. Villa acted, he was able to disarm him himself. . . . Besides this, he [Benton] committed other crimes previously. He was punished, not by Gen. Villa, but by the law."[98]

Fortunately for Villa, in a matter of several weeks the press furor abated in the United States. In the absence of any evidence to the contrary, Villa's word—spoken from many Constitutionalist promoters' mouths—was presented in the press at face value. And Villa may well have savored the propaganda victory. After all, the lies (that Benton had been tried), the disclaimers (that Benton had drawn on Villa), the boasts (that Villa had heroically disarmed Benton), and some of the invective heaped on Benton's character (he was "bad," which was never substantiated) had served a useful propaganda end. Villa had wriggled free of what initially appeared to be an intractable position. Moreover, the drawn-out military campaign, widely reported in the American press and culminating in the second taking of Torreón in early April 1914, drew media attention away from the Benton case.

FULL PRESS AT TORREÓN

Villa ably put the propaganda lessons of the Benton affair to work in the three-week-long showdown for the recapture of Torreón. Among other things, he more frequently employed the direct cable—which, though filtered through editorial decision-making, allowed speedy communication with a reading audience—and he used it to boast heartily of Torreón's imminent fall. The city's federal contingent capitulated on April 2, 1914, a surrender Villa had been boasting of as immediate for several weeks. His intent, which met with success, was to demoralize the federal troops.[99] He wired the *San Francisco Examiner* on March 20: "In fewer than three days Torreón will have fallen into our power and my following movements will be according to circumstances."[100] The Associated Press reported a Villa dispatch claiming that victory was not days but minutes away—fully four days before the city fell.[101] To belie this deception, he barred reporters from the front— as he had done before at Ojinaga in January 1914[102] and as he would do elsewhere that April[103] and June[104]—lest they reveal the falsity of his claims.[105]

Villa also employed strict censorship over the wires during his second Torreón campaign.[106] According to the historian Larry D. Hill, he also limited Carothers's dispatches to brief accounts lest the State Department, by publicly releasing the content of Carothers's cables, unwittingly undermine the intended demoralizing effect of Villista propaganda.[107] He denied reporters access to the telegraph until April 9.[108] "Not one word could be sent out," Associated Press correspondent Timothy Turner recalled. "The Villistas promised us facilities when the battle was over, but not before."[109] In an amusing anecdote, Turner recounted that the military censor, Major Santos Coy, was a drunkard, and reporters might easily have stolen dispatches past him once his inebriation gave way to slumber. Indeed, Turner had to flee for his life in a hail of bullets after being accused of sneaking information past the censor.[110]

By early 1914, Villa's propaganda had capably packaged him as a determined and resourceful warrior. The promotion and dissemination of such a framing continued with dogged perseverance through the Benton period and beyond. By the end of April 1914, Villa had added another weapon to his propaganda arsenal—his own propaganda organ in Mexico—and he redoubled efforts in the American press to highlight the pith of his "friendship" policy.

VERACRUZ AND *VIDA NUEVA*

It is a commonplace among scholars that Villa used the American seizure of Veracruz to considerable propaganda advantage.[111] Villa's multiple statements to the press, to special agent Carothers, to Secretary Bryan, and to President Wilson were designed to promote friendship. As the historian Alan Knight has noted, after the occupation began, "Villa took steps to cultivate a favorable image in the American press, and was solicitous for American interests within his domain."[112] Villa couched his friendship in terms of the righteousness of just revenge, sober responsibility, awed respect for the United States, and scorn for Huerta and dictatorship.

In an interview with a *New York Times* reporter, Villa remarked on the subject of the American seizure of Veracruz:

> No me molestería. . . . It is Huerta's ox that is being gored, and I am not worried about the outcome. I know Huerta as cowardly, and I do not think he will dare to defy the United States. As I see it from this distance, it is a matter between Huerta the traitor, and Wilson, the great President of the American people. . . . I believe that right will triumph. . . . We have offered American and other foreign property all the protection possible under war-time conditions. . . . Should the act of a drunkard and murderer be construed as an act of war and should war result, I can assure all Americans living within the bounds of the Constitutionalist territory that they will be protected, for such a war would be with a civilized nation, and the rules that were given to me by my good friend Gen. Scott will be observed by me.[113]

Additional Villa comments reported in the *San Francisco Examiner* colorfully punctuated the Times's note. The *Examiner* quoted Villa this way: "'Honest,' said the rebel general, between mouthfuls, 'I hope the Americans bottle up Vera Cruz so tight they can't even get water into it.'"[114]

Days later, the *Chicago Tribune* printed a Villa statement issued for general release:

> "We do not want a war with the United States," he said, "or with any other foreign nation. Mexico has troubles of its own,

and can settle them if it is given a little time. Personally I believe they are on the point of settlement now. I came to Juarez to meet with my good American friends; to extend to them a hand of friendship and to thank them for the great interest they have taken in the efforts . . . to restore peace to my country. . . . You may rest assured I will do all in my power to see that there is no change in our relationship. Why," he smiled, as he threw an arm about the broad shoulders of the government representative [Carothers], "all Europe would laugh at us if we went to war with you. They would say that 'Little drunkard, Huerta, has drawn them into a tangle at last.' Why does the United States want to pay any attention to that old drunken ass, anyway?"[115]

The promotion of Villa's foreign policy in the United States media ran on several tracks prior to the breakdown in relations with Carranza. At the outset, agents in the field promoted Villa. At the same time, during the period when he mouthed Constitution-alist loyalties, Villa also gained from the propaganda spread by Carranza's agents, as was shown by the Benton affair. In a general public-relations sense, then, prior to the autumn 1914 rupture in relations, what was good for Carranza and the Constitutionalists in the United States proved to be good for Villa. The same held true in Mexico, although the establishment of Villa's own propaganda newspaper, *Vida Nueva*, predated the official Villa-Carranza rupture by five months.

Censorship and ownership of publications by politicians was traditional and widespread in Mexico when Villa established *Vida Nueva* in April 1914.[116] The publication's full title—*Vida Nueva: Diario Político y de Información, Documentos para la Historia de la Revolución Constitucionalista: Periódico Official de Chihuahua*—implied Constitutionalist control, but the paper was firmly Villista. Funding came directly through the offices of the government of the state of Chihuahua, which Villa controlled.[117]

Vida Nueva was not the only newspaper Villa funded after his break with Carranza, but it was unique in that it was organized and run by Villistas specifically for the promotion of Villismo.[118] In Mexico, *El Combate*, published at Aguascalientes, and *El Monitor* of Mexico City reflected Villista sympathies, as *La Convención* of Aguascalientes[119] sometimes did.[120] In the United States, in addition to the *El Paso Times*, Villa allegedly funded seven other newspapers in Texas, from among which San Antonio's *La Prensa* stood out for the boldness of its pro-Villa rhetoric.[121]

Even before the Villa-Carranza rupture, Villa considered *Vida Nueva* as "our newspaper," designed to "offset Carranza's propaganda," according to one of his biographers.[122] On the day of its first issue, a front-page editorial read: "*Vida Nueva* promotes a new life for the nation, in these transcendent moments in which the people wage a moral struggle to conquer their enemies."[123] Manuel Bauche Alcalde, the publication's first editor, asserted that *Vida Nueva* could be instrumental in combating rival propaganda.[124] For example, the organ regularly published Villa's pronouncements—such as his disavowing of Carranza's leadership on September 23, 1914.[125] It also printed bald lies—such as a charge that Obregón had disavowed the leadership of Carranza in mid-June 1915.[126] Not surprisingly, Villa also used the paper to attack Huerta (and, after its recognition of Carranza, the United States).[127] In time, *Vida Nueva* portrayals reduced Carranza to the status of pirate,[128] revolutionary impostor,[129] and rebel/traitor.[130] They ultimately referred to him as the ex–First Chief.[131] A front-page editorial cartoon from March 1915 cleverly portrayed Carranza as an ass (fig. 1).

Villa established *Vida Nueva* with a seventy-thousand-peso grant,[132] and in 1914 the publication's average monthly costs totaled twenty-eight hundred pesos.[133] The paper claimed a readership of forty thousand in April 1915.[134] The initial issues tended simply to glorify Villa and attack Huerta, echoing the content of Villa's propaganda in the United States.[135] For example,

Figure 1. "Caricatura ingeniosa." Reproduced from *Vida Nueva*, March 11, 1915.

the paper's presentation of Villa's stand on Veracruz suggests a well-choreographed similarity with his statements reported in the American press. This is somewhat surprising. After all, one might expect the Mexican-nationalism component of his propaganda, which operated on a secondary track in the United States, to have received greater emphasis in Mexico. But with one exception it did not gain such treatment in *Vida Nueva*. On the matter of the Veracruz occupation, Villa noted in the organ that, first, he did not believe the occupation constituted an act of war against Mexico; second, all Americans would be protected in the event that the Huerta-Wilson standoff escalated into a wider conflict; and third, the occupation was a matter to be resolved between Huerta and Wilson.[136]

Vida Nueva did, however, publish an article headlined "The Intervention Is Unjustified."[137] It rationalized Villa's support for the occupation by reiterating his general assertion that the matter had been brought on not by American jingoism but by Huerta's folly. Villa expressed similar sentiments to Obregón in September 1914.

Vida Nueva expressed predominantly pro-American sentiments through 1914 and 1915, right up until Carranza received recognition. By the autumn of 1914, it began to heap scorn upon Carranza. In short, it echoed Villista propaganda in the United States.

CARRANZA AS OTHER

As Villa's relations with Carranza deteriorated over the spring and summer of 1914—in the press, ultimately, to the level of a street-fight—Villa employed a media strategy against Carranza similar to the one he used versus Huerta. First, Villista propagandists issued inexorably positive characterizations of Villa so that Carranza might pale in comparison (and he did; see chapter 6). Next, they insistently portrayed Carranza as Other—as embodying traits opposite to the hale virtues personified by Villa. If the two were opposites, the reasoning behind this construction held, then if Villa was America's friend, Carranza could not be.

When relations between the two leaders broke down irrevocably in the fall, diplomatic recognition became Villa's ultimate foreign policy aspiration. To win it, from a public relations perspective it made good sense to attempt to portray Carranza as the reverse of Villa—not just as unfriendly but as dishonest, immodest, immoral, and dictatorial.

Villista publicist John Roberts captured this sentiment precisely in a report published by the *San Francisco Examiner* just days after Villa's public disavowal of Carranza. He quoted Villa as saying:

> I don't want anymore war or bloodshed. I want peace, but Carranza does not seem to want it that way. I regret that affairs have so shaped themselves and have taken the only course left open to me. . . . Carranza has proved himself to be a liar and a despot. I have lost all patience with him. In the first place he repudiated his promise to the people of Mexico. . . . Mexico must have peace. We all want peace, except possibly Carranza, the imbecile.[138]

Villa's Chicago representative, E. A. Navarro, also released a statement to the press that stressed the common anti-Carranza themes of dictatorship, anti-democracy, selfishness, greed, and unmitigated ambition:

> The so-called carrancista faction, which has taken refuge at Vera Cruz, is led by a man who tried to impose a new dictatorship upon the Mexican people, refusing to abide by the decisions of the National Convention . . . [which] has the support of NINETY FIVE per cent of the Mexican people. . . . Such a rebellious action has made him an outlaw before the eyes of the people. . . . Carranza became a TRAITOR and threw

away the mask of democracy which had been concealing his selfishness and greed up to that moment.[139]

Even Carranza's own propaganda noted the Villa message. A Carrancista press release complained: "One of the most powerful forms of this work [Villa's propaganda] was spreading the idea in political circles and in the press and public opinion that Carranza was an enemy of the country as well as of impossible personal character." It added: "The principal incidents which helped to serve in spreading this false idea were the . . . Benton incident . . . [and] the Carranza protest against the occupation of Veracruz."[140]

Villa spent freely to gain his objectives. In May 1914, the Carrancista consul in Galveston, Juan T. Burns, insinuated that Villa had bribed the *Galveston News*.[141] By mid-August he was allegedly spending thirty thousand pesos on propaganda in New York alone (which the Carrancistas hoped to match).[142] At about the same time, in a note to Carranza, Manuel Carbajal noted "seditious" Villismo propaganda aimed at undermining the Constitutionalist banner.[143]

Prior to the Villa-Carranza rupture, Villa refrained from attacking Carranza directly in the American press. Yet he clearly alluded to Carranza in disparaging terms when he spelled out to the *New York Times* the moral reasoning behind his revolutionary position:

> Say for me that I have no personal feelings for or against Carranza. My interest is in the country and my people. I have shown this by allowing others the benefits for which I have fought. My position is that this country shall not be under a military regime again. . . . Read our Constitution and you will find that the army is second to the Constitution. . . . There has been too much personal politics. . . . Let the people rule. . . . There need be no fear because of me. I am simply representing the people who have never been represented before. . . . I desire morality.[144]

The concerted propaganda effort against Carranza began with Villa's public denunciation of the First Chief on September 23, 1914. His declaration was reported widely in the United States press: "In view of the attitude of Venustiano Carranza, which has been the cause of great injuries to our country and since he could never govern a republic nor make happy a country which aspires to a real democracy, a country which wants to have a government emanating from the people subject to an interpretation of the national feelings, we have been obliged to renounce him. . . . We are not in favor of personalism, but we are defenders of principles."[145]

The anti-Carranza campaign gathered steam as the two camps squabbled through the Convention of Aguascalientes in October. It again spilled into the open in November when a Convention government was established, an arrangement to which Carranza refused to agree. Villa's propaganda sketched clear battle lines: Carranza threatened Mexico with tyranny and despotism while Villa offered democracy and freedom.[146] As a result, the logic ran, Villa sought Carranza's ouster, in favor of, hyperbolically, almost anyone else.[147] Further, Villa championed democratic elections while downplaying his own ambitions as anything other than bringing peace to Mexico without, if possible, further bloodshed.[148]

In December 1914, as Villa prepared to co-occupy Mexico City with the Morelense revolutionary Emiliano Zapata, he also maintained strict censorship over cables emanating from the capital region.[149] At about the same time, from Gaston Schmurtz, the United States consul at Aguascalientes, came a report: "No newspapers have been allowed here from Mexico City for the past four days, presumably because they are favorable to Carranza."[150] And the Villa agitator and Mexican lawyer Roque González Garza expressed satisfaction with the results of the anti-Carranza media campaign. "These declarations have caused a very good effect," he wrote.[151]

With the dawning of 1915, the anti-Carranza element of Villa's propaganda began to take a backseat to the more standard Villa message of effusive praise for things American. The cause behind this shift remains uncertain, though it may have stemmed from three sources. First, Villa may have believed, as the American press seemed to, that Carranza was largely a spent force. Second, the American press's premature conclusion that Villa was the winner and Carranza the loser may have prompted editorial decisions that downplayed the anti-Carranza element of Villista propaganda. Third, Villa may have redirected the focus of his propaganda to offset potential American hostility toward his "taking charge" of the presidency. The *New York Times* printed a good example of the new propaganda emphasis in mid-January:

> Before I leave the border for the battle line I wish to say just one thing to the American press. . . . That one parting message is that as long as I have anything to do with the affairs in Mexico there will be no further friction between my country and my friends' country of the North. . . . To President Wilson, the greatest American, I stand pledged to do what I can to keep the faith he has in my people, and if there is anything he may wish I will gladly do it, for I know it will be for the good of my country.[152]

When Villa officially claimed a share of the leadership of Mexico on January 31, 1915, and declared himself "in charge" of the presidency, his explanatory rhetoric was carefully tailored to suit his long-standing outspoken opposition to dictatorship (though he governed as a dictator). He would rule, he claimed, as a caretaker of sorts, "in charge" of the presidency but not president.[153] One of his public statements read:

> On account of communications having been cut between the Convention Government and the division under my command, and as public service cannot be interrupted in the extensive zone which I control, I have found myself compelled to assume the political authority, creating three administrative

departments: The Foreign Affairs and Justice Department in charge of Attorney M. Diaz Lombardo; State and Communications, Don Luis de la Garza Cardenas; Treasury and Industry, Attorney Francisco Escudero.[154]

This statement clearly meant to suggest that altruistic motives inspired the measure ("I have found myself compelled . . . "). Villa implied that the assumption of authority—he was careful not to claim the presidency itself—was to be temporary ("communications having been cut . . . "). In the meantime, well-reasoned organization and the rule of law would prevail ("public service cannot be interrupted . . . creating three departments . . . ").[155] Censorship, too, was again strictly enforced behind Villista lines.[156]

As a positive omen, peace and prosperity reigned where Villa governed "temporarily," according to the Chicago agent, Navarro: "I would call attention to the reign of peace and prosperity initiated all over the territory controlled by the provisional government of Mexico with Gen. Villa as its temporary head, while in the small sections controlled by the Carranzistas there is nothing but anarchy, hunger, and riots, and the stubbornness of their chief, Carranza, is causing everlasting trouble to the American government and all foreigners."[157]

Villa's expressions of Mexican nationalism, in addition to trying to sell his dictatorship as temporary (and somehow democratic), again leaked through his pro-American rhetoric. Villa had been asked about reports that he would support American intervention if he were made "commander of such a move."[158] Villa refuted the allegation and told the Associated Press that he would join even with his Mexican enemies to forge a common front to combat any foreign aggressors.[159]

On another occasion he noted to the *Chicago Tribune:* "I manifest that my desires have always been that the Mexican people arrange all their troubles by themselves." Yet with the same breath he reaffirmed his support for the American occupation of Veracruz, although couching it in more practical terms than simple pro-Americanism. He advocated "that the American forces do not depart from the port of Veracruz, thus leaving it to the Carranza forces."[160] Villa's fortunes flagged steadily and swiftly after the losses at Celaya in April 1915, but his propaganda labored to disguise it. Still, evidence of a weakened Villa on the defensive can be read between the lines. Although over the winter of 1915 Villa invariably claimed victory in any and all engagements, his proclamations that he had routed Obregón at Celaya had an uncharacteristically muted ring. Under the auspices of the "Mexican Conventionist Agency," Villa reported: "The fighting at Celaya is progressing favorably to us. The enemy had tried to break the circle I have around him, but has failed in every effort. The decisive battle is not fought yet. News from Carranza about Obregon victory untrue."[161]

In an outright lie, days later Villa reported: "The recent engagements with General Alvaro Obregón's column at Celaya have resulted disastrously for the enemy who have suffered enormous losses in killed. . . . The enemy is completely demoralized . . . and the troops in the vicinity of Celaya . . . inform me that Obregón's men are constantly deserting him."[162] In fact the results were quite different: Villa had been crushed and his own troops demoralized.[163]

Villa continued to brag his way through stinging losses during the spring and summer of 1915, and his agents in Washington continued to play up his friendliness toward the United States. The tone bordered increasingly on the obsequious. Llorente announced: "General Villa certainly will give the most serious, attentive and practical consideration to any friendly suggestion reaching him from President Wilson, whose unselfishness of purpose he well understands and fully appreciates."[164] Further, in an effort to shore up support along the border, Villa secretly funneled ten thousand dollars into the *El Paso Times* in August and chipped in a two-hundred-fifty-dollar-per-week allowance to its Spanish-language edition.[165]

As late as the fortnight before the United States granted Carranza recognition, when Villa was advised of its imminent announcement, he mouthed a favorable view of the United States. The *Chicago Tribune* reported:

> "The war is just beginning," said Gen. Francisco Villa, with a broad grin upon receiving from his representatives at Washington late today [October 9] the news of the [impending] recognition of the Carranza faction. . . . "My enemies say I have a hoard of money in the banks. I have no money. I have only faith in my cause for which I am fighting. Please tell Americans this. . . . Despite the recognition of the so-called Constitutionalist government, the convention forces will continue as if nothing had happened. Carranza and his government does not represent the poor people."[166]

Even as Villa prepared to enter his most desperate hours, he plied the message of friendship with the United States—cloaked in the polite and humble finery of common-man democracy.

CONCLUSION

Villa's self-promotion in the media predated any strong tie to Carranza. His operatives in the United States championed him actively in the summer of 1913. Moreover, the tone and content of his media rhetoric during the period in which he swore allegiance to Carranza suggest that his loyalty was at best lukewarm and, further, contingent upon Carranza's willingness and ability to strive for the common-man theme Villa espoused. Additionally, the establishing of Villa's own newspaper, *Vida Nueva*, in April 1914, which frequently, if obliquely, challenged and criticized Carrancismo months before the formal rupture in relations, highlighted the fact that Villa's acceptance of Carranza was nominal.

Indeed, *Vida Nueva*'s very existence probably represented a threat to Carranza because it stood as a political counterpoint to strict Constitutionalism.

From the fall of 1913, the key to selling Villa's morality in and through the media rested on portraying him as a virtuous character—humble, honest, self-reliant, clever, friendly, democratic, brave, and fierce. Such qualities dovetailed nicely with a self-interest that was sold as congruent with that of the United States. The elements of morality and self-interest accentuated each other, and Villa's foreign policy pitch clearly suggested that his policy was the morally correct one to follow, especially if it also proved to be compatible with American interests.

Selling Villa and his policy as appealing to United States pragmatism by characterizing him as the inevitable winner rested in part on Villa's continued military success. In quasi-tautological fashion—given that Villa's policy had succeeded in terms of morality and self-interest—his foreign policy succeeded only if he succeeded militarily. And indeed, his mastery on the battlefield through the winter of 1915 continued to earn him goodwill from the Wilson administration, even though his military position declined precipitously in the spring and summer of that year.

For propagandistic ends, Villa charmed and cajoled reporters, funded publications both domestically and in the United States, censored outgoing reports by foreign correspondents, and pitched to the media a foreign policy rhetoric steeped in mythological Americana—self-reliance, personal courage, strength, reliability, and friendship—at almost every turn. Villa also sought to play himself off against the unflattering press depictions he promoted of Huerta and Carranza—to which both Huerta and Carranza responded energetically.

CHAPTER FOUR

MIXED PROPAGANDA REACTIONS

Huerta and Carranza

The story was invented right here in New York.

—Carrancista propaganda on Villa's positive image
in the American press[1]

*It is not true that Torreón fell [to the rebels] and it is not
possible that it might fall.*

—Huerta's minister of foreign relations,
two days before the city fell[2]

*Torreón remains under government control against all
danger.*

—Huerta's minister of foreign relations,
three days after Torreón fell to Villa's forces[3]

Villa's propaganda efforts intensified and complicated the struggle for political supremacy in Mexico. The perceived success of his media manipulation engendered bitterness in, and strenuous propagandistic reactions from, Huertistas and Carrancistas—furthering the proactive public-relations steps they had already taken. Both rival camps felt that Villa had cynically manipulated an

American press that unfairly supported and even promoted his cause. Huertistas and Carrancistas implicated the Wilson administration, too—albeit often imprecisely—in the alleged bid to promote a favorably persuasive Villa image in the press. To Huerta and Carranza, the White House's evident support for Villa seemed to lend direction to Villa's propaganda as well as to be swayed by it. In this chapter I examine first the efforts undertaken by Huerta and then those undertaken by Carranza to engage and defeat Villa on the propaganda battlefield.

HUERTA PROPAGANDA, PART ONE:
THE MEDIUM PROVES NOT TO BE THE MESSAGE

After Madero's death in February 1913, Huerta enacted a media strategy that included most of the elements of Villa's own tactics, with certain qualitative differences. Like Villa, Huerta bullied and censored Mexican publications and American news outlets in Mexico, and he closed down some Mexican publications. He funded and bribed others, both in Mexico and the United States. He also wired American publications directly in an effort to promote his case.[4] And he attempted, though with little success, to charm and coddle American news correspondents.

Controlling Mexico City afforded Huerta the means to intimidate, censor, and shut down opposition newspapers in the capital region to suit his ends—and in time he did, as the rebel threat in the north grew more serious. "Like all effective dictators, Huerta fully appreciated the value of a controlled press," the Huerta scholar Michael Meyer has observed.[5]

Mexico's "largest and most important dailies" generally threw their support behind Huerta. The Mexico City list included the partially subsidized *El Diario*[6] and *El Imparcial*,[7] as well as *El País*,[8] *El Noticioso Mexicana*, the *Mexican Herald*, *El Universal*, *La Nación*, *La Tribuna*, and *El Independiente*.[9] Occasionally, a critical anti-Huerta article appeared even among these publications. In such cases, the secretary of *gobernación* stepped in and replaced the author or editor with a more "obsequious" employee.[10]

In other cities, such as Guadalajara and Veracruz,[11] offending papers' directors were arrested. Still other publications—such as *La Opinión* (Veracruz), *La Unión* (Veracruz), *La Voz de Juárez* (Ciudad Juárez), and *El Dictamen* (Veracruz)—were forced to close their doors.[12] On at least one occasion Huertistas in Veracruz seized copies of the *New York Times* and refused to allow them to circulate.[13] Huerta also funded *El Eco de la Frontera* (Ciudad Juárez–El Paso) and *La Nueva Era* (Nogales) in an attempt to offset Constitutionalist[14] propaganda organs in the United States border region.[15]

Blatant misrepresentation of factual information made up a final element in the management of the pro-Huerta papers. Huertista victories in the field were exaggerated, whereas military setbacks were downplayed or ignored.[16] For example, a United States Navy officer noted that "Guaymas, a federal town, is naturally strongly partisan, and not much reliance can be placed in the war news given by it. Federal defeats are suppressed, victories exaggerated, and operations magnified."[17]

Woodrow Wilson's personal emissary, John Lind, noted Huerta's success in taking American diplomatic efforts aimed at pressing Huerta to withdraw and making them appear to be threats aimed not merely at Huerta but at the whole nation. The effects, Lind claimed, were outpourings of Mexican nationalism—and increased support for Huerta, at least in the capital region.[18] It was precisely this sort of public-relations tactic in Mexico—telling readers what to think, according to Lind—that Huertista propaganda sought to duplicate in the United States.

Huerta stubbornly pursued the construction of a favorable press image north of the border, and he kept a close eye on the sort of coverage he received in the American press.[19] He allegedly bribed

American reporters and editors in 1914 to the tune of four thousand dollars a week to plant false stories.[20] He also attempted to woo the foreign, especially American, press.[21] On one occasion he invited American periodicals to send correspondents to report from and about his regime.[22] He also sought to foster a favorable press image in other foreign capitals, and he kept a close eye on news reports from abroad.[23]

Despite dogged perseverance, Huerta's propaganda efforts in the United States largely failed. Press portrayals of the dictator tended to be unflattering and unforgiving. The *Washington Times*, for example, repeatedly condemned Huerta for his "butchery."[24] The *San Francisco Examiner* blasted Huerta for his lack of respect for the United States.[25] The *Chicago Tribune* presented him as a deplorable drunkard.[26]

With particular vehemence, the American press condemned Huerta for responsibility in the deaths of Madero and his vice president, Pino Suárez, in February 1913. The *Chicago Tribune* denounced him as a "savage,"[27] a "butcher," and a "renegade," labeling him "Judas Iscariot."[28] The *San Francisco Examiner* intoned that under Huerta, "all Mexico is weltering in murder and rapine."[29]

The *Denver Post* accused Huerta and his adherents of committing on Madero before his death "Atrocities that Cannot Be Printed."[30] And the *Post* saw in Huerta's actions evidence for his ultimate demise, because his regime was "beyond the pale of civilization. According to all the rules of international morality th[is] Mexican government is an outlaw."[31]

The press also censured Huerta for his defiance of the United States during the Tampico incident that led to the occupation of Veracruz, behavior that was portrayed as brazen and contemptible.[32] Notably, the *Los Angeles Times* deviated from the media tendency to condemn Huerta. Instead, this daily adamantly supported him, arguing that he had been unfairly maligned.[33]

HUERTA PROPAGANDA, PART TWO:
ENEMY? WHAT ENEMY?

Huertistas identified several sources for the unflattering image the American press cast of Huerta—and Villa was implicated in nearly all of them. Generally, Huertistas were convinced from mid-1913 on that Constitutionalists, and Villa in particular, were largely to blame for the negative media framing Huerta received in the United States.

Part of the Huertistas' problem stemmed from Villa's early seizure of the propaganda initiative. They were forced to play catch-up—and were unsuccessful, though they struggled gamely. In late December 1913, *The Nation* put it this way:

> Huerta's generals have taken a leaf out of the book by Pancho Villa, by enlisting the services of a propagandist. The Constitutionalist commander has always given notice of his strategic moves several days ahead. It is true that he has usually followed up his advance notice by attacking in quite a different place from the one designated and in a manner not outlined in his "release" copy. This is poor newspaper ethics. The efficacy of the method is undeniable, however, and is acknowledged by the other side [the Huertistas].[34]

A certain segment of the American press, Huertistas further believed, simply and without good reason harbored animosity toward Huerta. Consequently, Villa's propaganda in a sense played to a softened audience, already predisposed to support him. Add to this mix, Huertistas complained, Villa's apparent star quality and his willingness to foment anti-Huerta propaganda, and the results easily led to a misrepresentation of the truth, from which Villa emerged lionized and Huerta vilified. In the public-relations arena, then, the Huertista challenge was to overcome Villista propaganda on several fronts.

The Huertistas, however, suffered from two serious handicaps. First, Huerta's image had been effectively hamstrung from the beginning by the murder of President Madero and Vice President Pino Suárez. These political assassinations had sparked public outcry in the American press and prompted Woodrow Wilson to adopt an anti-Huerta policy. Further, in the United States the blame for the Tampico incident and the subsequent U.S. occupation of Veracruz was generally laid at Huerta's feet.[35]

Huertistas struggled gamely against enemy propaganda. Initially, Huertista propaganda tended to lump Villa with the rest of the Constitutionalists. For example, a front-page Huertista letter to the *San Francisco Examiner* in November 1913 simply lamented that Huerta had been "misunderstood." It made no reference to the Constitutionalists, let alone Villa (whose meteoric rise had only begun).[36]

Indeed, the absence of Villa and the Constitutionalists from the letter suggests that Huerta's strategy for dealing with Villa was one of calculated silence. To publicly ignore him represented good public-relations policy because it denied his importance. Villa's military successes over the winter and spring of 1914, however, rendered him impossible to ignore. The Huertistas' alarmed reaction to Villista propaganda waged during Villa's second struggle for Torreón in March and early April 1914 stands as probably their most strenuous and vocal response to any of Villa's propaganda campaigns.

Although internal Huertista correspondence repeatedly complained about the revolutionaries' manipulation of the press through and after Torreón, it seldom mentioned Villa by name. For example, in April 1914 the Huertista official José M. Luján penned a circular saying that "there exist in Veracruz individuals dedicated to making seditious propaganda and producing circulars that malign our good name as well as promoting the supposed victories of the infamous bandits of the Division of the North."[37] Villa here is damned only by association; he is not singled out.

HUERTA PROPAGANDA, PART THREE:
DEFEAT AT TORREÓN

Villa's media strategy for the second Torreón campaign employed censorship, telegraph blackouts, and exaggeration designed to demoralize federal troops. It met with some success (that is, positive assessments in the American media), in part because he ultimately captured the city for the Constitutionalists.

The early boasts, censorship, and blackouts also helped to establish a media frame for the story—Villa as an unstoppable force. This framing proved crucial, because Huertista attempts to counter it became lost in a sea of media pro-Villisms, generated in large part by the success of Villa's propaganda. Moreover, the facts as presented to the press by special agent Carothers, via the State Department, modestly bore out Villa's own reports.[38]

Within days of Villa's first assertions of success (the skirmishing began on March 10, Villa approached the city proper on March 20, and in the American press Villa's scripted exaggerations also arose by March 20), the Huertistas responded with numerous claims that Villa's forward progress had been stymied. But these counterclaims failed to effect a press reframing of the story. Of course Villa still had to deliver the city, but that he did so (the final assault began on March 27, and the city fell on April 2) only made the Huertista reaction sound hollow, bitter, and even groundless.

Villa had taken the propaganda initiative, and front pages across America spilled over with the story of his inexorable advance.[39] His bold claims of success during the prelude to the final assault forced the federal publicists back onto their public-relations heels. For example, Villa wired the *San Francisco Examiner* on March 20: "Within three days Torreon will be within our power and my next move will be according to circumstances."[40]

Forced to respond, Huertistas issued counterclaims of Villista failure that somehow rang untrue, not necessarily because Villa was advancing (although he was) but because his advance was framed by the press as inevitable and inexorable. Although within a week of Villa's first boasts of impending victory at Torreón, American dailies reported Huertista assertions that Villa's advances had been checked, the papers declined to reframe the story to reflect Huertista wishes.[41] Meanwhile, the Huerta-controlled press in Mexico City told only of federal successes, completely (and falsely) recasting the story—the federal forces in fact were slowly being defeated.

Throughout the later part of March and well into April 1914, Huertista correspondence expressed frustration and sometimes outrage at the effects of Villa's propaganda during the Torreón campaign. The two key issues were, unsurprisingly, Villa's exaggerated claims that the city was falling and, oddly, Villa's unwillingness (unsuccessfully portrayed by Huertistas as inability) to hold the city: he seized federal supplies, declined to waste firepower by leaving troops to hold the captured city, and moved on. Armed with these two issues, Huertistas unsuccessfully attempted to publicize the argument that the city had never really fallen.

In reports filed with the Huertista Ministry of Foreign Relations in Mexico City, Huertista consuls in the United States began citing American media reports that Villa had captured Torreón as early as March 24.[42] Huerta's secretary of foreign relations, José López Portillo y Rojas, responded simply, but not quite accurately: "Inexact news. Federal troops defeated Villa."[43]

From El Paso on March 27, meanwhile, Huertista official Miguel Diebold cabled a note to consuls around the United States claiming that the rebels were losing in a rout: "Rebels have suffered serious defeats in Torreón."[44] This came in the midst of an admission to a colleague that Diebold had had no word from General Joaquín Maas, one of the two Huertista commanders at Torreón, for more than twenty-four hours.[45]

Then, on March 29, 30, and 31, Maas wired Diebold instructing him to deny as "completamente inexactas" all press reports announcing the city's fall. But the cable was not wholly inspiring.

It went on, "The fighting continues and in all probability will end in our favor."[46] Diebold complied, issuing more denials to consuls.[47] Then he wired a similar announcement to the Ministry of Foreign Relations: "The news that could be acquired here with respect to the situation in Torreón is published by the rebels and is alarming and totally false. Since March 25 General Maas has telegraphed to me about various triumphs by our forces."[48]

Even after the city fell on April 2, Huertistas continued to deny it. The denials were issued in response to many inquiries Diebold received from Huertista consuls in American cities about the status of the battle.[49] Consuls elsewhere abroad, too, noted press reports of Villa's victory. The Mexican embassy in Berlin, for example, sent copies of notices from four different Berlin dailies that noted Villa's taking of Torreón.[50] Yet Diebold refused to admit that the city had fallen—and, after Villa abandoned it within days of the victory, sought to use his departure as evidence to support the claim that the city had never fallen.[51]

The American press's pro-Villa framing of the battle for Torreón prompted a Huertista official to single out State Department special agent George Carothers as one culprit behind the undesirable slant. The official claimed to have intercepted a note from Carothers to William Jennings Bryan, the American secretary of state, in which Carothers suggested that no news of the standing of the battle be released publicly because, according to historian Larry Hill, "any news might encourage the Federals to send in reinforcements."[52] Carothers, then, in the Huertista view, had duplicitously promoted Villa at Huerta's expense.

Huerta subsequently declared Carothers persona non grata in Mexico,[53] yet Hill explains that the Huertista official had "misinterpreted" the dispatch and unfairly blamed Carothers for writing the offending portion of it. In fact, the American customs inspector at El Paso, Zach Cobb, had added the clause in question— and had done so at the request of local Constitutional officials.[54] Hill writes: "They [the Constitutionalists] pointed out to him

[Cobb] that they allowed Carothers' dispatches to come out of Mexico on their telegraph lines as a courtesy; now they requested that the State Department refrain from releasing their contents to the press, because the battle was at a critical stage."[55] Bryan complied, too. The Constitutionalists had used their influence with Cobb to decided propaganda advantage.

The offending Carothers cable to Bryan had been brought to the attention of the Foreign Relations Ministry on April 1.[56] The following day, G. Fernández MacGregor, a Huertista foreign relations official, penned a cable to Mexico City: "It has been discovered that Carothers sent Bryan a message that Villistas had taken Torreón. I urge you to undertake a press campaign in order to publicize that Torreón has not fallen and will not fall; and that Villa's defeat has been fully confirmed."[57] Huertista consuls around the world reacted indignantly to the news of Carothers's cable, because they apparently believed the dispatches they had already received, and continued to receive, which held, in contradistinction to reality, that the city had not fallen.[58]

In one of many examples, R. S. Bravo, the Huertista consul at Laredo, filed a perplexed report complaining about the falsity of American press accounts of Torreón's capture.[59] López Portillo responded, urging Bravo to deny such reports locally and noting that "this government knows they [Villistas] are giving instructions to their agents to falsely promote them."[60]

López Portillo also alleged that he had "proof" that foreign correspondents had filed false reports favoring the rebel cause.[61] Although Diebold agreed, he also stressed the "rebel source" of much of the press disinformation.[62] A few days later Diebold was still identifying "rude attacks" by the American press against the Huerta government.[63] This Huertista anti-press invective continued through the middle of April.[64]

On April 4, however, an official from the Foreign Relations office noted the American press's news that Torreón had in fact fallen and cited a Villa telegram to Carranza to such effect.[65] Despite this,

López Portillo advised Huertista consuls that the city remained in federal hands,[66] and yet again, foreign Huertista consuls received the news warmly.[67]

Huertista propaganda after April 4 continued to meet with little success against Villa's media campaign. On April 8, for example, the Huertista consul in Chicago, César Canseco, issued a press release to nine Chicago-area dailies. It read in part: "The rebel forces have begun to run away from our soldiers; but the division . . . is trying to catch Villa in his retreat." Canseco complained that only one of the nine papers responded.[68] This was typical. The American press proved simply to be uninterested in much of what Huerta had to say. Moreover, within days, the Tampico incident filled the American press and all but suffocated Huertista propaganda.

When Huerta resigned in mid-July 1914, he left the media field wide open to only two serious contenders—Villa and Carranza. Their media struggle, like their struggle in the civil war itself, was waged on many fields and with an array of weapons.

THE CARRANZA MACHINE, STEP ONE:
IDENTIFYING THE ENEMY

From the summer of 1913 through the fall of 1915, Carrancistas fretted mightily over Villa's propaganda and strove to overcome it. Although Francisco Madero's death in February 1913 and the renewed fighting it gave rise to in Mexico attracted increased U.S. news interest in Mexican affairs in the spring of 1913,[69] Villa's military emergence in its own right drew many additional American reporters southward. Louis Stevens claimed that Carranza actually "hated" Villa for all his media popularity because "[i]t was around Villa and not Carranza that American newspapermen clustered."[70]

Carrancistas kept a close eye on American press reports, especially those emanating from New York.[71] Indeed, they were sensitive to the content and tone of American news reports as early as weeks before Madero's death.[72] They complained bitterly about the reports' content at the same time they sometimes relied upon the American press as a dependable source of accurate information. For example, within days of Madero's death, Carranza received a report from Los Angeles: "Press here reports uprising discovered in Mexico. . . . [Consequently] I believe it is urgent to establish our government in Chihuahua."[73]

The Carrancistas' worries stemmed from three basic sources: Villa's propaganda efforts versus those of the First Chief; American governmental sympathy for Villa (which, Carrancistas felt, reflected at least in part the success of Villista propaganda); and the "sensationalist" and "yellow" segment of the American press, which sometimes was manipulated by Villa, sometimes desired exciting news, and sometimes promoted hidden agendas such as, allegedly, the protection of publishers' business interests in Mexico. The image effects of Villa's propaganda, in the Carrancista view, created unflattering portrayals of Carranza while misrepresenting Villa in an unduly favorable light.[74] And so Carranza lost on both counts.

Carranza received negative press framing on several fronts. First, by association with revolutionary violence, he was implicated as a sneak and a thug.[75] The *Los Angeles Times* put it this way: "The aggregation of bandits and murderers who comprise the forces of Carranza and Villa have stolen everything they could."[76] The *San Francisco Examiner* was more pointed in a condemnation that asserted, "Carranza and his general [Villa] are all tarred with the same stick. They are simply organized brigands."[77]

Second, Carranza was depicted as vain and excessively opinionated.[78] To the *New York Times*, he was "hopelessly incompetent,"[79] "weak, vain and opinionated,"[80] and "impossible."[81]

Third, he was dictatorial.[82] Both the *San Francisco Examiner* and the *Los Angeles Times* charged, for example, that Carranza might use Villa's hard-earned territorial gains as the basis upon which to establish authoritarian rule.[83] As the *Chicago Tribune* had it, "Carranza, we suspect, seeks only the continuance of the aristocratic control of Mexico"[84] (a statement that implies oligarchy rather than dictatorship).

Fourth, he was frightened of Villa politically, and this fear might stem from cowardice. The *New York Times* suggested that Carranza preferred to "remain out of sight" rather than risk being overshadowed, if not supplanted, by Villa.[85] Echoing these comments two weeks later, the *Times* noted that Carranza "is not yet discernible to the naked eye."[86]

Finally, Carranza simply paled in comparison with Villa, "the Strongman of Mexico."[87] The *New York Times* captured the tone of the prevailing media sentiment in two editorials. The first chided Carranza for "hiding" from Villa: "CARRANZA is still out of sight. If Chihuahua is really the capital of his GOVERNMENT, there he should be, and the idea that he keeps away from there because he fears that he would lose even nominal authority [over Villa] if he left his hiding place is still general."[88] The second editorial damned Carranza for his want of personal vitality: "[T]he closest observers of Mexican affairs do not believe that there is any stability in CARRANZA or that his socialistic and confiscatory policy . . . would work. . . . He lacks the extraordinary personal force of VILLA."[89] The *Los Angeles Times* referred to the First Chief as "that pretender and failure V(egetable) Carranza."[90]

The Carrancistas fingered Villa as the primary instigator of the American media's disparagement of Carranza. As early as January 1914, allegations surfaced in the Carranza camp that Villista agents in the United States actively sought to discredit the First Chief and promote Villa.[91] As the Villa-Carranza relationship unraveled, such charges gave rise among Carrancistas to a sense of anxiety and urgency that gathered a rhetorical momentum. In August 1914, for example, the Carrancista official Rafael Zubarán Capmany related an allegation to Carranza that Villistas were fomenting pro-Villa propaganda in Tampico.[92] The cable insinuated that if press copy promoted Villa, then somehow it denigrated Carranza by comparison.

A more serious example can be seen in a September 1914 telegram to Carranza from Zubarán that charged Villa with bribing New York reporters and, with open arms, receiving support from Científico elements as part of a campaign to discredit Carranza.[93] Such charges, unsurprisingly, traversed a two-way street. In August 1914, Villa complained bitterly to Carranza about the tone and content taken toward him by an article published in the Carrancista paper *El Progresso*.[94]

The unflattering image of Carranza in the American press—and hence, it was held, in the minds of the American public, other "ignorant people,"[95] and politicians[96]—made the First Chief appear, foremost, to be anti-American. Further, Villa's policy of friendship with the United States itself warranted condemnation for being based on opportunism and not on principle—or so it was publicly argued. During the summer of 1915, Villa's most desperate hour, the Carrancista consul in El Paso, Andrés G. García, expressed the sentiment precisely. Villa's "policy," and the promotion of it, represented a cynical ruse, he said, "which very clearly shows the attitude he has toward the American people and their government. If you will remember I told you long ago that Villa only pretended to be a friend of the American people only for reasons of policy and that he was not a real friend of the Americans at all. Time has proved this up."[97]

Carranza's Veracruz stand, too, had made him an easy American media target and fueled the portrayal of him as anti-American. Again and again Carranza felt compelled by negative coverage to deny that he harbored anti-American sentiment. In a public statement, Carranza's man in Washington, Eliseo Arredondo, penned a good example of the frustration felt throughout the Carrancista camp:

This shows one instance of how exaggerated and false are reports in daily newspapers, giving space in the news to sensationalized stories, without care for their origin and their connection to Señor Carranza's enemies and the foreigners allied with them, and it has the sole objective of producing an alarming and misleading scandal in the American public's mind. . . . Señor Carranza has just telegraphed to this agent that these attempts . . . that have produced exaggerated and alarming news reports are intended only to excite popular opinion. [98]

This undated news release expresses the central anxiety felt by Carrancistas about the First Chief's image for almost the entirety of the 1913–1915 period. It claims that Carranza has been presented in a false light, but rather than focusing on virtues in Carranza that might belie the negativity, the passage wallows in complaint—the common tenor of Carrancista charges about Villa's propaganda. The blame is laid upon two enemies: the inherent sensationalism of the press and Carranza's foes, who have been conspiring with shadowy foreign interests. (Villa goes unnamed, which in all likelihood dates the release to between mid-April and late September 1914.) The result, the passage asserts, contributed to an excitement of public—and hence political—opinion in the United States.

In another example of Carrancista frustration over press treatment of the First Chief, scarcely six months before Carranza received de facto recognition from the United States, Andrés G. García, the Constitutionalist consul at El Paso, received a gripe from an official of the Carrancista Pan-American News Service. It read: "I wish it clearly understood once and for all that this government is not anti-foreign in its tendencies. My highest pleasure will be to treat foreigners with careful and considerate justness."[99]

Villista propaganda had been able, other Constitutionalist dispatches alleged, to manipulate the American government into taking an unfavorable view of Carranza. For example, a Constitutionalist biography of Carranza offered to the American press maintained that "it is nevertheless a fact that the wily bandit [Villa] took [advantage of] the petty prejudices and futile grudges of the American government against Carranza."[100] Regarding Villa's favorable casting in the American press, a Carranza propaganda dispatch claimed: "The story was invented right here in New York."[101]

Carrancista assertions about American governmental complicity in Villista propaganda were not always so restrained (and they may have served to delay recognition of the Carranza regime). On one of many occasions, it was alleged "that the efforts of the reactionaries are backed by high officials of the American government residing in Mexico, who are sending to the American Department of State false information regarding the situation in Mexico."[102]

On the other hand, Carrancista propaganda itself sought directly to influence opinions and actions at the highest levels of American government. This had been true since the summer of 1913. For example, in a cable to Carranza dated August 1913, propagandist Herbierto Barron clearly articulated the intent of his efforts in the United States: to favorably influence Woodrow Wilson.[103] As was the case with Villa's propaganda, this element of Carrancista policy never changed.

Through the spring and into the fall of 1915, Carrancistas worried about the disruptive effects of Villa's propaganda. For example, in June, Carrancista newspapers were advised to publish reports to correct the "absolutamente falsa" impressions caused by Villista military claims.[104] In another case, in September, Carranza was notified that Villistas in Washington were waging an intense disinformation campaign against the First Chief.[105] Even as late as October 25, 1915, six days after Carranza had been granted de facto recognition, the Carrancistas worried about Villa's press efforts.[106]

The Carrancistas also repeatedly lamented the undesired portrayal the First Chief received from the sensationalist "yellow" press. The American State Department official Leon Canova agreed, and he attributed the problem to the two kinds of correspondents sent to Mexico. The first kind, he observed, was inexperienced, knew little about Mexico, and suffered from an exaggerated sense of his own importance. The second type—notably the Hearst reporter—was under "instructions" to agitate for and slant all reports toward the goal of United States intervention. Further, both types were inclined to view Carranza unfavorably because Carranza, the administrator, was boring and dull, whereas Villa, the warrior, was exciting and charismatic. As a result, Canova reasoned, Carranza received less coverage than Villa in absolute terms, but also more negative coverage.[107] Carranza responded, in part, by keeping close tabs on Hearst reporters.[108]

The Carrancistas' complaints against the American press, which spanned the 1913–1915 period, were typically aired internally, but they became especially pointed and vocal outside the Carrancista camp after the Villa-Obregón engagements at Celaya in April 1915. Carrancista correspondence is full of frustrated complaints about bad press. In one eight-week period during the summer of 1915, for example, Carranza complained about Villa's "false" propaganda and Hearst's "false" news, and he railed at "false" press reports of General Pablo González's defeat near Mexico City. At the same time, from information gained via news reports, Arredondo reported to Carranza from Washington word of Villa's military resurgence. He also cited press reports as indicative of official Wilson administration policy moves, and he concluded that the American government was formulating policy following the lead of "a group of reactionaries and traitors."[109]

Over the summer and early fall of 1915, the Carrancistas engaged in a letter-writing campaign to American newspapers in Washington, D.C., and New York and to officials highly placed in the United States government, in an effort to undo the perceived pro-Villa bias in the American press. In a September letter to Robert Lansing, by then the acting American secretary of state, Arredondo took aim at the collusion between the "sensationalist" and "insidious" press and Carranza's "enemies," who sought to portray Carranza falsely as anti-American.[110] Propagandist Herbierto Barron, meanwhile, wrote to Wilson to argue that Villa's cause was lost. He cited an article in the *New York Sun* to support the claim.[111] The implication Barron drew from the *Sun* report was that Carranza merited official American support as a consequence of Villa's diminished fortunes. Curiously, five days later, providing no evidence, Barron declared to Carranza that he had succeeded in influencing Wilson.[112] At about the same time, Barron outlined for Carranza his own letter-writing campaign to New York City dailies.[113]

Carrancistas also attempted to tap personal connections to lend weight to the argument that Villa had cynically managed to capture Wilson's ear.[114] For example, George F. Weeks, a former American correspondent who would later become a part of the official Constitutionalist propaganda operation out of New York,[115] wrote to his old friend Franklin Lane, United States secretary of the interior, to press the Carrancista case at the White House. He accused Villa of having engineered Carranza's unseemly depiction in the American press.[116] Lane dutifully passed the note he received to Lansing—with one important addition. The complaint now had the sanction of an important figure in government. Lane wrote: "Here is a note from a man I have known for some twenty-five years. He is a newspaper man with whom I formerly worked, and who I have always thought is a very level-headed fellow."[117]

Villa was not the only adversary that Carrancista propaganda had to overcome. The American media were also considered to be enemies. For example, some press portrayals of Carranza were seen to be slanted because certain American publishers maintained large estates in Mexico and consequently felt threatened by the Revolution. Publisher opposition typically translated into editorial opposition and therefore into unfavorable framing.

The reaction from the Carrancista side was predictable. William Randolph Hearst, owner of publications such as the *San Francisco*

Examiner and the *New York American*, as well his information agency, the International News Service, gained the most virulent denunciation. His publications were excoriated for wallowing in sensationalism, and an American official, who declined to provide a signature ("for obvious reasons"), told Carranza that he believed Hearst provided the major rhetorical and financial support Villa relied upon in the United States.[118] Other dispatches labeled Hearst the Constitutionalists' "most irritating enemy,"[119] and his publications, thoroughly "yellow" (*amarillo*).[120] Carranza agreed.[121]

Harrison Gray Otis, owner and publisher of the *Los Angeles Times* and owner of vast landholdings in Mexico—some of which were protected by heavily armed and well-provisioned employees[122]—also earned the enmity of Constitutionalists.[123] The *Los Angeles Times* supported Huerta and, like the *Examiner*, called for United States military intervention in Mexico. In October 1913, one Carrancista charged Otis and Hearst with seeking to provoke United States intervention in the hope of American annexation of the Mexican states of Sonora, Chihuahua, and Coahuila.[124] On another occasion, Pesqueira asserted that Otis and Hearst stood behind Villa "in every move he makes."[125] In time, the *Examiner* and the *Los Angeles Times* threw their weight behind Villa—but well before the rupture in relations between Villa and Carranza, which clearly rankled Carrancistas.[126]

Finally, the media strategies of Villa partisan and Sonora governor José Maytorena also raised the ire of, and generated reactions from, the Carranza regime. By mid-spring 1914 they precipitated a vitriolic "newspaper fight." Maytorena had allegedly paid an El Paso newspaper (probably the *El Paso Times*) to attack Pesqueira and Obregón,[127] and Maytorena's official personal propaganda organ, *La Voz de Sonora*, repeatedly attacked Carranza.[128] Equally damning were charges that he was destroying opposition (that is, Carrancista) newspapers in Sonora, accepting antirevolutionary Científico support, and buying up newspapers and using them to promote Villismo at the expense of Carrancismo.[129]

In part, according to Louis Hostetter, the American consul at Hermosillo, Maytorena was simply responding in kind to scurrilous attacks against his character leveled by Carrancista press organs.[130]

THE CARRANZA MACHINE, STEP TWO: ORGANIZING THE ANGER

The Carranza camp found it necessary to establish a propaganda machine from the ground up, in part because of the perceived depth of Villa's propaganda success and the perceived hostility of the American press to Carranza.[131] In some ways its activities simply mirrored those of the Villa propaganda machine. For example, Carrancista consuls disbursed thousands of dollars to support and bribe news publications in Mexico and the United States.[132] On the other hand—and this represents one of the two key differences between Carranza's and Villa's propaganda operations—Carranza's superior organization, encompassing news bureaus, wire services, and many propaganda organs, considerably surpassed Villa's, which tended to operate ad hoc, without a news bureau or wire service and with relatively fewer propaganda organs at its disposal. The second crucial difference between the two propaganda machines lay in the content of the packaged product. Villa provided a more exciting, saleable, and likable product.

Carrancistas considered American wire services and newspapers hostile and unreliable, even while sometimes employing them as sources of valid information.[133] Partly as a consequence, Carranza dispatched lobbyists and press agents to the United States to generate favorable publicity for himself and his Constitutionalist cause. This step benefited Villa so long as Villa remained a Constitutionalist—but it and subsequent Constitutionalist media actions aimed first to promote Carranza.[134]

Sherburne Hopkins served as the first key Constitutionalist man in Washington in 1913. At the same time, Adrián Aguirre Benavides, who employed the services of two "co-religionists," fomented Constitutionalist propaganda in New York in the spring of 1913.[135] Felix Sommerfeld, too, promoted the cause in 1913, but the depth of his loyalty to Carranza was thought (accurately, as it turned out) to be suspect.[136] Carrancista agents began to monitor his behavior in early July 1914—and extended the surveillance to include apparently all members of the Constitutionalist contingent in New York.[137]

Like Sommerfeld, Hopkins and Benavides jumped ship and sided with Villa in September 1914. Others stood ready to take their places. These included Robert V. Pesqueira and Modesto Rolland, who launched competing news agencies to promote the Constitutionalist movement. Charles A. Douglas, a Washington lawyer,[138] replaced Hopkins as legal adviser,[139] while Eliseo Arreondo stepped in as Carranza's confidential agent in the American capital.[140] The American lawyer Richard Cole also promoted Carrancismo from cities around the United States.[141] Samuel Belden served as a key propagandist in the United States, especially in the transborder region.[142]

Rolland worked with Carlo de Fornaro to co-found the Mexican Bureau of Information in August 1914. Free of charge, the bureau provided English-language press copy (that is, propaganda) to more than five hundred publications. Further, it published the biweekly *Mexican Letter*, which heartily promoted Carrancismo and bitterly and methodically opposed Villa. The bureau also sent propagandistic communiqués to politicians, including President Wilson, and other public officials.[143]

Pesqueira, meanwhile, established the Pan-American News Service (PANS), ostensibly an unbiased international wire service. In fact it served Carrancismo in much the same way and tenor as did the local-level dispatches of the Mexican Bureau of Information. Pesqueira sought to link all consulate cities through PANS.[144]

In Mexico, G. H. Velásquez founded the Oficina Central de Información y Propaganda Revolucionaria, the agency responsible for formulating and circulating propaganda within the Constitutionalist organization.[145] In 1915 it circulated bulletins throughout Carrancista territory promoting Carranza and decrying his enemies.[146] The tone of the circulars suggests that they served both as founts of information and as morale boosters.

Pesqueira proved unequal to the task of using PANS to foment effective pro-Carranza and anti-Villa propaganda, and on at least one occasion he expressed frustration to Carranza that the propaganda war was being lost to Villa.[147] Reacting to accusations against the service on counts of inefficiency, squandering funds, and failure to cast an image consonant with its propagandistic raison d'être, Carranza looked to replace Pesqueira. Pesqueira's most glaring error had been an inability to dissociate the service publicly from the Carranza movement. A newly revamped PANS, designed to "maintain an appearance of absolute independence," was to be headed by the New Orleans journalist and Villa propaganda "neutralizer" Joseph Branyas,[148] but it failed to get off the ground when Branyas died unexpectedly.[149] Still, despite the limited success gained under Pesqueira's directorship, the PANS anti-Villa message had at least been consistent. PANS had attacked Villa without let-up on many fronts and lauded Carranza as the opposite of all the evil represented by Villa.[150]

During the summer of 1915 a Carranza aide recruited Timothy Turner, the former *El Paso Times* and Associated Press reporter, to reorganize and head the Mexican Bureau of Information, which would include PANS. Turner, who had funneled information to the Constitutionalists since as early as May 1914,[151] put together a plan to professionalize the bureau by staffing it with former newspapermen and distancing itself, at least ostensibly, from the Carrancista movement. Somewhat hyperbolically, Turner claimed: "The function of the bureau would be to create through constructive channels of publicity a true understanding of Mexican affairs. . . . The New York director and his assistants would work in similar corporation." The key to establishing effective propaganda, Turner asserted, was the appearance of disinterest. "The news thus given out as official statements would be more eagerly received by the American press and lack entirely the appearance of artificial propaganda."[152]

Turner's goal of appearing disinterested met with failure. For example, a February 1915 attempt to disguise Carrancista propaganda offered to the American Press Association of New York stirred the association's president, Hartland Smith, to write to Secretary Bryan inquiring about the legality and ethicality of using such material. The material itself—as effusive in its praise of Carranza as it was dismissive of Villa—came free of charge and camera-ready to print from the so-called Western Newspaper Union of Chicago. In addition to situating the union, a Carrancista creation, far from the hubs of revolutionary propaganda—New York and El Paso—the Carrancistas attempted to cast it as quintessentially American by tombstoning in its letterhead lists of Midwestern American cities subscribing to its services.

Yet the propaganda clearly failed to sway Hartland Smith, who noted to Bryan that the association had also received requests from "other factions in Mexico" to distribute and print propaganda. Bryan responded by acknowledging the Carrancistas' legal right to circulate such information, and he suggested to Smith that publications inclined to print it be advised to inform readers of the source.[153]

Meanwhile, the revamped PANS bureau began operations quickly and energetically. Other Carrancistas spoke highly of it. Alfredo Breceda, who had served as Carranza's private secretary, lauded Turner's work (and also charged that Arredondo's press agents were a waste of money and that Pesqueira was incompetent).[154] By August 1915, the bureau was handling virtually all serious news releases—just in time to celebrate Carranza's recognition in October.[155]

Like Villa, Carranza funded and bribed news publications. While Villa personally had *Vida Nueva* (Chihuahua City) and received positive coverage from *El Combate* (Aguascalientes), *El Monitor* (Mexico City), *La Convención* (Aguascalientes), and the *El Paso Times*, Carranza maintained his own stable of propaganda organs. These included *El Constitucionalista* (published in Ciudad Juárez, Chihuahua City, Saltillo, and Monterrey; founded in 1913),[156] *El Demócrata* (Mexico City, Piedras Negras, San Luis Potosí, and Monterrey; 1913),[157] *El Diario Official* (Chihuahua City; 1913), *El Dictamen* (Veracruz; 1914), *El Pueblo* (Veracruz; 1914),[158] *La Opinión* (Veracruz, Mexico City; 1914),[159] *El Liberal* (Mexico City; 1914),[160] *La Justicia* (1914), *Los Sucesos* (1914), *El Legalista* (1914),[161] *Churubusco* (1914), *El Libertador* (Querétaro; 1915),[162] *La Revolución* (1915),[163] and *El Nacional* (Mexico City; 1915).[164]

It is worth remembering, too, that prior to the rupture in Villa-Carranza relations, all Constitutionalist organs, at least ostensibly, promoted Villa as well as Carranza. Their resources and pro-revolutionary, anti-Huerta messages overlapped. For example, Herbierto Barron proudly noted to Carranza in May 1914 that the pro-Villa *El Paso Times* was printing articles he had written to promote the more general Constitutionalist cause.[165] At the same time, and suggestive of how unbridgeable the Villa-Carranza schism would later become, from El Paso Andrés G. García sought either increased funding for *El Paso del Norte* or funds to establish a new organ to combat Villista propaganda in the *El Paso Times*.[166]

Carranza also funded and bribed media in the United States. The list included, but likely was not limited to, *El Eco de México* (Los Angeles),[167] *El Paso del Norte* (El Paso),[168] the *El Paso Herald*,[169] *La Prensa* (Los Angeles), *El Progreso* (Laredo),[170] the *Record* (Laredo),[171] *Revista Mensual Ilustrada* (New Orleans),[172] *La Raza* (San Antonio),[173] *La Lucha* (El Paso),[174] *El Mefistóles* (San Francisco), *El Rebelde* (Los Angeles),[175] the *San Antonio Light*,[176] and the *Tucson Citizen*.[177] Carrancista agents distributed the bribes. For example, Arredondo cited Carrancista agent Francisco Elias's "urgent" need for "press" money in Washington in the spring of 1915.[178] Shortly afterward, in New York, Elias received two thousand dollars "for press expenses."[179]

Like Villa, Carranza demonstrated a willingness to censor outgoing news reports. The practice occurred frequently, and Carranza defended it on both legal and moral grounds. He argued that such measures fell within the rights of action of a sovereign (that is, Constitutionalist) nation in defending itself from calumny.[180] Censorship became more common after the Villa-Carranza split. "Rigid censorship" became the norm for cables emanating from Veracruz after Carranza established the seat of his claim to the Revolution there following the American military withdrawal in November 1914.[181]

In another episode, in Mexico City in February 1915, Carrancistas found it necessary to close down rival newspapers in an effort to silence criticism generated by reports of widespread starvation in the capital.[182] This step was taken after censorship apparently proved unable to stem the tide of negative reports.[183] Obregón, whose forces occupied the city, attempted to deflect criticism of the strict measures he had taken by offering to meet with representatives of the press. But the offer was a ruse on Obregón's part, according to Cardoso de Oliveira, Brazil's minister to Mexico and State Department confidante—nothing more than an attempt to bully the journalists by forcing them to submit to impossible standards of conduct.[184] American correspondents, with one exception (the correspondent for the *New York Sun*), boycotted the meeting.[185]

Carranza also employed an itinerant physician, Krum Heller, to promote his cause by speaking to salons and other small gatherings in cities around the United States, most often in the Southwest.[186] While the specific contents and effects of Heller's speaking engagements remain unclear, at least part of his mandate included attacking Villa. For example, he sought funds to combat Villista propaganda in Brownsville in 1915.[187] By most Carrancista accounts, Heller's efforts were successful, and his work apparently did not lack for funding.[188]

Finally, one avenue of propaganda not explored by the Carrancistas with the interest shown by Villa was the moving picture. Although Villa's efforts with the Mutual Film Corporation did not deliver the expected dividends, the films still received modest screenings in New York, and photographs taken from newsreel stills got wide circulation. Further, newsreel footage shot by several American and Mexican enterprises and shown around the world (though primarily in the United States) generated modest publicity for Villa and Carranza alike.[189] In March 1914, Carranza granted to unnamed cameramen the rights to film the Constitutionalists in action.[190]

THE CARRANZA MACHINE, STEP THREE: GETTING EVEN

The key goal of Carranza's propaganda—indeed, probably of most political propaganda—was to generate public and hence political support. Carrancistas clearly predicated their U.S. media strategy upon the assumption that they could influence the American media's agenda vis-à-vis the Revolution.[191] The American public and American politicians would then, ideally, fall in line.

Carrancistas fashioned an organization designed to serve these ends. But two major roadblocks stood in the way: the relatively favorable, sometimes glowing, media image of Villa, achieved in some measure by Villista propaganda, and the relatively unflattering media image of Carranza, also fostered in no small part by Villa propaganda. An examination of the contents of Carrancista propaganda illustrates the perceived importance of overcoming the Villa image.

The *Mexican Letter*, which was sent to more than five hundred media publications free of charge, provides probably the best example of Carranza's anti-Villa propaganda.[192] The publication itself was organized loosely. Typically two or three typed pages in length, each issue might touch on three or four topics that would be separated by asterisks and supplied with appropriate headlines. Bylines identifying the author appeared occasionally.

The *Mexican Letter* painted Villa with strokes quite similar to those used by Villistas to portray Carranza. Villa was maniacally dictatorial, obsessed by presidential ambitions, unyielding in a mad and violent opposition to democracy, and bitterly anti-American in a duplicitous guise. Where Villa propaganda played up Villa's humble, man-of-the-people origins, the *Letter* cast him as an ignorant, uneducated, dangerous buffoon, unfit for public office.

Early copies of the *Letter* frequently rebuked the United States government for undue Villista sympathies. Reflecting Carranza's eagerness for the occupying American troops to withdraw from Veracruz, in September 1914, for example, the *Letter* charged President Wilson with "unconsciously playing into the hands of the reactionary elements of Mexico."[193] Although Villa went unnamed, in part because the official rupture in relations was still a week away, the barb implicated him, too, albeit allusively.

The *Letter* also pounded Villa indirectly by attacking his association with other Carranza enemies—notably Maytorenistas and Huertistas. For example, in October 1914, in the midst of the attempted Villa-Carranza rapprochement at Aguascalientes, the *Letter* called on Villa to curb Maytorena's wanton disregard for the international border separating Mexico and the United States.[194]

In more measured tones, the same release also accused Villa of bad faith at Aguascalientes: "I . . . call your attention to the fact that press reports emanating from El Paso contain many false reports relative to the personnel of the constitutionalists, many of these containing bitter personal attacks directed at our First Chief and also at our constitutionalist army. So it might be well for general Villa to have his agents desist."[195]

The tenor of the anti-Villa contents of the *Letter* became increasingly bitter as it became ever more apparent that the Villa-Carranza rupture might prove irreconcilable. In mid-November the *Letter* published a Carranza statement to the convention:

> I am now of the conviction that the true cause of the difficulties which the country is now encountering is the natural reaction which follows the triumph of every revolution. . . . It is . . . reactionary elements [that] always endeavor to exert their influence upon some one of the most conspicuous revolutionary chiefs, exciting his personal ambitions of command in order to rally around him and thus secure his protection. . . . There is greater ambition than that of being President of the Republic and that is to preserve such a military omnipotence as will permit a man to control all the powers of the country. The insistence of General Villa in preserving the command of a military division considered to be omnipotent which at the same time pretends to re-establish a constitutional government under the basis of the old regime and to designate a civilian for the Presidency of the Republic, clearly indicates that it is the dream of this chief to constitute himself arbiter of the destinies of Mexico.[196]

(A later edition of the publication dismissed the convention as a "blind to deceive the American Press.")[197]

The mid-November issue of *Mexican Letter* also leveled a variety of other barbs. One was aimed squarely at convention president Eulalio Gutiérrez, who was portrayed as both a man "of great honor" and a Villa puppet.[198] It also lashed out at "Washington jingoes" for portraying Carranza in the United States press as anti-American. In fact, the *Letter* claimed, "it has always been Carranza's aim to establish closer and friendly relations with the United States."[199]

Not only was Gutiérrez condemned for being Villa's lackey, but Villa, too, earned censure for being little more than the agent of the "Mexican-American junta in New York." Moreover, Villa "has to obey orders or he won't get any money to buy arms and ammunition."[200] Framed in this way, Villa is at once dominatingly manipulative with regard to the convention authorities yet childishly dependent on pseudo-foreign interests.

A December 1914 copy of the *Letter* stressed that a lack of substance belied Villa's propaganda claims. The publication cynically noted Villa's "picturesque" quality but tarred him as having "become an unconscious tool within the hands of the enemies of Mexico. He has allied himself with the reactionaries and the científicos." Ironically, considering the *Letter*'s point of origin (that is, penned largely by Americans in New York), it also attempted to smear Villa by commenting that the promotion of his policy-making "savours of press agency."[201]

A colorfully worded, if slightly oblique, assertion in another issue echoed this last point but also suggested that Americans' gullibility contributed to Villa's popularity: "Barnum said that the American people liked to be humbugged. In the case of Mexico the Americans are being humbugged but it is doubtful if they like it."[202]

Yet again in January 1915, Villa and the American press came under attack. "The press campaign in favor of Villa (as the ipse [*sic*] facto ruler of Mexico) is only a continuation of the press campaign carried on during Huerta's regime in his favor. The Villa publicity campaign has made Pancho Villa the most interesting figure in Mexico for American readers. . . . [However,] Villa's fame [is] essentially a manufactured American article."[203]

But the Carrancistas, too, attempted to ply the American press with messages like those found in the *Letter*. Though initially less successful than the Villistas in promoting public-relations material as news, in time the Carrancistas achieved their goal. For example, echoing the increasingly bitter tone of the *Letter*, a statement by Rafael Zubarán Capmany printed in the *New York Times* claimed:

We have every reason to believe the accredited report that the American agent, George C. Carothers, has sold out to Francisco Villa, alias Doroteo Arango. This is his true name. He has assumed the name of Francisco Villa for reasons known to himself, and history alone will tell what crimes his true name of Doroteo Arango may hide. . . . At the very moment that he was openly declaring friendship for the United States he was threatening to invade this nation at El Paso . . . [and] when a few months ago Arango was declaring that the conduct of the United States was justified in the Vera Cruz matter he was at the same time swearing vengeance upon this nation.[204]

This press release covers many insinuating bases: the American government's complicity (via Carothers); Villa's general unreliability (he changed his name, probably to cover criminal tracks); Villa's true anti-American feeling (cynically disguised as friendship); and his dangerousness (he had planned to attack the United States).[205]

The Carrancistas enjoyed greater success at placing stories in American publications after Villa's stinging defeats at Celaya. For example, in early May 1915, the *New York Times* reported and commented on its editorial page about a story claiming that Felipe Angeles, architect of Villa's military operations, was a closet Huertista. Moreover, the story noted the existence of collegial correspondence between Angeles and Porfirio Díaz after the latter had gone into exile.[206] Villa agents hotly denied the allegations and claimed the letters had been fabricated by Carrancistas.[207]

The Carrancistas scored a minor propaganda coup in late May 1915 when Luis Aguirre Benavides, formerly Villa's private secretary, deserted Villa and threw his allegiance behind Carranza. Among other allegations that surfaced in American press reports was Benavides's charge that Benton had never received a trial but had been summarily executed after quarreling with Villa. Only the physical interposition of Villa's wife, Luz Corral, had saved Benton from instant death by Villa's own hand. Rodolfo Fierro, Villa's bodyguard, had shot Benton through the head at close range, according to Benavides, which was why the body had never been turned over to the widow.[208]

By mid-July the *New York Times* was citing a Carrancista message that bore marked resemblance to Villa's media statements of the previous eighteen months. A headline read, "CARRANZA BIDS FOR RECOGNITION, Gives Out Statement Telling His Plans for Jeffersonian Rule and Praising Wilson, DESIRES OUR FRIENDSHIP."[209] Still, Carranza struggled to shake his media reputation for cowardice. It remained "one of his marked traits," according to the *New York Times*.[210]

A Carrancista dispatch from the summer of 1915 drubbed Villa for systematically striving to misrepresent Carranza since the early winter of 1914. It sought to identify Villa with "the rotten elements of Mexico such as the Cientificos," and it went on to say:

> One of the most powerful forms of the [Villa propaganda] work was spreading the ideas in political circles and in the press and public opinion that Carranza was an enemy of the country as well as of impossible personal character. The principal incidents which helped to serve in spreading this false idea were . . . the Benton incident [and] the Carranza protest against the occupation of Veracruz . . . and in a minor degree all the international exchanges have served for the purpose of presenting him in a color not in keeping with his true character.[211]

In late September 1915, the American Carrancista sympathizer Willard Simpson wrote to Carranza: "Your enemies are making their last stand and it will, in my opinion, amount to nothing. That you have upheld the dignity and sovereignty of your own country, is now admitted generally by the American press, and it is conceded that the Constitutional Government will receive some form of recognition soon."[212] Simpson was correct on one count—that Villa was finished as a serious contender for the Mexican throne. On a second count, that the American press tended to embrace Carranza, Simpson missed the mark. Villa's stature in the American press had clearly declined while Carranza's had improved, but neither Carranza's level of press approval nor his media popularity ever matched Villa's.

The Carrancista propagandist Herbierto Barron attributed Villa's media demise and Carranza's improved media stature to the Carrancistas' successful and truthful propaganda. Villa's power had been thoroughly quashed, he correctly pointed out in a cable to Carranza, but he also asserted that Carrancista propaganda had proved to be effective in convincing the Wilson regime both of Carranza's greater suitability to govern Mexico and of the reality of the situation—Villa was finished.[213] He had written to Wilson in mid-August and asked the president to pay particular attention to a news report from the *New York Sun* (which he reproduced in the letter) concluding that Villa was a spent force.[214] A week later Barron wrote to Carranza and claimed he had influenced Wilson against Villa, although he provided no evidence for it.[215] In fact, Barron had widely overstated the effectiveness of Carranza's propaganda. Carranza had gained recognition largely because he defeated Villa militarily.

CONCLUSION

In some ways, the competing propaganda machines—Huerta's, Carranza's, and Villa's—used similar tactics. They all employed censorship liberally, wired cables directly to American newspapers, attempted to charm and coddle American reporters, exaggerated military gains, and downplayed or lied about military setbacks.

Carranza, however, developed and maintained an operational edge over Huerta and Villa. His public relations machine became organizationally more sophisticated than its rivals, with the establishment of two news agencies, a wire service, and more propaganda organs funded both in the United States and in Mexico. Carranza also had greater financial resources at his command than did Villa—a gap that grew more pronounced with time.

Yet, on balance, Villa's propaganda operations must be judged far more effective than Huerta's or Carranza's. Why? The first major reason is that Villa had seized the propaganda initiative by the fall of 1913—and held fast to it. Because Villa spread his messages first and effectively, Carrancista propagandists fought an uphill battle through 1915. Even during his military collapse, Villa maintained higher levels of support from and popularity in the American press. Indeed, newspapers such as the *Los Angeles Times* and the *San Francisco Examiner* preferred to agitate for United States military intervention in Mexico after Villa's eclipse than to throw support to Carranza. Both had initially been anti-Villa, anti-revolutionary, and, in the *Times* case, pro-Huerta.

The second major reason for Villa's propaganda predominance derives from the content of Villa's messages, which, for the sake of comparison with Huerta's and Carranza's media efforts, can be broken down into seven themes—friendship with the United States, congruent self-interest, the pragmatism of supporting a winner, Villa's morality, his "common man" image, his physical attractiveness, and his adherence to democracy. In these areas Villa promoted himself with far greater facility than did Carranza or Huerta, while portraying his two rivals as virtual opposites of what he claimed to represent.

Villa repeated his message of friendship for the United States seemingly at every opportunity, whereas Carranza and Huerta, to different degrees, did far less to promote a theme of friendship. There was, indeed, little that Huerta could do to overcome the disastrous public relations effect with which the murders of Madero and Pino Suárez saddled him. His 1913 propaganda messages were intermittently friendly—for example, he offered olive branches to American business interests—but also defiant. And the actions he took with regard to the Tampico incident in April 1914, which contributed to the American occupation of Veracruz, were clearly and intentionally hostile.

Carranza's "friendship" became a staple of his propaganda message increasingly in 1915. Yet it won him few rewards in the United States press (although it probably contributed to feelings of reduced anxiety in Washington as Villa, Washington's favored revolutionary, faced military collapse over the spring and summer). Carranza's problem stemmed from the pith of his earlier propaganda message, which had championed Mexican nationalism, often at the expense of friendliness. Where Villa expressed a desire to accommodate U.S. concerns, Carranza's message put the United States at arm's length and made it clear that the First Chief sought to placate Mexican concerns.

In terms of self-interest, Villa promoted a foreign policy that closely paralleled U.S. policy while portraying Carranza as self-serving and uninterested in either cooperating with the United States or truly serving Mexico's national interest. Carranza himself chose to promote a line of self-interest that suited his promotion of Mexican nationalism. He gained little by it—as is best evidenced by his initial stand on the Veracruz occupation—and ultimately discarded these tactics in 1915 when he adopted a policy of rhetorical friendship with the United States. Huerta's self-interest was promoted as solely Mexican and only added to the ill will he gained by Madero's death and the Tampico incident.

Villa wanted to persuade Washington through his propaganda that supporting him made good sense pragmatically because he was likely to be the winner in the Revolution. Carranza, too, sought to promote himself as a winner, but through 1914 the message often got lost in his unbridled Mexican chauvinism. In 1915 he took steps to portray himself as a winner and the likely victor of the Revolution. Again he gained little by it, not because it was untrue but because, first, the message was inconsistent with the framing he had gained in the press as vain, prideful, and sneaky and, second, it represented a major shift from his earlier postures and the position Villa had cast him in.

To speak of Huerta's pragmatism is almost an oxymoron, because Huerta never argued that he was a winner or that he was destined to emerge triumphant over the revolutionaries. Instead, he proffered an unappealing argument that he should be supported because he occupied the presidential chair. Neither the press nor the Wilson regime paid much attention to it. And what about Madero's death? He simply denied responsibility for it.

Villa's propaganda cleverly tied his morality to Villista perceptions of American self-interest. His was not merely a question of "What's in it for me?" but rather, "Is it the right thing to do?" Carranza's morality, like his self-interest, was steeped in virulent Mexican nationalism. Consequently, and in contradistinction to Villa, the "right" thing for him seldom resembled America's self-interest.

As for Huerta's morality, in the United States it was another oxymoron. He was a cold-blooded murderer of Mexicans and hostile to the United States. He was deemed immoral before he had a chance to promote morality.   ·

The theme of the "common man" provided much of the glue that held the elements of Villa's message together. His propaganda depicted him as a quintessential "little guy," a man of the people, of humble origins, who had raised himself up by dint of sheer perseverance and abilities and now wanted nothing so much as to uplift Mexico's downtrodden. Villa promoted land reform, among other things, because it was the right thing to do—and conveniently for America's self-interest, land reform appeared to offer political stability to Mexico.

Huerta was a dictator. He had no pretensions to the contrary, in the prevailing American depictions, nor did his propaganda evince any interest in portraying him as a "little guy." Neither did Carranza attempt to portray himself as a common man. He did advocate land reform, but of a measured and cautious variety. Villa, meanwhile, portrayed him as a high-handed, haughty aristocrat.

In another theme, Villa successfully promoted himself as aesthetically attractive—as an athletic, active, hands-on leader, a fearless warrior, vital, robust, and possessed of uncommon horse-sense. Neither Carrancista nor Huertista propagandists, by contrast, attempted to present their leader as physically appealing. Carranza's public relations stressed his experience, but, in conjunction with Villista barbs, Carranza usually emerged as old, clumsy, and ineffectual—because of both his age and the inherent obtuseness of aristocrats. Promotion of Huerta ignored this issue, although Villa effectively tarred him with being a drunkard.

The theme of democracy was probably the key political ingredient of Villa's propaganda. He advocated grass-roots democracy and the end of personalism and military influence in government. His common-man origins made this element of his propaganda especially compelling. And he cast Carranza as his political opposite—dictatorial, aristocratic, and elitist.

Carranza's message was democratic, although decidedly less ebullient in this respect than Villa's. And his democratic impulses took a backseat to profusions of Mexican nationalism—at least through 1914. In 1915 the message targeted democracy and how Carranza embraced the concept of it, but the language was often stiff and unenthusiastic. He championed the law, whereas Villa championed the people. Huerta, of course, as dictator made no pretensions to being democratic.

Although surpassed in organizational sophistication by the Carranza public relations machine, the Villa propaganda operation's more effective messages were better tailored to achieve the ends all three leaders sought—diplomatic recognition, financial backing, public support in both the United States and Mexico, and material backing to fight their enemies. Villa won all of these struggles, save the one for recognition.

Villa was packaged and sold as exciting, daring, brave, clever, a man of the people, humble, democratic, and friendly. Carranza was portrayed both by Villista propaganda and, in many ways, by his own public relations materials as the opposite of Villa—dull, cautious, obtuse, aristocratic, dictatorial, and unfriendly. Huertista propaganda, meanwhile, had never been able to recast the unflattering portrayals the dictator received as a result of his involvement in the death of Madero and the events that precipitated the Veracruz occupation.

CHAPTER FIVE

THE TROUBLE WITH MEXICANS

Villista, Carrancista, and Huertista propagandists not only vied with one another in the mass media but also, at a very basic level, grappled with widely held American visions of Mexico and Mexicans. Often hackneyed, ethnocentric, and even racist, these images permeated press representations and often undermined the propagandists' best efforts. Some of the standard American frames for understanding Mexico and Mexicans dated back centuries, and they often devolved into stereotypes. In this chapter I briefly chart the etiology of Hispanic, Indian, and Mexican (that is, *mestizo*) imagery in the United States, and I examine three themes commonly used by the American press in its treatment of Mexicans: their supposed backwardness, racial limitations, and moral decrepitude.[1]

The prevalent American visions developed as loose composites of three overlapping types—Hispanic, Indian, and, mainly, *mestizo* (which I refer to as Mexican). It is useful to break the Mexican rubric into its two main *mestizaje* components—Hispanic and Indian—because, although each was denigrated in the United States as dangerously immature and given to extreme intemperance, their constituent characteristics lent different shades and sometimes different attributes to the perceived mongrel they engendered—that is, the Mexican. The Mexican, the dominant image, became in part a conflation of the Hispanic and the Indian, but it also evolved as more than that. From the early days of the United States, Mexicans have been portrayed as a separate category combining the worst elements of the Hispanic and the Indian.

HISPANIC-MEXICANS AND THE BLACK LEGEND

The Hispanic component of the Mexican character—which I refer to as Hispanic-Mexican—derived from anti-Spanish sentiment (sometimes referred to as the Leyenda Negra, or Black Legend), which had its roots in sixteenth-century England.[2] Because English colonists carried anti-Spanish attitudes to the "New World" like so much cultural baggage, a similar sentiment took root and flourished as the colonies, and later the United States, shared a frontier with Spain and then Mexico. In the nineteenth century, as Mexico gained its independence from Spain and as the United States began its geographical expansion toward the Pacific Ocean, many Americans readily applied anti-Spanish sentiment to Mexico because of its partly Spanish heritage.

The Hispanic-Mexican appeared to Americans to represent the antithesis of everything they held dear about themselves.[3] Americans tended to be Protestant; they viewed and valued themselves as thrifty, hardworking, and peace-loving and as upholding the virtues of cleanliness, egalitarianism, technological advancement, and abstemiousness.[4] Hispanic-Mexicans, by contrast, were Roman Catholic (read, religiously corrupt) and were seen as exemplifying thievery, laziness, uncleanliness, untrustworthiness, cowardliness, and hierarchy. To Americans they were scoundrels, liars, unprogressive, cruel, decadent, lecherous, greedy, treacherous, sexually promiscuous, comfortable with incest, and fond of violence.[5]

Anti-Hispanic-Mexican sentiment peaked twice, with the United States' two major foreign wars of the period—the Mexican

War (1846–1848) and the Spanish-American, Cuban War (1898). The public sentiment expressed during both conflicts has served for historians as a barometer for the contours and, to some extent, the depth of anti-Hispanic-Mexican feeling in the United States.[6]

In the twentieth century the Mexican image has fared somewhat better than it did in the nineteenth. Yet while the discrete Hispanic component of the image has largely faded from view, many of those themes have appeared in somewhat different form in anti-Indian portrayals.

INDIAN-MEXICANS: GOOD SAVAGES/BAD SAVAGES

The anti-Indian component of American estimation of the Mexican character stems from general American racial and cultural antipathy toward American Indians.[7] Early European contact set the stage and established the tradition of anti-Indian sentiment in American culture. Although Indians first represented curiosities to "New World" Americans (née Europeans), they quickly became objects of disdain—ultimately to be seen, as Raymond Stedman puts it, as "the enemy."[8]

Like Hispanic-Mexicans, Indians have been represented as a "reverse or negative model" to the predominant American culture.[9] American portrayals have tended to ignore Native Americans' cultural diversity, "conceiving of Indians in terms of their deficiencies according to white ideals rather than in terms of their own various cultures."[10]

The un-American characteristics of Indians have included intemperance, sexual promiscuity, lust, lechery, venality, warmongering, polygamous practices, and fiendishness, as well as an inclination for cannibalism, human sacrifice, personal filth, cruelty to captives of war, laziness, cowardice, and deceit.[11] Stedman, who has examined the Indian image in American film and fiction, asks rhetorically:

[D]o the Indians of a book or movie seem to belong to the human race? Do they have homes? Families? Emotions other than mindless fury? Anxieties not connected to warfare? Aside from the menacing chief or the lovely princess, do the Indian characters have personal names? Daily tasks? Amusements other than drinking or torturing? In sum, are they seen in anything resembling full dimension? When they are not and incidental white characters are, the implication is obvious, the cliché imminent.[12]

Less prominent by far, the positive attributes of the "noble" Indian include being friendly, courteous, and hospitable and having the qualities of great stamina, physical endurance, and bravery, as well as tenderness toward family members.[13] Virtually all of the nominal characteristics of Indians would surface in American press depictions of Mexicans between 1913 and 1915, with the general exception of Indians' positive attributes.

THE MESTIZO: MEXICAN MONGREL

Since Mexico achieved independence from Spain in the early 1820s, Mexicans have been portrayed in the United most commonly as the products of blended Spanish and Indian heritage—as *mestizo*, in short. This Hispanic-Indian admixture has been twisted in the United States into a creature that adds up to less than the sum of its half-breed parts.[14]

While the Hispanic was held to be racially and culturally superior to the lowly Indian, Mexicans were viewed as "mongrels" who represented the worst and most depraved extremes of both races and cultures:

The mixed blood was widely assailed as the most despicable of human types. . . . Precisely because he was a mixed-breed,

the Mexican was ranked . . . below the Indian and the Negro
on the scale of inferior races. The Mexican's "mongrelization"
carried cultural as well as racial implications. Trapped in a
cultural limbo, the Mexican seemed to possess none of the
European's [read, Latin's] intelligence nor any of the Indian's
primal serenity and sensitivity to nature.[15]

Depictions of Mexicans became increasingly unfavorable
during two periods: first, that of Manifest Destiny (1830–1850),
perhaps highlighted best by the Mexican War (1846–1848),[16] and
second, the later nineteenth century and early twentieth century
(1890–1920), when Social Darwinism sank deep roots into the
American Zeitgeist, as was well expressed during the Spanish-
American-Cuban War (1898).[17]

Early-nineteenth-century American depictions of Mexicans
came from travelers, adventurers, frontiersmen, and soldiers. Yet
"they did not simply describe Mexican life as they found it, they
passed judgment over it."[18] And the sentiment expressed was that
which the British had earlier employed versus Spain: that Spaniards—
and now their half-breed descendants, Mexicans—were lazy, cruel,
and treacherous.[19] As Cecil Robinson put it: "Pioneer America
could find little to approve of in the Mexican society it collided
with, being affronted in all its major concerns by Mexican attitudes,
real or imagined."[20] (By Philip Wayne Powell's reckoning, in this
passage "Britain" could substitute for "Pioneer America," and
"Spanish" for "Mexican"; and by Stedman's account, "Britain"
might be substituted for "Pioneer America," and "Indian" for
"Mexican.") Mexicans were seen, Robinson continued, as "imprac-
tical yet cunning, mystical but erotic, fierce yet evasive, obsessed
with a concept of honor but, to the Americans, seemingly incapable
of truth in the homespun, American sense of the word."[21]

In the twentieth century, American popular depictions of
Mexican attributes remained mostly unchanged and unchallenged,[22]
though there has been a tendency since the 1920s to portray

Mexicans increasingly more realistically.[23] The general tenor of the treatment, however, remained dismissive through the 1980s.[24]

Also, in the twentieth century Mexicans have been seen as less a mixture of Spanish and Indian blood and tradition and more as a separate entity—although the characteristics falling under the half-breed rubric have remained largely consistent with those of the nineteenth-century mongrel (and the combined worst elements of Black Legend Spanishness and savage Indianness).[25] Given the continuity of the prevalent American vision of Mexicans as irascibly backward, morally depraved, and racially limited half-breeds, it is unsurprising that such sentiments infiltrated American press treatment of the Mexican Revolution, but with revealing variations.

THREE SCARLET BADGES

In order to address the question of Villa's propaganda successes, I examine two sets of pertinent American images of Mexicans and Villa. The first set, the subject of the rest of this chapter, consists of images appearing in selected American press organs. The second, the subject of chapter 8, comprises images resonant in the American diplomatic record.

In its portrayals of Mexico and Mexicans during the Revolution, the press drew selectively (and sometimes unconsciously) from the pool of long-established characteristics of Mexicanness. In this sense, images of Mexicans in the American press between 1913 and 1915 maintained continuity with historical representations of Mexicanness, with certain qualitative differences. For example, the press played up the Indian component of the mongrelized Mexican, an admixture that received scant attention elsewhere. On the other hand, the press evinced little interest in nominal Mexican religious corruption, an important ingredient of more general American visions of Mexico. Press treatment also eschewed the

Mexicanness topic of sexual depravity—yet this matter was duly noted in American diplomatic reports coming from Mexico. Press treatment of Villa and Mexico, then, both derived from and contributed to deeply internalized, widespread American cultural visions of Mexico.

Three general themes stand out in the way the American press treated Mexicans during the Revolution. First, the theme of backwardness, usually manifesting environmental influences, typically included Mexicans' being stuck in the material circumstances and retrograde mindset of earlier centuries, as well as exhibiting immaturity and tendencies toward violence. Second, racial limitations, deriving from Mexicans' perceived genetic inferiority, included mental unsophistication (even stupidity) and a weakness for pleasures of the body that contributed to a hedonistic delight in pillage and chaos. Third, the theme of moral decrepitude incorporated dishonesty, a love of excessive (often gratuitous) violence, innate cruelty, an inclination for theft, and a propensity for sneakiness.

To assess and explore the consonance between American historical visions and American press treatment of Villa, I focus on the contents of leading newspapers in six major American markets—Chicago, Denver, Los Angeles, New York, San Francisco, and Washington, D.C.—as well as on eleven news magazines with national circulations.[26] Villa's, Carranza's, and Huerta's propaganda vied with prevalent American visions, and this struggle was manifested in these and other publications. Also, because media content to some extent reflects and to some extent influences public opinion,[27] examining how the American press depicted Mexicans provides a framework against which specific images of Villa, Huerta, and Carranza might be assessed.

The *Chicago Tribune*, founded in 1847, was steeped in muck-raking in the 1910s. It took on "spectacular crusades," according to one author, who added, "One never knew where the *Tribune* was going to stand."[28] Yet during the Mexican Revolution, the paper served as a reliable barometer for the middle-of-the-road media position on the conflict—more friendly and less hostile than some, less friendly and more hostile than others.

The *Denver Post*, established in 1895, had a reputation as a "notorious yellow journal" during the early twentieth century.[29] The *Post* generally supported both Villa and the Revolution. It tended to rely heavily—as countless other papers did—on wire services for its revolutionary news. The *Post* lacked a bona fide editorial page, although it occasionally ran front-page opinions. Cartoons—again, sometimes received from the wire services— typified its editorial coverage.

The *Los Angeles Times* fell under the control of former Union soldier Harrison Gray Otis in the 1880s. After purchasing a one-quarter interest in the daily in 1882, Otis bought a controlling share of the paper in 1886. He actively directed and shaped editorial policy at the *Times*. Under his directorship the paper "had a reputation for biased news presentation."[30] One author has described him "as a man always looking for his next enemy and his next fight."[31] Otis owned large tracts of agricultural property in northern Mexico, and his paper espoused vitriolic anti-revolutionary sentiments. Villa ultimately won endorsement and praise from the Los Angeles daily, although it continued to call for United States military intervention in Mexico. Among the media examined here, it remained the most unrepentantly racist in its portrayals of Mexico and Mexicans.[32]

The *New York Times*, "the greatest of American newspapers . . . [because it] is a newspaper of record, first and foremost," according to one author, was established in 1851.[33] During the Mexican Revolution the *Times* provided the most even-handed and, at the same time, favorable coverage of Villa and the Revolution among the media examined here. Its editorials tended to adhere closely to President Wilson's policy.

The *San Francisco Examiner*, the flagship of William Randolph Hearst's media empire, at first took a strong anti-Wilson and anti-

Villa position on Mexico. In time, however, the paper lauded Villa as the likely savior of Mexico. Hearst, like Otis, owned vast tracts of land in Mexico. The *Examiner* actively promoted United States military intervention in Mexico.

The *Washington Times* was purchased and fell under the editorial direction of publisher Frank Munsey in 1909. Munsey had fashioned a media empire from inauspicious beginnings. It began with the establishment in New York in 1882 of the *Golden Argossy: Freighted with Treasures For Boys and Girls*.[34] During the Revolution the *Washington Times* acted as a Wilson administration mouthpiece.

Evidence used in this chapter to assess how the press constructed Mexican images is drawn from three basic sources—news stories (and their headlines), editorials (and their headlines), and editorial cartoons (and their captions). Each was the product of an often complex, sometimes collaborative process on the way to publication. News stories reflected a mixture of opinion and interpretation that might include the input of one or more reporters and one or more copy editors. The accompanying headlines were the handiwork of an editor—who might or might not have read the news story fully or closely and who might or might not have agreed with the view(s) presented in it. Editorials represented a publication's official opinion yet did not necessarily reflect the sentiments expressed either in news stories or in news headlines— or, for that matter, in editorial headlines, which might have been written by someone other than the author of the editorial itself. Editorial positions were typically staked out by a committee composed of competing voices. Further, shifting influences such as publisher pressure or even personnel turnover might affect the content, tone, and consistency of editorial comment. Editorial cartoons reflected the cartoonist's perception of and reaction to editorial direction (which varied by publication). They also reflected the contents of news stories and headlines, as well as the cartoonist's personally held views, which might be the product of nonmedia influences.

Internal media influences that affected content included editorial policy, the political ideologies of reporters and editors, prevalent journalistic norms, advertising, and ownership. While it is usually difficult to tease out specific influences on selected content, ownership is worthy of special consideration. For example, the owners of the most vehemently anti-Villa publications examined in this chapter, the *San Francisco Examiner* and the *Los Angeles Times*, maintained large landed estates in Mexico and consequently had good reason to fear any potential shake-up of the political order. In both cases the publishers—Otis and Hearst—actively directed editorial policy at their respective papers.

News stories, editorials, and editorial cartoons, with their respective headlines or captions, provide the grist for the exploration of American press depictions of the Mexican Revolution. Press treatment of the conflict employed a three-pronged Mexican typology of backwardness, racial limitations, and moral decrepitude. These three components surfaced continually, coloring depictions of Mexico and recasting and distorting the Revolution.

BACKWARDNESS

The basic features of backwardness included being stuck in the material trappings and primitive thinking of earlier times. According to press portrayals, Mexicans eschewed progress and advancement in favor of stasis and cultural rot; violence was endemic in Mexico because the mongrels had not evolved enough culturally to embrace sensibly peaceful ways. Further, because Mexico had never experienced progress and orderliness, it stewed in chaos. Arnoldo De León put it this way: "Where whites were energetic, Mexicans seemed backward; where whites were ambitious and aggressive, Mexicans seemed apathetic and complacent; where whites considered themselves inventive, Mexicans seemed anachronistic; and where whites knew their direction, Mexicans appeared to be going nowhere. . . . [W]hite culture appeared more advanced, more progressive, and more civilized."[35]

Expressing a sense of urgency, a mid-February 1913 cartoon in the *San Francisco Examiner* exemplified the press's concern with Mexicans' inability to advance (fig. 2). In it, the Mexican hope of "progress" slips away like the setting sun while the Mexican people (cartoon Mexicans were almost always male, and the whole population was usually represented by a single character) misuse precious time engaging in mayhem and violence—symbolized by the smoking pistol and fiery torch, both of which also suggest moral limitations. The man's face is hidden, but he seems by the energy of his exertion to be enjoying himself.

And Mexico's elusive pursuit of progress is likened to running on a treadmill—much energy expended without discernible advancement. The suggestion is that Mexicans will not advance until they willingly give up their lust for violence (the pistol) and anarchy (the torch). They must become calmer and more orderly—the antitheses of which are also signified by the man's costume (spurs, sombrero) and his wasted energy. Last, the picture also maligns the Mexican character by linking it to the diminutive mutt running alongside the treadmill.

Couching its sentiments in a bastardized expression of geographical determinism, the *Chicago Tribune* observed: "On one side [of the Rio Grande there exists] shiftlessness, poverty, slovenliness, laziness; on the other side enterprise, energy, prosperity, and thrift. It is as if we were stepping from one century to another."[36] And small wonder, the *Los Angeles Times* explained: "The Mexican seems to have gained little or nothing in civilization in 400 years."[37]

A late March 1914 cartoon in the *Los Angeles Times* portrayed similar sentiments in reference to "Mexican anarchy," pondering, "How Long Will It Continue?" (fig. 3). The suggestion was that "it" had been going on for a very long time. The answer seemed simple enough: it would continue until the Mexican decided to put down that bottle and torch and devote his energy to something

Figure 2. "REVOLUTION!" Reproduced from the *San Francisco Examiner*, February 17, 1913.

productive. Then order might replace chaos, and abstemious diligence might stand in for drunken revelry.

One implication of the cartoon is that the mayhem might well continue indefinitely because the backward Mexican so thoroughly enjoys chaos, as is suggested by the evident mirth on the caricature's face. This portrait also raises the issue of Mexican racial and

Figure 3. "How Long Will It Continue?" Reproduced from the *Los Angeles Times*, March 30, 1914.

moral limitations. The man's dark-skinned face radiates a devilish insouciance born of drunkenness (he is spilling his bottle of "polque" [*sic*]), and he is apparently ready to commit "anarchy" (again, a fiery torch).

A pictorial in the *San Francisco Examiner* cast Mexico in the grip, literally, of "anarchy," "riot," "revolution," and "demoralization" (fig. 4). While the depicted Mexican struggles to be free, the hold of these elements appears firm and in possession of greater strength than his (judging by the immensely larger size of the hand). The setting—the blazing sun, the buzzards in flight (associating the Mexican with rottenness), the character almost melting in the heat, and the basic inequality of the struggle—suggests an environmental weakness in Mexico of almost Sisyphean proportions and futility.

Why, the picture seems to query, might the Mexican remain "in the grasp"? The only elements of evidence available to answer the question are, first, his dress—the sombrero (a ubiquitous signifier of backwardness), the pistol (another signifier of backwardness and sometimes moral depravity), and the charro's jacket (it completes the backward outfit)—and, second, his tautological and thoroughly backward activity—he is fighting to be free of something from which he can never free himself by fighting. He really is "in the grasp."

The *Los Angeles Times* and the *San Francisco Examiner* routinely excoriated all sides in the Mexican Revolution by lumping them together as essentially "uncivilized" because of inherent backwardness. A *Times* article, for example, warned Americans to be wary of their southern neighbors because Mexicans "will hate . . . [and] his [their] prisoners will be the prisoners of Indians no more civilized than the Indians who tortured our grandfathers a hundred years ago or the Indians who spiked the heads of our fathers and brothers in the Philippines."[38]

Indians were seen not simply as backward but in some cases as actually incapable of civilization, as the term was used by some of

STILL IN THE GRASP

Figure 4. "STILL IN THE GRASP." Reproduced from the *San Francisco Examiner*, November 25, 1913.

the media. The *North American Review* asserted: "Mexico is not, in fact, a nation, but a country peopled by many tribes of Indians of varying degrees of development, none reaching what we would call civilization."[39] Even more ominously, American Indians, too, according to a late June 1914 cartoon in the *Los Angeles Times* (fig. 5), might, if the logic of President Wilson's Mexico policy were applied to the United States, expect the United States to be given "back" to them.

The cartoon makes its point ironically. It charges that "It Would Be Just As Reasonable" to return the United States to the American Indians, but the point is that giving the land back to "the poor Indian" in Mexico would be just as futile and ridiculous as it would be to give the United States back to his American counterpart. Further, in the sketch the Indian character, on behalf of all American Indians, appeals to the "Great White F(e)ather"—a jibe at Woodrow Wilson's reluctance to be as firm with Mexico as the newspaper often demanded. Again, clothing helps to signify backwardness: the Indian is draped in a pseudo-traditional blanket and feathered headdress while Wilson sports a suit and tie.

In two cartoons of late April 1914, the *Chicago Tribune* highlighted the superiority of American culture by comparing backward Mexico and the progressive United Sates. In the top portion of the first cartoon (fig. 6), inhabitants of the former Mexican territories of California, Nevada, Utah, Arizona, Colorado, New Mexico, and Texas are clearly fashioned as characters retrograde (clad in sombreros, spurs, and patched clothing), passive, and inclined toward violence and perhaps crime. This is suggested by their sidearms (pistols and knives), downtrodden demeanor (as if they lack the confidence to look you in the eye; they may also have something to hide—perhaps a crime), and passive stances. Below, the same territories under American influence are represented by characters exuding the trappings of progress—smart modern clothing, assertive body language, and confident visages. Only "Mexico" remains unchanged—still armed, still meek (and possibly

Figure 5. "It Would Be Just As Reasonable." Reproduced from the *Los Angeles Times*, June 29, 1914.

Figure 6. "CIVILIZATION FOLLOWS THE AMERICAN FLAG." Reproduced from the *Chicago Tribune*, April 23, 1914.

sneaky), still uncivilized. Suggesting that Mexico's problem might stem partially from a congenital infirmity, the Mexico character is pigeon-toed in both representations.

In the second *Tribune* sketch (fig. 7), United States superiority is directed particularly at Spanish influence in Latin America. The cartoon again raises the theme of fundamental backwardness

Figure 7. "WHAT THE UNITED STATES HAS FOUGHT FOR." Reproduced from the *Chicago Tribune*, April 26, 1914.

while seeming to imply a link between racial characteristics and culture. Before the United States rescues them "from their oppression," the Philippines, Hawaii, Puerto Rico, Cuba, and Panama all labor under slavery or some form of Spanish tyranny. This is invoked not only by their shoddy clothing but also by their apelike stances (hunched over, knuckles curled under, arms dangling, hands at or below the knee).

While a literal reading of the cartoon suggests an obvious case of Latin American backwardness, the apelike appearance of the first line of characters also implies that Spanish cultural influence could physically transmogrify otherwise tractable and teachable citizens into little more than subhumans. American influence (unapologetically referred to as "intervention"), on the other hand, offered "sanitation," "education," "prosperity," "self-government," and "health."

As the foregoing cartoons suggest, Mexican backwardness had clear political implications, too. Indeed, the *Saturday Evening Post* noted that Mexicans' general "ignorance" had led to a situation in which "[t]he people are incapable of working out a constitution like ours. They hardly even know what it means."[40] And *Collier's* snidely chipped in: "Some of the rebels in the north call themselves Constitutionalists. This is a joke."[41]

Some publications held out the possibility that Mexicans might be trained to emulate civilized behavior as a first step on the road to progress. As *Everybody's* confidently asserted: "We must teach them how to respect us. . . . Then we must teach them how to behave."[42]

Press analyses sometimes conflated issues of Mexican backwardness, which usually was associated with learned behavior, with race. For example, the *Los Angeles Times* explained Mexicans' inferior racial makeup in part by associating their behavior with "ferocious" Aztecs and "barbarous" Spaniards.[43] It is unclear whether the alleged behavior was believed to be learned or inbred.

Elsewhere the Los Angeles publication likened Mexicans to animals and disparaged the notion that they might be taught even the rudiments of civilization, such as reading and writing. It commented that "75 percent of the Mexicans can neither read nor write, are without moral perceptions, are as utterly unfit to intelligently exercise the right of suffrage as so many coyotes, and . . . to give them the power to vote would be to perpetuate the conditions of brigandage which have for so many months desolated Mexico."[44]

The animal reference also raises the second theme of media representations—the racial limitations of Mexicans.

RACIAL LIMITATIONS

In addition to their backwardness, Mexicans were portrayed in the United States press as racially inferior to Americans. The two main ingredients in this deterministic soup were the alleged racially derived stupidity of Mexicans and their genetically based penchant for mayhem and violence. Such a priori conclusions were consistent with traditionally held notions about how Spanish and Indian obtuseness and love of violence had combined to make the mongrel Mexican even dumber and more inclined to violence than his constituent ancestors. In the middle of the nineteenth century, it was commonly believed, for example, that Mexicans' cognitive inferiority stemmed literally from thick skulls.[45]

One consequence of being daft and destined to revel in violence was that Mexicans did not have the sense to throw off backwardness in favor of progress and forward thinking. Their brains did not—could not—work that way.

A letter to the editor of *The Nation*[46] aptly captured the prevailing media sentiment: "The average [Mexican] peon is mentally a child and morally a savage. . . . Villa, Zapata, Orozco et al are simply savages of superior intelligence . . . [and] they take the field because it affords them an opportunity to murder, rob, and torture."[47] A *Chicago Tribune* editorial explained the problem genetically: "Brigandage is . . . in the Mexican blood."[48]

Echoing these conclusions, and bemoaning the disastrous implications of Mexico's Aztec ancestry, the *Chicago Tribune* expressed alarm about "the savagery of the hybrid Aztec-Indian-Spaniard race."[49] Readers of the *Tribune* might not have been surprised at this. After all, they had also been informed that the practice of cannibalism was not uncommon in northern Mexico (although it is unclear whether this practice was considered learned or inborn).[50]

The American novelist and reporter Jack London, who reported from Mexico for *Collier's*,[51] expressed the prevailing American press sentiment about the effects of *mestizaje*:

> Mexico is an Indian country. . . . Sixty-five per cent of the inhabitants are pure Indians; 15 per cent are pure Spanish, Americans, English, and other foreigners. The remaining 20 per cent are mixed Indian and Spanish. . . . And it is precisely this 20 per cent half-breed class that foments all the trouble, plays childishly with the tools of giants, and makes a shambles and a chaos of the land. . . . The "breeds" are the predatory class. They produce nothing. They create nothing.[52]

In providing an explicit comparison between Mexicans and Americans, the magazine *Forum* exemplified the widespread media judgment.[53] It juxtaposed the defining elements of the two nations' racial makeup. Charging that Mexicans were natally "inclined toward crime,"[54] and claiming that Mexicans' "mixed" racial makeup predisposed them to civil strife, the magazine complained that the Indian component of Mexico's "mixed" blood had long since washed away any beneficial effects that might have been gained from Spanish lineage—which was itself weak and listless when compared with northern European bloodlines. Yet, oddly, the six features that characterized the Mexican were more cultural than racial in origin. Mexicans were

1. Mainly of Indian type;
2. Illiterate;
3. Mainly of illegitimate birth;
4. Inefficient as workers;
5. Intemperate;
6. Quarrelsome.[55]

Americans could be summed up in four lines:

1. Loyal submission to the will of the majority;
2. Candid recognition of the inalienable rights of the minority;
3. A cool, sober judgment;
4. A very high standard of education and morals.[56]

In short, in dialectical fashion, Mexicans function here as the antithesis of American normality.

Mexicans' sanguinary inadequacy had far-reaching political and foreign policy implications. "Mexico has always been run by a despot," charged the *San Francisco Examiner*.[57] The *Chicago Tribune* agreed and observed, "The main reason for the present condition of Mexico is the innate selfishness of its people."[58] The *Examiner* joined in, laying the blame squarely on the "inherent" defects of the Mexican: "Look at the cause, the racial and personal characteristics [of the] ignorant class of so-called peons. . . . [A]bout one-half of these are pure Indian. . . . The peon is the negative, not the positive man. He assimilates, often readily, but does not create. He is a follower, not a leader. Leading means taking the initiative and shouldering a responsibility. This he will not do. Procrastination is inborn in him."[59] Also seen as inborn, not to mention closely aligned with backwardness, was Mexicans' moral depravity—the third main theme of the media depictions.

MORAL DECREPITUDE

To Americans, it appeared that Mexican appetites knew few boundaries. This was natural both culturally and racially, according to the press, because backwardness set few limits on immodest or extreme behavior and because by blood Mexicans were inclined to be physically indulgent. In this media vision, mayhem and wanton behavior were endemic to Mexico, and sensible heads seldom

Figure 8. "OUR EYES ARE ON THEM." Reproduced from the *Chicago Tribune*, February 13, 1913.

prevailed because Mexicans had developed neither a moral intelligence nor any particular measure of self-control. The root of the problem was moral weakness. Arnoldo De León observed: "Throughout the [nineteenth] century, whites [in Texas] spoke of Mexican docility, ignorance, decadence, mediocrity, antagonism toward work, submission to vice, and hedonistic proclivities. . . . [B]iological difference was only one aspect to the total image."[60]

One effect of Mexican moral depravity was that the United States had to keep a close eye on Mexican affairs, as was suggested by an editorial cartoon in the *Chicago Tribune* in mid-February 1913,

WILL HE HAVE TO OPERATE?

[Copyright: 1913: By John T. McCutcheon.]

Figure 9. "WILL HE HAVE TO OPERATE?" Reproduced from the *Chicago Tribune*, February 19, 1913.

days before Madero was killed (fig. 8). The rendering suggests Mexican volatility (the smoking volcanoes), timidity, and sneakiness (small figures hiding, even skulking, behind a sign reading "Mexico"). It also ponders United States intervention (the big cannons as eyes). At the very least, suggested another pictorial a week later (fig. 9), Mexico was such a pain in the neck that Uncle Sam might have to "operate" on it (read, intervene).

One common manifestation of moral decrepitude was an intemperate fondness for drink. By culture, blood, or both, as indicated in newspaper cartoons (see fig. 3), Mexicans regularly imbibed to excess. They simply could not help themselves.

Frequently, again as shown by editorial cartoons (figs. 2, 3, and 4), Mexicans delighted in chaos and violence. *Forum* magazine reasoned that Mexicans "are likely to be quarrelsome and inclined towards crime"—at least when they had the energy to commit it—because "[t]he Mexican temperament . . . is without ambition and his efficiency is low indeed."[61]

Media portrayals sometimes rolled two or more of the elements—backwardness, racial limitations, and moral decrepitude—into one collective assault. For example, upon the outbreak of World War I in Europe in August 1914, the *Los Angeles Times* printed a cartoon in which Mexicans were dismissed as little more than crybabies (fig. 10). The intemperate toddler in the picture wails for lack of attention from an indecisive Uncle Sam (sitting on the proverbial fence), whose interest is suddenly taken up by events in Europe. The infant also represents backwardness, because an infant (that is, Mexico) is less developed than an adult (the United States). Not unexpectedly, given the temperamental vices of backwardness, the child remonstrates by flailing its arms. Further, the infant-versus-adult theme implies racial limitations; nonwhites were portrayed frequently as childlike, and the child clearly is not white. This combining of the elements of Mexicanness also provides a ready sense of continuity between press depictions and the ongoing historical treatment of Mexicans in the United States.

CONCLUSION

During the Mexican Revolution, the American press tended to portray Mexicans much as they had already been portrayed for more than one hundred years in the United States—as given to backwardness, racial limitations, and moral decrepitude. Within these broad themes, Mexicans were cast as cruel, greedy, dishonest,

Figure 10. "The Interesting Game." Reproduced from the *Los Angeles Times*, August 8, 1914.

Figure 11. "THE BANDITS' FOE; MEXICO'S SAVIOR!" Reproduced from the *San Francisco Examiner*, April 30, 1914.

stupid, grasping, and underhanded.[62] No Mexican revolutionary leader proved wholly able to escape being tarred with these three brushes, although some fared considerably better than others. Neither Huerta, Carranza, nor Villa could stand the shining light of civilization, suggested a *San Francisco Examiner* cartoon of late April 1914 (fig. 11). Moreover, when the three themes were applied to Huerta and Carranza, their confluence produced two compelling archetypal Mexican figures—the Savage (Huerta) and the Sneak (Carranza).[63]

In press depictions, Carranza and Huerta, along with Villa, assumed the basic characteristics of Mexican racial and cultural inferiority, but unlike Villa, they were virtually straightjacketed by being typecast as immutable archetypal examples of Mexicanness. In contrast, the press, while tarring Villa with some elements of Mexicanness, also lauded him, sometimes nearly allowing him to shed his Mexican skin and become U.S. Americanized.

CHAPTER SIX

THE SAVAGE AND THE SNEAK

Huerta and Carranza in the American Press

Despite their dogged propaganda efforts, Huerta and Carranza, in different ways, were each tainted by American images of Mexicanness in the United States press. Huerta was cast as a prime example of the archetypal Mexican Savage—barbaric, cruel, dishonest, vicious, disrespectful, oafish, and depraved. Carranza was framed as the consummate Mexican Sneak—slightly barbaric, oafish, egoistic, haughty, defiant, and disingenuous. The press also tended to dismiss Carranza by contrasting his sneakiness with Villa's more favored character as the archetypal Warrior.

HUERTA THE SAVAGE

Savage, n. a man of extreme, unfeeling, brutal cruelty; a barbarian.
> —*WEBSTER'S NEW UNIVERSAL UNABRIDGED DICTIONARY*

The application of several key characteristics of historical and prevailing press treatment of Mexicans proved to be especially damning to Huerta. He was categorized principally as a Mexican savage. The two subcategories of this incarnation—beast and barbarian—derived from the general historical pool of the three American cultural frames of Mexicanness: backwardness, racial limitations, and moral decrepitude. In particular, Huerta was condemned for butchery, obtuseness, murderousness, drunkenness, cruelty to prisoners of war, love of violence, and disrespect (for the United States).[1]

"SAVAGES IN CONTROL," a *Chicago Tribune* headline announced after Huerta had engineered President Francisco Madero's death and assumed the presidency in February 1913.[2] Huerta was a "butcher . . . [a] renegade," the Chicago daily intoned. Tagging Huerta with an almost bestial brazenness as well as insufficient cleverness to have at least covered his tracks, the paper added: "Madero is murdered in the streets by a stratagem so transparent that through it Huerta can be seen giving orders." The *Tribune* further impugned Huerta by labeling him "Judas Iscariot Huerta."[3] "All Mexico is weltering in murder and rapine," the *San Francisco Examiner* warned.[4]

The *Washington Times* repeatedly denounced Huerta's "Government by Butchery." In late July 1913, the paper juxtaposed its condemnation of Huerta with its support for the revolutionaries: "There seems to be nothing there [in Mexico] now but anarchy and chaos; and anarchy and chaos founded on a purpose of restoring liberty and order would at least be preferable to the anarchy and chaos which represent the treachery and assassination program which ushered in Huerta."[5]

The *Denver Post* reported, "MADERO HORRIBLY TORTURED BEFORE BEING SLAIN" and expressed great alarm at the heinousness of the acts because they were, the headline announced, too horrible to be revealed in print.[6] But in a macabre about-face days later, the paper did sketch the torture Madero suffered before being shot: tied to a chair, the president had his eyes gouged out with a knife—while Huerta's colleague Felix Díaz (nephew of Porfirio Díaz, the dictator

Figure 12. "WHAT CAN MEXICANS EXPECT . . . ?" Reproduced from the *Denver Post*, February 21, 1913.

Madero had unseated in 1911), sat idly by strumming a guitar and singing inflammatory "sonnets."[7]

"WHAT CAN MEXICANS EXPECT OF A NEW GOVERNMENT WHOSE FIRST ACT IS MURDER?" queried the title of a late February 1913 cartoon in the *Denver Post* (fig. 12). This sketch fashions Huerta as nearly bestial: smoking rifle in hand, evincing a defiant and triumphant posture, he stands with a foot on the chest of "THE BROTHER OF MADERO." One implication to be drawn was that Mexico might expect little good to come of Huerta's power grab, as is evidenced by Huerta's flag, which reads, "I HAVE OVERTHROWN THIS GOVERNMENT, THE FORCES ARE

WITH ME AND FROM NOW ON PEACE AND PROSPERITY WILL REIGN." The word "peace" is crossed out.

Huerta's perceived lack of respect for the United States also earned him censure. One cartoon in the *San Francisco Examiner* (fig. 13), for example, depicted Huerta in black garb (meant to suggest evil by color) clasping a bloody sword in one hand while, with the other, taunting Uncle Sam "RIGHT UNDER HIS NOSE." The depiction suggests that the United States would be justified in intervening in Mexico because Huerta's insolent, murderous actions actually invited it.

A more moderate, even blackly comical, interpretation of Huerta's character appeared in a *Chicago Tribune* cartoon (fig. 14). In it Huerta is lampooned as a Mexican jumping bean. This depiction denies him a full measure of self-control and intelligence. It suggests that Huerta's erratic behavior (symbolized by the bean's jumping) will end in resignation (that is, the bean will fall into a hole of oblivion, judiciously watched over by President Wilson).

Reflecting a typical Mexican tendency toward intemperance, Huerta also drank too much alcohol, according to the press. Two *Chicago Tribune* editorial cartoons stressed the point. Both were published in the later part of April 1914, in the midst of the Tampico incident, with the Veracruz occupation looming. In the first (fig. 15), Huerta's inferiority vis-à-vis the United States is shown by the significantly greater size of Uncle Sam, who prepares to spank Huerta with a shoe—presumably to punish him for the Tampico incident, though no specifics are provided. Huerta stands not just defiant to the United States but exaggeratedly so. The barb of alcoholism is registered by Huerta's counselor, "Colonel Cognac," whose advice—"DICTATE YOUR OWN TERMS, MY GENERAL"— is drunkenly misguided.

In the second cartoon, the *Tribune* attempted in three frames to belittle with humor Huerta's predilection for drink (fig. 16). In the first two frames, Huerta offers to diplomatically "treat" with

Figure 13. "RIGHT UNDER HIS NOSE." Reproduced from the *San Francisco Examiner*, February 18, 1913.

representatives of foreign governments—that is, to engage in a diplomatic dialogue. Huerta's real intention is revealed in the third frame. By "treat," according to the cartoon, he means to provide alcoholic beverages free of charge. His slackened posture and greedy countenance in the third frame suggest that Huerta would

Figure 14. "THE MEXICAN JUMPING BEAN." Reproduced from the *Chicago Tribune*, January 28, 1914.

like nothing better than to get drunk. By contrast, the diplomatic figures display shock at this lack of protocol.

The *Los Angeles Times* disagreed strongly with anti-Huerta depictions. It professed admiration for Huerta. For example, in October 1913, a typical editorial opined: "President Huerta is a brave soldier who has succeeded in preserving the government of the republic of Mexico from utter destruction, American property from seizure, and many Americans from torture and death."[8] Almost a year later the news organ still agitated for Huerta. In an

Figure 15. "HUERTA HAS A BAD ADVISER" Reproduced from the *Chicago Tribune*, April 18, 1914.

early February 1914 editorial that reeked with anti-Wilson sentiment, the *Times* explained its position: "He [Huerta] has shed blood, but he has fought for his life and his country to show what he could do in the way of reorganization: from the first he has been harried by his enemies and bedeviled by President Wilson."[9]

Yet in spite of the *Times*'s support, the Mexican savage rubric plagued Huerta from the day of Madero's death. The foundation

Figure 16. "HUERTA MAY NOT BE RECOGNIZED BUT . . ." Reproduced from the *Chicago Tribune*, April 18, 1914.

of his image rested upon his cruelty and his viciousness, which reflected historical Mexican backwardness, racial limitations, and moral decrepitude. Fleshing out his character, the press portrayed him as alternately incontinent (for example, he was drunken, or morally depraved), obtuse (for example, he did not acknowledge American superiority, which showed his racial limitations and backwardness), and childishly volatile (for example, he was represented in cartoons as a jumping bean, in need of a spanking, or smaller in stature than Uncle Sam, all symbolizing racial limitations and moral decrepitude).

Despite Villa's own Mexican heritage, this rendering of Huerta presented Villa with the opportunity to play himself off against it—which he did. The press responded, as I discuss in detail in the next chapter, in part by casting Villa as the reverse of Huerta, albeit incompletely so—he was partially stricken with watered-down elements of the Savage but was balanced by a backdrop of American-like virtues.

And what of Carranza? Unlike Villa, but like Huerta, the First Chief was thoroughly damned by his Mexicanness. In this case, the American press fashioned Carranza as an archetypal Mexican Sneak.

CARRANZA THE SNEAK

Sneak, n. a person who sneaks; a stealthy underhanded contemptible person.
— *WEBSTER'S NEW UNIVERSAL UNABRIDGED DICTIONARY*

Carranza was a sneak—and exhibited many standardized Mexican behaviors to prove it, American press treatment showed. He was cowardly, vain, disrespectful, and defiant (to the United States). He was slightly savage, had a thieving nature, and repeatedly represented himself in a false light. All of these traits, to varying degrees, reflected the three basic Mexican frames of backwardness, racial limitations, and moral decrepitude.

Prior to Huerta's resignation in mid-July 1914, Carranza the sneak received less media attention than Huerta the savage, for three reasons. First, Huerta garnered more headline news because he was president. Second, Huerta engaged the interests of the United States media and the United States government with particular passion from the day of Madero's death—an event that shocked the American press and official Washington. Carranza, on the other hand, gained little media attention until the fall of 1913, when the rebel military advances began to represent a visible and increasingly viable threat to Huerta's regime. Yet even then, Huerta as savage probably provided more exciting news copy than Carranza as sneak.

Rebel advances in the fall of 1913 and winter of 1914 raise the third reason for Carranza's relatively less prominent media standing compared with Huerta's in the period from Madero's death through Huerta's resignation. That is, Villa got the lion's share of the credit for the victories and therefore received wider coverage in the American press. Villa's propaganda operations through the spring of 1915 had promoted him in the United States more effectively than Carranza's propaganda had promoted the First Chief. Further, cast as a conquering warrior in the press, Villa presented a far more exciting media commodity than did Carranza, cast as an armchair general.

By the summer of 1915, however, as it became apparent to the American press that Villa's days were numbered and Carranza represented the only bona fide political alternative in Mexico, most of the media examined here extended to Carranza a marginally more favorable portrayal. He was still a sneak, but the media began to couch new assessments of him in quasi-fatalistic terms— that is, upon Villa's decline, Carranza had become Mexico's last best hope for salvation.

Like Huerta's American press image, Carranza's was culled from the pool of long-standing American visions of Mexicanness— with qualitative differences. In four key variants of sneakiness, Carranza typified Mexicanness, in the estimation of the American press. First, he was slightly savage; second, he was disrespectful and defiant toward the United States; third, he presented himself in false light, in part to disguise his cowardice; and, fourth, his behavior was contemptible.

Initially, press portrayals tainted Carranza by allusion: Constitutionalists were no good; Carranza was a Constitutionalist;
therefore, Carranza was no good. In a late March 1913 editorial
titled "SAVAGERY," the *Los Angeles Times* ridiculed the Constitutionalists—implicating Carranza, who, as First Chief, led the rebel
cause—for engaging in warfare that amounted to little more than
"savagery."[10] In December, another editorial echoed these
sentiments. The rebels, the *Times*'s commentary claimed, "are
plundering and murdering like any other brigands."[11]

On another occasion, the *Times*'s opinion page dismissed
Carranza as the leader of rebels who fought not for "liberty" but
for "plunder." The *San Francisco Examiner* agreed, noting that
"Carranza and his general [Villa] are all tarred with the same stick.
They are simply organized brigands."[12] One result of this brigandage, the *Times* chimed in, was that "[n]o man will dare till his land
for he will not know what day his crops will be destroyed, his
home burned, his wife and daughter violated and himself tortured
to death."[13]

That Carranza was implicated by the actions of subordinates
was sometimes made more explicit. Again, an editorial from the
Los Angeles Times illustrates the point: "The aggregation of bandits
and murderers who comprise the forces of Carranza and Villa have
stolen everything they could reach."[14]

A March 1915 editorial cartoon in the *Denver Post* directly
fingered Carranza in what it viewed as the Mexicans' predilection
for revolutionary violence (fig. 17). American tolerance for such
behavior has about run out—"IT'S REACHED MY LIMIT," Uncle Sam
warns. Carranza, a smaller figure than Uncle Sam (suggesting
lesser importance), meanwhile appears befuddled and cross-eyed,
and he clings to a smoking pistol and blood-soaked dagger.

Serving to mitigate the image of Carranza as savage, the *Chicago
Tribune* generally provided a more flattering counterpoint to the
Los Angeles Times's assessments of the Constitutional rebels. In the
fall of 1913, the *Tribune* suggested that early recognition of the

Figure 17. "HE'S GOT UNCLE'S GOAT AT LAST!" Reproduced from the *Denver Post*, March 9, 1915.

Constitutionalists' belligerency status against Huerta represented the best path of diplomatic action for the United States.[15] Such a course, the paper stated without further explanation, would serve both American self-interest and morality.[16]

The *Tribune*'s conditional support of Carranza derived from its view that the rebels represented a better alternative than Huerta for United States strategic interests. Carranza's character still lacked the moral strength and fiber of the American character, though. For example, when Carranza bristled at United States insistence that the body of Benton, the Briton who had been killed while under Villa's care in late February 1914, be released for

American examination, his attitude was portrayed as petulantly defiant. A headline read, "CARRANZA FLOUTS BRYAN." The story explained how Carranza's "Ruffled Dignity" made him oblivious to reasonable American demands. Indeed, his exaggerated pride made the United States "Look Ridiculous."[17] The next day a self-righteous editorial concluded, "Carranza is irritating, but it is grotesque to suggest what he does can touch American honor. . . . [The United States] can afford to use the patience of greatness."[18] This forbearance came despite Carranza's inclination to "put [his] thumb to [his] nose and point [it] in our direction."[19]

Not surprisingly, Carranza's anti-occupation stance on Veracruz elicited bitter commentary from American media. "Carranza more than Huerta has called an American army of occupation into Mexico," snorted an editorial in the *Chicago Tribune*.[20] The *San Francisco Examiner* agreed, charging that "Carranza and Villa are equally guilty with Huerta of insults to the American flag and outrages upon, and murders of, American citizens."[21]

What was a newspaper reader to make of such allegations? An editorial in the *New York Times* announced in January 1915: "CARRANZA, who once seemed be the coming man, has proved himself 'impossible.'"[22] The *San Francisco Examiner* agreed, citing Carranza's problematic "ATTITUDE" and "defiance."[23]

While an editorial in the *New York Times* accepted Carranza's right to protest the American invasion of Mexican territory, it termed the First Chief's outrage, expressed in a letter from Carranza to Secretary of State Bryan, "foolish." Further, it ridiculed Carranza for having had to rely on Villa's more sensible reaction to the occupation, which had demonstrated Villa's better understanding of Wilson's anti-Huerta motivations. Remember, the *Times* admonished, Villa's open support for the limited invasion had helped to defuse a war scare.[24]

The *San Francisco Examiner* reported almost gleefully about Carranza's initial reaction to Wilson's decision to send troops into Veracruz. "CARRANZA'S THREAT FALLS LIKE BOMBSHELL . . . CARRANZA'S

THREAT IS WARLIKE," one banner headline announced.[25] A day later an editorial cooed, "The war [with Mexico] has well begun, with a wise step at Vera Cruz."[26]

Media concern about Carranza's predilection for dictatorship surfaced in the fall of 1913, despite his democratic propaganda rhetoric. While the *Los Angeles Times*, for example, noted Villa's personal hold on most of northern Mexico,[27] the paper expressed mild alarm that Carranza might use Villa's hard-won terrain as the basis upon which to establish a dictatorship.[28] A *Times* editorial in late February 1914 also suggested that Carranza was generally "not to be trusted" to establish democracy in Mexico, though it provided no rationale for this conclusion.[29] The *New York Times*, meanwhile, saw Carranza's behavior at the Convention of Aguascalientes in October 1914 as indicative of a future dictatorship.[30]

The *Chicago Tribune* echoed the *Times's* misgivings about Carranza's taste for dictatorship. Juxtaposing a portrayal of Villa as democrat, the Chicago daily cast Carranza in the political mold of Huerta. "What was wrong in Huerta," an editorial warned, "is not right in Carranza."[31]

By late September 1914, an *Examiner* editorial headline enthusiastically declared Villa "the Strongman of Mexico."[32] Notably, also, from the summer of 1914 through early April 1915, the paper endorsed Villa and did not continue to press for further United States military intervention. By late April 1915, however, as it became apparent to the *Examiner* that Villa's military position had been seriously undercut at Celaya, the daily began again to call for United States intervention.[33]

Even when Carranza appeared to receive occasionally favorable assessments in the media prior to the spring of 1915, the media simultaneously damned him. For example, an editorial in the *Los Angeles Times* noted, "Everybody concedes his [Carranza's] integrity and ability," but it also noted that his revolutionary campaign was a largely worthless, "programless one."[34] Moreover, this relatively warm assessment of Carranza was penned in the fall of 1913, slightly before the time the press began to express its clear preference for Villa, and before Carranza had been tagged with being a sneak.

Ostensibly more favorable toward Carranza was a *Los Angeles Times* editorial penned the day after Huerta resigned in mid-July 1914. The opinion cited Carranza's "more humane" character, versus Villa's, as probable cause to warrant United States "endorsement" of the First Chief. Yet the best solution to the Revolution remained joint United States–European intervention—a call that clearly undermined any intent to favor Carranza.[35]

Generally, though, most approbatory media readings of Carranza stemmed from a rubbing-off of favorable assessments of Villa. For example, the day following Huerta's resignation the *Chicago Tribune* editorial observed: "The first chief with a Latin soul and Saxon mind, Gen. Carranza, and the military genius of the revolution, Villa, a bandit grown reformer and a first class fighting man, may have their triumph and hear their bands play in Mexico City."[36] In this passage, not only does Carranza bask in an unearned light—the glow of Villa's military achievements—but the very words used to describe the First Chief—"Saxon mind" and "Latin soul"—had been lifted directly from a Villa quote in a *Tribune* article of April 24, 1914.[37] Further, it suggests that Carranza had ridden to prominence on Villa's military coattails rather than having achieved anything admirable in his own right.

The *New York Times* framed Carranza quite favorably in comparison with Huerta, but the First Chief's image as a revolutionary leader paled in comparison with Villa's. An examination of headlines from the month of November 1913 illustrates this point. The *Times* cast Villa as an active, virile, courageous warrior. Headlines read: "VILLA MOVES ON CHIHUAHUA, Will Attack With 9,000 Men To-day,"[38] "FIGHTING AT CHIHUAHUA, Rebels Under Villa Attack Again," "VILLA DYNAMITES TWO FEDERAL TRAINS,"[39] "VILLA ROUTS FEDERALS AT JUAREZ . . . Federals in 'Disgraceful Retreat' the Rebel Leader Reports,"[40] "REBEL ADVANCE ON HUERTA FORCES IS NOW

GENERAL . . . VILLA'S VICTORY OPENS WAY,"[41] "Villa's Vanguard Starts South."[42]

Carranza also received less headline coverage than Villa, and the *Times* tended to cast the First Chief as a dandy and as less active than Villa. Headlines read: "LIFT THE [American arms] EMBARGO, CARRANZA'S PLEA,"[43] "CARRANZA GIVES A BALL, Entertains Townspeople,"[44] "Carranza Changes Campaign Plan."[45] A garbled cable from Carranza to the *Times*, printed on the front page, further suggested that a proud, touchy First Chief led the Constitutionalists. In part the cable read: "I would not accept for any reason or under any conditions the cooperation of the United States Government for fighting Huerta until he is driven from the post which he has usurped."[46]

The tepid support granted Carranza by the *Times* contrasts with the unflattering treatment the paper afforded Huerta. Some of the few Huerta-damning headlines read: "FEDERALES LOOTING GUAYMAS,"[47] "ALLEGED 'ELECTION ORDERS', Huerta Instructions to Nullify Balloting," "HUERTA GAVE ORDER TO FIRE ON EL PASO,"[48] "Huerta Government Admits the Fall of Victoria."[49] Huerta is guilty by association—"Federales looting"—for gerrymandering an election, for firing on innocents in El Paso, and for losing.

Yet the bigger problem for Carranza remained Villa, the *New York Times*'s coverage suggests. By comparison, Carranza cut a poor figure—and comparisons continued to be common. A February 1914 editorial captured the tenor of this treatment:

> CARRANZA is still out of sight. If Chihuahua is really the capital of his GOVERNMENT, there he should be, and the idea that he keeps away from there because he fears that he would lose even nominal authority if he left his hiding place is still general. With CARRANZA in view as the actual head of the so-called constitutional revolution, and VILLA really subservient to him, that particular branch of the Mexican rebellion would gain in respectability.[50]

More plainly spoken, this passage might simply have queried, "What kind of leader can Carranza be if he cannot even exercise control over his own government? Is he really so frightened of Villa?" Another *Times* editorial two weeks later echoed this suggestion of cowardice and again chided Carranza for not being "discernible to the naked eye."[51] In late October 1914, the *Times* criticized Carranza as "weak, vain, and opinionated." This same editorial lauded Villa as "the best hope of Mexico."[52] As late as June 1915, even after reporting that Villa was militarily and politically spent,[53] the daily's editorial page continued to express misgivings about Carranza, commenting that "the closest observers of Mexican affairs do not believe that there is any stability in CARRANZA or that his socialistic and confiscatory policy . . . would work. . . . He lacks the extraordinary personal force of VILLA."[54]

During the winter of 1915, when Villa's power reached its apogee in the estimation of the American press, Carranza received particularly dismissive treatment. The *Los Angeles Times* expressed the general media hope that Villa would "succeed in restoring peace to Mexico." As leader of Mexico, it continued, Villa "[i]n any event . . . would be an improvement upon that pretender and failure V(egetable) Carranza."[55]

Carranza's media representation improved somewhat after Obregón's forces soundly defeated Villa's at Celaya in April 1915. Headline reports of the outcomes of the two military engagements augured a change in the tone of subsequent Carranza coverage: "VILLA FORCES DEFEATED . . . Carranza Troops Victors,"[56] "CARRANZA DEFEATS VILLA,"[57] "VILLA MEN ROUTED CARRANZA REPORTS,"[58] "FIRST ROUT OF VILLA,"[59] "HEAVY BLOW TO VILLA,"[60] "REPORTS VILLA ROUT WITH LOSS OF 14,000,"[61] "VILLA DEFEATED, OFFICIAL REPORT,"[62] "VILLA'S HOPES ARE SHATTERED."[63] But these headlines spoke more to Villa's failure than to Carranza's victory.

By the summer of 1915, as the press began increasingly to report news of Villa's military and political eclipse by Carranza, some publications began to call for de facto diplomatic recognition of the First Chief. Any other course of action, the *Chicago Tribune* believed, would "merely result in another revolution"—hardly an endorsement of Carranza.[64] The *New York Times* disagreed in August, claiming Carranza's pronounced cowardice made him a poor candidate to gain recognition.[65]

By early October 1915, some newspapers warmly greeted rumors of Carranza's impending recognition, which came on October 19. The *Chicago Tribune*, after calling for United States military intervention in early September,[66] by mid-October supported Carranza's recognition and expressed hope that the First Chief would prove to be "strong enough" to maintain himself in government. But neither the *Los Angeles Times* nor the *San Francisco Examiner* threw support behind Carranza. With Villa's eclipse, both papers felt it ever more imperative that the United States embark on a full-scale intervention in Mexico. On the other hand, the *Denver Post*, the *New York Times*, and the *Washington Times* supported Wilson's decision to grant Carranza de facto recognition.

CONCLUSION

Both Huerta and Carranza were damned in American press reports—Huerta primarily as a savage, and Carranza foremost as a sneak. To varying degrees, they shared the Mexican qualities of dishonesty, inherent deceitfulness, and cruelty. And these attributes were in line with historical American visions of Mexican backwardness, racial limitations, and moral decrepitude. Why the press condemned Huerta with greater vigor than it did Carranza seems clear enough—a murdering barbarian is worse than a cruel, conniving liar.

But what of Villa? That the press chose so often to couch its denunciations of the First Chief by comparing him with Villa suggests that for the American press, Villa may have at least partially and temporarily escaped his own racial, moral, and cultural Mexicanness.

CHAPTER SEVEN

THE WARRIOR

Villa in the American Press

Warrior, n., a man experienced or engaged in warfare; a fighting man.

Villain, n., one who is guilty or capable of gross wickedness or crimes; a vile wretch; a scoundrel; a rascal.

Hero, n., any man admired for his courage, nobility, or exploits, especially in war; the central figure in any important event or period, honored for outstanding qualities.

—WEBSTER'S NEW UNIVERSAL UNABRIDGED DICTIONARY

An image of Francisco "Pancho" Villa as an archetypal Mexican Warrior cut a swath through the pages of the American press during the fiercest hours of the Mexican Revolution, 1913–1915. This press treatment consisted of two overriding but unequal components—the lesser of which was fundamentally Mexican and the greater of which was quintessentially American, at least by media reckonings.

In his Mexican guise, Villa was cast as the Warrior-Villain—a fighting man who personified a watered-down version of savagery typified by innate wickedness and inherent brutishness. In the press's framing of Villa as American, he was fashioned as Carranza's other—the First Chief's inverted image reflection—and endowed with the characteristics of forthrightness, responsibility, honesty, courage, athleticism, love of democracy, and friendliness. In this guise Villa became the Warrior-Hero, an admirable fighting man. As warrior-hero Villa nearly escaped inclusion in the gallery of types condensed from the elements of Mexicanness.

In this chapter I examine the chronological devolution of American media portrayals of Villa and his foreign policy through five familiar settings: his emergence as a media darling in the fall of 1913 and early winter of 1914; the Benton case in mid-February 1914; Villa's public stand on the American occupation of Veracruz; his taking "charge" of the presidency in late January 1915; and his steady decline after the defeats he suffered beginning at Celaya in April 1915.

VILLAINOUS BEGINNINGS:
THE WARRIOR TAKES THE STAGE

Villa burst onto the media scene in the fall of 1913 amid concurrently admiring and disapproving media reports of his battlefield exploits. In the early approbatory portrayals, the general tended to be cast as friendly, ambitious, aggressive, active, an effective leader, and a winner. Headlines taken from the *New York Times* in the autumn of 1913 capture the sentiment of these initial pro-Villa expressions: "REBELS FAVOR AMERICANS,"[1] "VILLA MOVES ON CHIHUA-HUA,"[2] "Rebels Under Villa Attack Again,"[3] "VILLA DYNAMITES TWO FEDERAL TRAINS,"[4] "VILLA ROUTS FEDERALS AT JUAREZ,"[5] "VILLA'S VICTORY OPENS WAY,"[6] "VILLA TO ATTACK CHIHUAHUA,"[7] "Villa's Vanguard Starts South,"[8] "'ON TO MEXICO!' VILLA'S WAR CRY,"[9] "SEVEN GENERALS DESERT HUERTA; READY TO SURRENDER TO THE REBELS: ENVOYS IN JUAREZ TO MEET WITH GEN. VILLA . . . .VILLA PROMISES MERCY,"[10] "Villa Boasts 20,000 Rebels Will Surround Huerta's Capital By Christmas."[11]

At the same time, the anti-Villa press played up Villa's short-comings and military defeats, casting him as a cruel, vicious, and ineffective leader—what amounted to a watered-down version of the Savage archetype. Selected headlines from the bitterly anti-Villa *Los Angeles Times* of 1913 serve to make the point: "VILLA'S REBELS IN RETREAT, Backbone of Revolution is Broken in North,"[12] "MASSACRE [under Villa] AT TORREON,"[13] "HOSTAGES IN DANGER, Rebels [led by Villa] Hold Them as a Foil,"[14] "SCORE REBELS FOR ATROCITIES,"[15] "VILLA IS EXECUTING ALL FEDERAL OFFICERS,"[16] "Villa, the 'Executioner' (with photo),"[17] "GEN. VILLA IS ALARMED . . . Gives Him Cold Chills While Preparing for Attack on Chihuahua,"[18] "MAY FIGHT CARRANZA, Villa at Outs With His Chief,"[19] "SPANISH PRIESTS, NUNS, VICTIMS OF VILLA'S MEN."[20] Villa, in constructions of this sort, tended to be cast as unnecessarily violent, lacking in sound judgment, impetuous, vicious, egoistic, and a poor leader.

Despite the incongruity between the ways in which Villa was presented in the *New York Times* and the *Los Angeles Times* in the fall of 1913, the two papers—indeed, all the publications examined for this study—agreed on one thing: Villa was a warrior, a fighting man. But was he a fighting man whom the press would admire (the hero) or whom it would despise (the villain)? The answer was both, depending very much on the particular time in question.

Like Carranza, Villa was sometimes vilified simply because of his association with the rebel forces. A November 1913 editorial in the *San Francisco Examiner* put it this way: "There is no safety in parley with these revolutionists. Behind all their parleys is a deep-seated hatred of the United States . . . in this mad, so-called republic of Aztec Indians, who have grown to be feudists [*sic*] and revolutionists by practice and profession."[21] An editorial in the *Chicago Tribune* expressed similar sentiments: "They go around to every one of substance in the neighborhood. They take whatever they can find in the way of money, clothes, provisions, and liquor, especially liquor. If thwarted, they kill."[22]

Sometimes Villa was smeared by the application of historical Mexican stereotypes. The *Saturday Evening Post* noted: "Probably a majority of Mexicans are of pure, or mixed, Indian blood. . . . They are animals, señor; they are not people. That is the real problem in Mexico."[23] In other cases Villa was denounced as "savage,"[24] fighting not for the glory of "liberty" but for the barbaric love of "plunder."[25] In late January 1914, the *Los Angeles Times* put it that way, calling Villa "as unscrupulous a ruffian as ever murdered a friend."[26]

THE WARRIOR'S ESCAPE: THE BENTON AFFAIR

The death of British national William S. Benton on February 17, 1914, as we have seen, precipitated a full-blown international diplomatic incident. After several public-relations missteps, Villa held fast to a rendering of events in which he had disarmed Benton and then had him tried before a military tribunal, sentenced, and shot. The affair largely dissipated when the United States, in part for lack of any solid evidence to the contrary, accepted Villa's version of events.

Benton's death temporarily solidified media positions on Villa. Those publications inclined to take a relatively favorable view of the general tended to accept his explanation for the execution or else reserved judgment. Those media outlets opposed to Villa tended to become even more rhetorically hostile. But these positions proved malleable.

The *Los Angeles Times* took the lead against Villa on Benton's death, depicting him as a villain and a sneak. It spit invective at Villa, Wilson, and Bryan. Villa was a "bandit and a murderer." Wilson earned the epithets "obstinately stupid . . . [and] obstinately wicked."[27] Secretary of State William Jennings Bryan gained a larger stage. "Bryan's Childish Faith in Villa Makes Him the Laughing Stock of Europe," the paper mockingly charged.[28]

The *Times* also published an artist's fetching portrayal of the rancher Benton that highlighted a benevolent aspect—doleful eyes and a humble expression (fig. 18). A March headline charged Villa with a cover-up attempt: "VILLA FOOLS CARRANZA; HOODWINKS BRITISH; Makes a Bluff at Torreón to Divert Attention from Benton Case."[29] Indeed, according to the *Times*, Villa's efforts to recapture Torreón—the city he had first captured in early October 1913 and then abandoned shortly after—served as part of a "well-formulated scheme" to redirect the media's focus away from the Benton imbroglio.[30]

The *San Francisco Examiner* used the Benton case as a rallying point in its call for United States military intervention in Mexico.[31] The paper also accepted the official American position, which took Villa at his word, ruefully commenting: "Just what occurred may never be known."[32] A headline hinted at the reasoning behind simultaneously accepting Villa's version of events and calling for intervention: "Must We Buy Britain's Consent to Govern Ourselves?"[33] In fact, the Hearst syndicate's flagship hotly resented what it identified as British meddling in American affairs, manifested by the official British reaction to the Benton case. The *Examiner* had championed the cause of intervention as early as it had concluded that Madero's fortunes were lost in Mexico.[34]

The *New York Times*, too, initially took a dim view of Villa's assertions about Benton. A bitter anti-Villa missive penned by a group of El Paso residents appeared prominently on the front page. In part it read: "The career of Francisco Villa, a man who has been an outlaw and murdered for many years, and who is now leading an arbitrary and despotic reign of terror over Northern Mexico is more cruel and barbarous in his methods than any tyrant in the world's history."[35]

A *Times* editorial published the same day largely agreed with these sentiments, albeit draped in more politic language. Calling Benton's death a "murder," it noted Villa's excuse that Benton had

His Passing on a Cause Celebre.

WILLIAM S. BENTON
DRAWN BY HIS FRIEND
FA SOMMERFELD · OF
ELPASO

Figure 18. "His Passing on a Cause Celebre." Reproduced from the *Los Angeles Times*, March 12, 1914.

tried to kill him "will not be seriously considered, we infer, in Washington or in London."[36]

But Washington did consider Villa's excuse—and accepted it. Just two days later the paper conceded: "The prevalent belief in official circles is that in the absence of any satisfactory evidence to the contrary, it will be difficult for this government, at least, to reject

Villa's version."[37] Yet although the *Times* then largely followed the White House's lead, it did not do so with complete equanimity.

On one hand, the *Times* vilified Villa for "murder," while on the other it acknowledged his right of self-defense. On at least one occasion the New York daily attempted to treat the issue humorously. A fictitious Chicago Irish saloonkeeper, "Mr. Dooley," was made to say in mid-March 1914:

> Our relations with Pancho is most corjal an' just what ye'd want th' relations iv a gr-eat civilized republic with wan iv th' most notorious burglars now in public life to be. . . . We're justly proud iv our little frind [Villa], an' he loves an' respects us. P'raps he holds us in too much awe an' veneration, but that is no more thin nachral in a meek an' modest half breed who has gone into partnership with wan iv th' most po'ful nations in th' wurrild.

"Dooley's" piece goes on to liken Villa to a mixture of Jesse James, Sitting Bull, Geronimo, and the "Apachy Kid."[38] In one sense, this passage may have exonerated Villa for his "savagery." After all, he was fighting, as *Everybody's* put it, a "ruthless Indian war."[39] What might one have expected?

The *Times* also reported that Villa had complained to George Carothers, the State Department special agent, that he, Villa, should be able to kill whomever he liked, provided the victims were not American. "What difference does it make to you what I do to the Spaniards and other foreigners?" the paper, without providing a source for the quote, reported Villa as having told Carothers.[40] The next day the paper reported that Carothers hotly denied the conversation with Villa had ever taken place; he attributed the source of the story to Villa's enemies.[41]

Generally, however, the *Times* fell into step behind the White House and began to fashion Villa as a warrior-hero by establishing his military acumen. For example, Villa's "natural genius . . . as a fighting man" warranted comment.[42] More importantly, the paper granted Villa the opportunity to address the charges against him directly. As a case in point, it published a "Statement to the *Times*," in both English and Spanish, in which Villa proclaimed his innocence by couching his actions as legally justified self-defense, pure and simple.[43] In other words, Villa was not a warrior-villain. But did that mean he was a warrior-hero? Not necessarily.

The *Denver Post* began its Benton coverage in a measured, dispassionate manner: "William S. Benton of El Paso, a wealthy Scotchman, subject of Great Britain, was shot to death Tuesday by order of a rebel court-martial. He was accused of conspiracy to take the life of General Villa."[44] This prosaic tone did not change appreciably throughout the affair. The paper presented a full airing of "facts" as they became known. In due course, the publication noted the news of the Briton's death, Great Britain's reaction, Villa's changing story, Villa's refusal to give up the body, and Carranza's establishment of an inquiry board—all with little of the rhetorical fanfare evinced in some other publications.[45]

On the other hand, an editorial cartoon in the *Post* (fig. 19) suggested that Villa's actions, when combined with Huerta's, merited United States intervention—"UNCLE SAM'S NEXT STEP!" In the pictorial, Huerta has sunk from the level of dictator to that of drunkard, and Villa from "hero" to "butcher." Both characters are portrayed as oafs wearing startled and dumb countenances. Each is armed with a blood-drenched dagger. Mexican inferiority vis-à-vis the United States is shown by the enormous size of Uncle Sam's boot and the ease with which it might trample Huerta and Villa.

From the beginning, the tenor of the *Post*'s coverage reflected a mild anti-British bias that prevailed over a still weaker and inconsistent anti-revolutionary sentiment. The basic Villa position, as the paper presented it, derived from two sources—the *Post*'s acceptance of the rebel claim that Benton had been naturalized in Mexico and the clever rebel observation that ordering Benton's death fell squarely within the rules of war. In the latter case, the

Figure 19. "UNCLE SAM'S NEXT STEP!" Reproduced from the *Denver Post*, February 25, 1914.

paper quoted from—and accepted—the argument of a Pesqueira dispatch:

> Benton entered Villa's apartments very unexpectedly, demanding protection of his interests and bitterly insulting Villa and the rebel army. General Villa told him that he considered him an enemy to the Constitutionalist cause and that in order that he might not continue to work against it, he, Villa, was going to pay him the value of (Benton's) property in the state of Chihuahua. Benton became exasperated at this and drew his

revolver, intending to kill the general, but the latter immediately knocked him down, disarmed him and sent him to jail. Benton was afterward tried by a special military court and sentenced to death and duly executed, all in accordance with the laws and usages of war.[46]

The *Chicago Tribune*'s coverage began with the publication of juxtaposed versions of Benton's death. According to one, Villa himself killed Benton. The rancher had angered Villa by charging: "'Damn you, Pancho Villa. I am as good a man as you are . . . ' [so] Villa struck him with his revolver and felled him." A variant of this story embellished the tale: "Villa cursed and slapped him and Benton drew back to strike. . . . Benton's death followed."[47] In the second scenario, Villa simply ordered Benton's arrest and execution, which, according to a report several weeks later, was gleefully carried out by Villa's bodyguard, Rodolfo Fierro.[48]

Contrast the foregoing passages with a commentary from the *Tribune* penned about two months after Benton's death: "[T]he murderer of Benton, is no better than Huerta, the murderer of President Francisco Madero. . . . The everlasting issue of civilization versus savagery is joined. . . . The bandit leaders must all be reduced."[49] Here the *Tribune* marginalizes Villa by lumping him with the "savage" Huerta, who, like any Mexican mongrel, stood in direct opposition to the influences of civilization.

The propagandistic damage control Villa engaged in, fashioned in part by Carrancistas and redounding to Villa's benefit, argued in the press that Benton was not a foreigner—that he had been naturalized in Mexico and thus his death was solely a Mexican affair. In an attempt to defuse the issue by labeling Benton a Mexican rather than a Briton, Federico González Garza, Villa's legal adviser, argued in a report cited by the *Denver Post:* "We have heard that Benton held several small offices under President Diaz and that he once was mayor of a small settlement on his own estate. He could not have held office without being a Mexican citizen and the records of Chihuahua City are being searched to establish the facts."[50] How that search, if it ever took place, turned out, and just how the media assessed this argument, remains unclear.

The anti-Villa representations had been unable to make stick the charges that Benton had been murdered. So, while Villa's actions were deplored by some press outlets, press reactions to the Benton affair demonstrated on the whole that Villa's press image had improved slightly. Villa had been able to justify the death of a foreign national to the satisfaction of an American press inclined to stereotype Mexicans as savage (like Huerta), sneaky (like Carranza), or backward, racially limited, and morally decrepit.

It is worth remembering, too, that during the Benton affair Villa took a measure of refuge in the staunch public support Carranza offered him, both diplomatically and in the press. Carrancista agent Luis Cabrera wrote to Robert Pesqueira that "we need to convince press and Washington government that commission appointed is quite reliable and means serious investigation . . . not merely made to avoid irregular and intrusive investigation contemplated by foreign commission. . . . [P]lease make declaration along these lines and assure Washington and press . . . that action will be taken."[51] If the propaganda actions taken were not immediately successful—Pesqueira wrote to Carranza that "public opinion in both the United States and Europe continues to be very unfavorable"[52]—an essentially favorable media depiction, molded by Constitutionalist propaganda, shortly carried the day.

From a public-relations perspective, Villa ably escaped the Benton affair. A cartoon in the *Denver Post* (fig. 20) reflected one general sentiment about the source of Villa's ongoing favorable reception in the media: he was eliminating Huerta, and he was a winner. As a result, the potentially dampening long-term effects of the Benton case tended to be downplayed.

With the bad taste of the Benton killing behind, the press's representations of Villa and his foreign policy moved toward their

IT IS SLOWLY BUT SURELY TURNING HIS PICTURE TO THE WALL!

Figure 20. "IT IS SLOWLY BUT SURELY TURNING HIS PICTURE TO THE WALL." Reproduced from the *Denver Post*, March 26, 1914.

penultimate and sometimes radiant transformation in April 1914. A cartoon in the *Chicago Tribune* echoed these sentiments (fig. 21). Dark, menacing, and ominous, Villa, saber in hand, prepares to engage a sinister-looking and angrily surprised Huerta. "AH! HERE COMES MADERO'S FRIEND!" bemoans Huerta.

WELCOME TO VERACRUZ: VILLA AS WARRIOR-HERO

When Huertista soldiers arrested a group of American sailors in search of gasoline at Tampico in April 1914, an international

Figure 21. "MEXICO'S TWO STRONG MEN." Reproduced from the *Chicago Tribune*, April 4, 1914.

incident erupted, leading to the American seizure and occupation of Veracruz. But Villa jumped in to save the day with a loud and tactically brilliant profession of support for the American action— completely overshadowing Carranza's strident and aggressive opposition to the U.S. presence. With Villa's public stand, and with a subsequent rhetorical backing-off by Carranza, the war scare dissipated. Villa's statements riveted the popular press in the United States. Where the Benton killing had hardened American media positions on Villa, his decision to publicly back Wilson softened the tone of his media opposition.

The *New York Times* led the cheer for Villa on Veracruz. "VILLA REPUDIATES HUERTA'S DEFIANCE . . . SAYS 'ME NO MOLESTERIA' . . . Or as a New Yorker Put It, 'I Should Worry!,'" chortled one headline.[53] Then the paper happily announced Villa's orders to his troops to execute anyone who instigated an anti-American demonstration in Ciudad Juárez.[54]

For the *Times*, one of the transformational effects of Villa's public stand was that it generated a greater willingness on the newspaper's part to take Villa at his word. With Villa's increasing popularity, the *Times* seemed to be more willing to grant him a channel to speak directly to readers, thereby affording him enhanced power both to act as the architect of his own image and to woo readers on terms of his own choosing. This dovetailed neatly with the new editorial approval that Villa's Veracruz stand had wrestled from the publication. For example, in the story headlined "VILLA REPUDIATES HUERTA'S DEFIANCE," Villa explained: "Should the act of a drunkard and murderer be construed as an act of war and should war result, I can assure all Americans living within the bounds of the Constitutionalist territory that they will be protected."[55]

Villa also availed himself of such rhetorical opportunities to play up his preference for peace and nonviolence and his bitter opposition to Huerta, the "usurper." For example, on April 24, 1914, the *Times* quoted the general on its front page (which Villa sometimes seemed to own): "Mexico has enough troubles of her own, and is not seeking a war with any foreign country, certainly not the United States. I have come to the border for the purpose of conferring and seeking advice from my good American friends. . . . Say for me that we want no war, are seeking no war, and wish only the closest and most friendly relations with our neighbors of the North."[56] Two days later another dispatch reaffirmed the common foreign policy themes and not so discreetly disparaged Carranza: "Carranza's message was a great mistake. . . . My personal wishes are that the United States continue the blockade of the Huerta ports. . . . I will personally make Huerta offer a full and satisfactory apology to the United States."[57]

To Villa's good fortune, the *Times*'s editorials throughout the first weeks of the crisis echoed his dissatisfaction with Carranza's attitude. Indeed, adopting an aggressive, muscular posture, the paper suggested that Carranza's protest might have been taken more seriously if only he had had the military clout to back it up.[58]

For the *Times*, Villa's Veracruz position proved almost cathartic. The paper seemed to welcome the new certainty about Villa that his Veracruz stand, in the *Times*'s interpretation, appeared to offer—Villa was a friend, and he might be trusted.[59] The paper simultaneously railed against Carranza's defiant Veracruz stand and warmly greeted Villa's pro-Wilson posture: "If ever a rebel chieftan and pretender was in the position of having a powerful friend to pull his chestnuts out of the fire it was CARRANZA up to the point of dispatching his foolish note to Secretary BRYAN."[60] For the *Times*, doubts about the moral fiber of Villa's character appeared to wane. This, in turn, lent a moral authenticity to his overtures of friendship—one key message of his propaganda. Although the paper had hardly declared an end to the Revolution or anointed Villa king of Mexico, after Villa declared for Wilson on Veracruz the publication embraced him as a trustworthy friend. Of course, given Villa's eager propaganda, this naturally redounded to his favor.

In a story partially headlined "VILLA'S INFLUENCE SEEN," a *Times* dispatch noted: "To assure his friends on the American side and throughout the United States, Villa hastened to Juarez and issued a statement that Carranza's position was not the position of the revolution and was not held by him. He admitted that the Carranza note was a grievous mistake and the outcome of bad advice from political friends."[61] This passage not only closely matches Villa's own words quoted above but also portrays Villa's friendship as a fait accompli ("to assure his friends on the American side and throughout the United States").

Another *Times* example illustrates the press's casting of Villa as American friend while alluding to Carranza as possibly cowardly: "Villa hurried to Juarez, angry and snorting because Carranza and his non-fighting diplomatists neglected to confer or counsel with him or Gen. Felipe Angeles, the military brains behind the revolution."[62]

In the two preceding passages, the *Times* embraced some of Villa's foreign policy posturings and presented them as reflecting the truth as the paper understood it. The passages cast Villa as friendly to the United States and Americans, physically hearty, possibly dangerous, worthy of respect, and in charge. By contrast, Carranza figures as duplicitous, possibly cowardly, and unfriendly. In the *New York Times*, Villa had become a warrior-hero while Carranza remained a sneak.

Much like the *New York Times*, the *San Francisco Examiner* proved receptive to Villa's flair for rhetorical drama. For the Examiner, this occurred even before Veracruz. For example, by mid-March 1914 Villa had begun his second campaign to take Torreón. Headlines read: "VILLA TAKES TORREON'S OUTPOSTS IN HARD FIGHT,"[63] "VILLA'S TORREON ATTACK SCHEDULED FOR TO-DAY,"[64] "TORREON TAKEN BY GEN. VILLA,"[65] "FOUR DAYS FIGHTING ENDS IN VICTORY FOR VILLA, Rebels Led By Intrepid Chief,"[66] "FINAL ASSAULT THRILLING, VILLA INDEFATIGABLE."[67] Not only were these headlines, according to the stories' attributions, based largely on Villa's own claims, but throughout the campaign Villa's image shone as never before. Approved the *Examiner*: "General Villa, grimy with dust and sweat, a red bandanna handkerchief about his neck, participated. He rode up and down the lines swearing and cheering, cursing and calling upon the saints."[68]

An *Examiner* cartoon expressed a sense of relief that Villa had so ably quashed Huerta's forces at Torreón (fig. 22). In it, Villa, menacing though he may appear, promises to overturn Huerta's dictatorship by lassoing him. The cartoon remains ambiguous, however, about the role of dictatorship for Mexico. Dictatorship is represented as a bull that Huerta is unable to ride. Villa's presentation as a well-adorned caballero suggests that once Huerta is removed, perhaps Villa will prove able to tame and ride it effectively.

But if Villa seemed increasingly intrepid and successful, the *Examiner* had no compunction about making an abrupt about-face within days of the Tampico arrests and the news of Carranza's objections to the American occupation. The paper turned suddenly cold on Villa and lumped him with the rest of the dreaded Constitutionalists. One editorial opined: "It has been charged against this [Wilson's] Government that because of their hostility to Huerta we have been unable to see Carranza and Villa as they really are— savage, cruel insurrectionists with quite as much blood guiltiness upon them as has Huerta."[69]

Days later, the publication began to reverse course once more, albeit less peremptorily, when Villa started issuing his pro-occupation pronouncements.[70] Too, like the *New York Times*, the *Examiner* increasingly granted Villa a more direct channel to speak for himself. By increasing the frequency of direct quotations, the *Examiner* gave Villa's voice increased exposure. One report quoted him as saying, "But why talk of war with the United States? It would be extremely foolish for two reasonable and intelligent men to fight over a drunken man, and would it not be the height of folly for the United States and Mexico to come to blows over a man like Huerta? It seems to me that the entire civilized world would laugh should this come to pass."[71] Later, an article titled "VILLA TAKES FIRST DRINK IN TOAST TO WILSON," found Villa hyperbolically mouthing his foreign policy message of friendship flavored with admiration for President Wilson and a recitation of Villa's own humble origins, his earnestness, and his integrity:

> I am nothing but a plain soldier and the words you will hear me utter now will be the words of an uncultured man. . . .

THE MAN BEHIND

Figure 22. "THE MAN BEHIND." Reproduced from the *San Francisco Examiner*, April 1, 1914.

Senors, for the first time in my life I am going to propose a toast, and for the first time in my life I am going to drink a toast, and it will be the first time that I ever willingly let liquor pass my lips. . . . You gentlemen should be proud that

you are Americans; that you represent the press of the greatest
nation on earth, ruled by the greatest man alive, President
Wilson.[72]

The *Examiner*'s editorial page countered the news columns,
however. It accused Villa of being in cahoots with Huerta and
predicted a large-scale Mexican-American war.[73] Another editorial
accused "Carranza and Villa [of being] equally guilty with Huerta
of insults to the American flag and [of committing other] outrages."[74]

This contrast between portrayals on the editorial page and those
elsewhere in the *Examiner* raises some intriguing questions. Was it
the result of disagreements among newspaper decision-makers?
Or was an editorial decision taken to provide space to contrasting
points of view? Might different editors with different interpretations of Villa have been responsible for different sections of the
paper? Might it simply have been an oversight? Might no one at
the paper have noticed or cared? To some extent, it did not matter
how the "facts" portrayed Villa, because up until April 1914, press
interpretations tended to forge him from the elements of Mexicanness—usually (though not always) as a warrior-villain.

The *Los Angeles Times*'s portrayals of Villa and his foreign policy
during this period exemplify the point precisely. If the *Examiner*,
the Hearst flagship, appeared unsure what to make of Villa in
March and April 1914, its ambivalence paled in comparison with
that expressed in the *Los Angeles Times*. Throughout those two
months the *Times's* news stories granted Villa both quasi-hero and
near-demon status, while the editorial pages both bitterly opposed
him and left the door open to gestures of friendship.

A reconciliation of these sometimes stark differences of opinion
can be found in the forceful and rigid application of the Mexicanness template that the paper employed in its editorials. It amounted
to this: no matter how successful Villa appeared to be, in the final
analysis he was just a half-breed; he could not break the shackles
of that stereotype. Hence the paradoxical position: elements of

heroism filled columns of print, but they conflicted with an expressed editorial inclination that simply refused to acknowledge much in Villa's behavior except the Mexican proclivity for villainy. Mexicanness held only limited room for heroism.

Many of the *Times*'s news presentations about Villa at this time bordered on the outlandish and sensational. Perhaps this occurred in part because interpretations more closely fitting the factual reality of Villa's military heroism were anathema in terms of the stereotypes the paper employed. Headlines read: "SEES VILLA LUSTING IN HIS LAIR, Finds Tiger Lusting For Blood . . . And His Head Looks Like a Bullet That Has Never Been Fired,"[75] "Villa is not fighting for a principle . . . he is fighting because he has a price on his head,"[76] "Mrs. Villa has seconded her husband's ambition to go down in history as a military genius,"[77] "[Villa] believes he will eventually be able to uplift the common people of his country . . . [Villa is a] second Napoleon,"[78] "[Villa is a] rude genius . . . miniature Napoleon, courageous, resourceful and indomitable."[79] Then, taking a swipe at Villa's propaganda, a *Times* editorial complained that it was "impossible to distinguish between [that] which is sincere and that which is subjected into publicity merely to win popularity in Mexico and to create partisan admiration abroad." In a tender moment only the day before, however, the newspaper had reported warmly about Villa's future plans. A headline read in part, "[Villa] Pictures Uplift of the People and an Equal Distribution of Land."[80]

Continuing its ambivalence, the *Times* noted in late April that Villa wore a "sneer on his lips," "enjoyed venting his spleen," and "demonstrated a pronounced hostility to Americans."[81] Yet the same day a *Times* editorial suggested that Villa might indeed prove to be America's friend—though it warned that "he does not enjoy a reputation for veracity." His friendship needed to be proved from day to day.[82]

In sum, the central concern for the *Los Angeles Times*—which, of all the publications examined here, expressed the most stentorian opposition to Villa but which was also inconsistent in its appraisals of him—revolved around Villa's perceived lack of morality and his predilection for violence and treachery. If he was not a savage of Huerta's proportions, then he was certainly a villain. The morality issue, to the extent that the paper employed a template of Villa as a violence-loving Mexican, was stacked against him. The Mexican-ness framing wrote him off in advance.

Yet the paper's inconsistency in stereotyping Villa left room for a second strong current in its interpretation—he was also a warrior-hero. After all, the paper had reported that Villa stood for land reform and uplifting the downtrodden of Mexico, and he was willing to risk his life in pursuit of these objectives. As a consequence, Villa had some room to maneuver diplomatically—provided he toe the American line (as the *Times* interpreted it) and act friendly. Such actions might not fully humanize him, but they might grant him measured support. And so he was cast also as a warrior-hero.

As the Veracruz crisis unfolded, Chicago newspaper readers might have been confused if they had read the *Los Angeles Times* before turning to the *Chicago Tribune*'s portrayals of Villa and his foreign policy. Like the *New York Times* and the *San Francisco Examiner*, the *Tribune* evinced little skepticism about the premature reports of victory at Torreón in March[83]—although on at least two occasions, citing Huertista sources in Mexico City, it also reported stinging losses for the rebels.[84] Yet on the whole, Villa's image gained favor in the Chicago portrayals during April.

After the conflicting reports about the outcome of the battle for Torreón, Villa emerged triumphant. He ultimately took the city because, as news photographer John Dornan explained after returning from the front, "Gen. Villa is a fighting man. He was everywhere, and his greatest delight was to join the assaults on foot and throw hand grenades himself." Further, the *Tribune* suggested that the federal general defending Torreón was "insane."[85]

As a *Tribune* cartoon happily depicted it, Villa's military might now threatened Huerta's grip (fig. 23). Although the cartoon shows

Figure 23. "BETWEEN THE DEVIL AND THE DEEP SEA." Reproduced from the *Chicago Tribune*, April 16, 1914.

Villa with the usual pistol in one hand and bloody saber in the other, his portrayal has a more appreciative side, too. He is physically active, and his quarry, Huerta, is contemptible enough to warrant the violence Villa clearly threatens him with. Moreover, Villa is on the side of the good—Woodrow Wilson symbolically leads an American flotilla whose purpose is similar to Villa's.

Carranza's anti-occupation statement abruptly changed this warm mood toward Villa in the *Tribune*. Suddenly an editorial reported that Villa, "the murderer of Benton, is no better than Huerta, the murderer of President Francisco Madero. . . . The ever-lasting issue of civilization versus savagery is joined. . . . The bandit leaders must all be reduced."[86] Days later, however, echoing the flip-flopping evident in New York and San Francisco, the Chicago paper began to recast Villa as a friend after all. In doing so, it in part allowed the general's voice to speak directly to readers: "'I didn't want war, and I am sure your people don't. We have always been good friends haven't we? Why shouldn't we continue that way? . . . Why does the United States want to pay any attention to that old drunken ass, Huerta, anyway?' Villa himself is a teetotaler."[87]

Yet in keeping with the front page–editorial page disagreements of the *Los Angeles Times* and the *San Francisco Examiner*, on that same day the *Tribune* inaccurately editorialized that Villa and Carranza constituted nothing more than Huerta's "hired" guns.[88] In mid-May, one more editorial shift began. Villa re-earned respect by virtue of his "clear and definite idea of what he wants. . . . He wants Mr. Huerta."[89]

In sum, Villa's pro-occupation stance was widely cheered. Coupled with his accumulating military successes and his seizure of opportunities to promote himself, Villa's media image rebounded healthily from the damage inflicted upon it by the Benton imbroglio. With minor exceptions, he was now generally considered to be America's friend, albeit a volatile one and (inconsistently) of inferior Mexican makeup.

The *Literary Digest* nicely expressed the new mood in which Villa's morality flourished—a generous mood, granted in part because his morality tended to ride the same wave as his military fortunes. The *Digest* purported, if hyperbolically, to speak for the entire press of the United States.[90] A headline announced, "THE RISE OF VILLA'S STAR." The article championed his "born genius as a strategist and commander" and emphasized how "tremendous is the personal triumph of Villa."[91]

Figure 24. "THE DILEMMA OF THE LION OF MEXICO." Reproduced from the
Chicago Tribune, July 5, 1914.

THE WARRIOR'S FINAL ASCENT:
UNCLUTTERED HEROISM

Villa's stature in American press reports continued to thrive
throughout 1914 and well into 1915. His complimentary rendering
relied heavily on his military successes, his fascinating character,
and Carranza's supposed shortcomings. A *Denver Post* cartoon
representing Villa symbolically as a lion and his rival generals as
ravening wolves (fig. 24) illustrated the favor in which Villa stood
in some of the press—especially when compared with Carranza.

After all, Villa could legitimately claim chief responsibility for the Constitutionalist victory. He could tally the abdication of Huerta in mid-July 1914 among his numerous military achievements. And by August 1914, the helmsmanship of the nation appeared to lie at his feet. He was clearly the successful Warrior.

After the formal rupture in relations between Villa and Carranza in the autumn of 1914, Villa continued to receive approbatory press coverage. In part, the Villa-Carranza split contributed to his good press because the American news media had framed Carranza as a sneak. Further, both the press and Villa's propaganda tended to portray Villa and Carranza as dissimilar, sometimes to the point of being opposites. While Villa was heroic, for example, Carranza could not be; if Villa was friendly, Carranza was unfriendly; while Villa fought, Carranza cowered; where Villa oozed charm, Carranza offered blandness.[92] Moreover, if Carranza as sneak represented an American Other construction, and if Villa represented the opposite of Carranza, then Villa became, in a sense, American. Indeed, some of his attributes as a warrior-hero fell clearly outside the pale of historical American cultural views of Mexicanness.

In a pictorial (fig. 25), the *Denver Post* cast Villa as a sincere land reformer who wanted to uplift the "MEXICAN PEOPLE"—and also as the real power in Mexico. Not only is Villa larger (read, more important) than Carranza in the cartoon but he is also forcing the First Chief's hand to do the right thing for "the people." Villa's source of authority, meanwhile, derives from his military position—shown by his army outside the window. Yet his army might, by its numbers, also represent the people of Mexico and thereby signify Villa's democratic inclinations.

That Villa had to be a successful military leader in order to gain a commendatory media portrayal had been apparent since the fall of 1913. The *Fortnightly Review* made the importance of this relationship explicit. The logic was simple: winning is a prerequisite for positive media portrayal. (Of course the spirit of democracy, as suggested by the preceding cartoon and as stressed

Figure 25. "'I HAVE DONE MY PART—NOW FOR YOURS.'" Reproduced from the *Denver Post*, July 19, 1914.

repeatedly by Villa's propaganda, also contributed.) But this was not quite the whole story. After all, Benton's death had initially threatened to stain Villa's image permanently, despite his battlefield successes. (And Huerta, it will be recalled, had been framed unfavorably not because of any military failure but because of the murders of Madero and Pino Suárez and his position on Veracruz.)

The *Fortnightly Review* captured the prevailing media sentiment succinctly. Villa merited support because of his military victories and in spite of the fact that "the story of his life from the late [1880s] to the present time would be little more than a recital of cold-blooded murders, thefts, torturings, and atrocities of an even worse description." The catch was this: "Will he carry out orders he receives from Washington?" If so, then support should follow.[93]

The *Los Angeles Times* and the *San Francisco Examiner* echoed the logic of matching support for Villa with his military fortunes. The *Times*, never Villa's friend, did eventually come to express admiration in its interpretation of his forceful style of leadership. As they would in New York and San Francisco, Villa's public pronouncements seemed to make inroads against the Los Angeles daily's proclivity to prejudge him as a Mexican.

On one hand, by early 1915 a front-page *Times* story called for U.S. intervention to save Mexico "From Herself." In fact, the article boasted, "[m]any Mexicans secretly desire it."[94] On the other hand, weeks later an editorial spoke warmly of Villa, observing that he "demonstrated by his utterances that he is a friend of the common people of Mexico." Manifesting a remarkable change of heart, the paper went so far as to "hope that he will succeed [in] restoring peace to Mexico." In short, the dissonant pro-Villa and anti-Villa voices in the *Times* thrived. One result was that while Villa may have been many good things, he could not entirely shed his Mexicanness. But then, neither could Carranza, whom the *Times* denounced mockingly—which in turn led to relatively increased Villa support. "In any event," an editorial intoned, Villa "would be an improvement upon the pretender and failure . . . Carranza."[95]

In the *San Francisco Examiner* throughout 1914 and into 1915, Villa continued to serve as probably his own best image choreographer. For example, he cabled the paper in May 1914: "I have no aspirations. I will go back to work as soon as I drive out that drunkard, Huerta. I am only a poor man. I wish only to see my countryman freed from tyranny. I am a patriot. Yet I am the man whom they call the bandit Villa. If I wanted money I could be the richest man in the world, for I have walked among gold, silver, and jewels."[96] Such presentations, rife with elements championing honesty, abstinence, humble origins, the virtue of work, and a healthy suspicion of ill-gotten gain, fit well with the *Examiner*'s sweetening assessments, which lauded Villa for his power, his "genius," his political acumen—and his ruthlessness.[97] Villa was almost American.

In September 1914 the paper named Villa the most potent, capable, and popular force in Mexico.[98] In an expression of explicit publisher input into editorial affairs, unique among the publications examined here, William Randolph Hearst, owner and publisher of the *Examiner*, also expressed a liking for Villa. He wrote:

> The one man in this Mexican conflict and crisis who has appeared to tower over all others in personal power and capacity, in the magnetism to lead, the mastery to command and the ability to govern, is Francisco Villa. There are many men in Mexico more cultivated than Villa, many better educated, many more trained in diplomatic services and in the gentler arts of government. But these qualities are not what is required. . . . A strong hand is needed, a determined purpose, a masterful mind, an experience gained from personal contact with the mass[es]. . . . These qualities Francisco Villa possesses as no other man in Mexico.[99]

Autumn headlines reinforced Hearst's view: "VICTORY IS SCORED BY VILLA,"[100] "VILLA IS DECLARED RIGHT MAN TO RULE IN MEXICO."[101]

The *New York Times* and the *Chicago Tribune* agreed. On the basis of Villa's military prowess, the *Times* noted: "The signs now point to Villa as the most competent to restore law and order. . . . [A]lthough he is known as a dangerous man, it is obvious that he has more skill, larger power over his followers, and a clearer idea of the needs of the country than GEN. OBREGON or GEN. CARRANZA."[102] Further, and perhaps most importantly, Villa deserved to be rewarded because "he has behaved handsomely toward us."[103] But make no mistake—this was only another way of repeating what the *Fortnightly Review* had already stated in less equivocal terms: if he follows America's lead or orders, then let him be supported. Like the *Fortnightly Review*, the *New York Times* made it clear that Villa warranted support under no other conditions.

The *Chicago Tribune* applauded Villa because "he seems to be keeping with his original direction." That "direction," however, went unexamined.[104] Further, it will be recalled that earlier in 1914 the *Tribune*, like other publications, had expressed confusion about how to interpret Villa. No matter. As part of the Chicago daily's ostensibly charitable reinvention of Villa, the former bandit had become a populist leader and "the military genius of the revolution."[105] An insightful commentary noted further:

> It is not to be wondered at that the personality of "Pancho" Villa, with its strange contradictions, is one that appeals to the imagination to a greater degree than any other man now in the public eye. . . . Perhaps it was this appeal that drew newspaper writers around him and thus gave him a publicity which other big figures in Mexican affairs have missed. . . . [I]t is about him that are woven the most romantic and fantastic stories, all interesting and some true. . . . He is good "copy" anyway you look at him.[106]

In spite of this candid analysis, the *Tribune*, too, fell increasingly under the charm of Villa's public pronouncements and tended to present them as factually accurate.

Villa's favorable press coverage, then, was rooted firmly in his ability to conquer. He compounded that success, from a public-relations standpoint, for the very reason the *Tribune* pointed out: he was "good copy." His story was "good" for the business of selling newspapers and magazines. Villa's public statements— sometimes issued by his propagandists, sometimes delivered in interviews—also clearly worked to embellish the way the popular press presented him, in part because his military successes lent his claims an air of authenticity.

As "good copy," Villa exhibited several key traits. For example, he gained kudos through January 1915 for disavowing any interest in becoming leader of Mexico. All the publications examined for this study highlighted the story of Villa as politically unambitious. Typically, the framing included references to his humble origins, his self-reliance, his commitment to formal education and to uplifting the downtrodden, his love of democracy, his admiration for Woodrow Wilson and things American, and his violent opposition to authoritarian rule (read, Huerta and Carranza). In short, he was framed under rubrics of Americanness.[107]

On one of many occasions, in late September 1914, just days after Villa formally disavowed Carranza, the *New York Times* reported, "VILLA WON'T RUN FOR PRESIDENT."[108] How believable was this claim? The *Times* argued: "For the present, he is entitled to the benefit of the doubt [for] Villa is a Mexican of an unusual type."[109] The "savage," the "murderer" of Benton, had come a long way in six months.

An example culled from the *Chicago Tribune* drives home the point that the press tended to hold Villa increasingly in favor. After Villa took "charge" of the presidency, a *Tribune* editorial defended his action:

> Villa has been driven by necessities. . . . This is not a regency, protectorate, dictatorship, or tyranny. It is an office we shall understand by likening it to the superintendency of [an] asylum for the insane. It is both custodial and curative. . . . [W]herever Villa is, there is the presidency. He is not the embodiment of it, but the custodian of it. . . . Villa has always been controlled by a sense of his own unfitness for the presidency, and his sincerity is attested by the fact that he now does not take the office, but merely charge of it.[110]

THE STAIN OF MEXICANNESS

On the eve of the decline in Villa's military fortunes in April 1915, the general stood in the American press as a figure brave like a lion, clever to the point of genius, and powerful like Napoleon Bonaparte. He appeared to be a resourceful self-promoter with an amiable willingness to mold his policies to reflect and, if necessary, bow to the interests of the United States.

The Nation expressed mild astonishment at Villa's public transformation from warrior-villain to warrior-hero:

> [Villa's] rapid and steady emergence from the reputation of being the worst of cutthroats to patriotic leader, as well as a military captain of remarkable ability, is one of the most extraordinary phenomena we can recall in the history of any public age. A year ago, if anybody had said that the people of this country . . . would be able to find in the doing of "Pancho" Villa a bit of real comfort and solace amid the general gloom, he would have been regarded as the silliest of jokers. . . . [I]t seems that his [Villa's] conduct ever since has been that of a loyal citizen and a friend of peace and orderly government.[111]

The Nation did not intend to lionize Villa. Instead, it alleged that his most substantive foreign policy accomplishment had been his manipulation of the American press—to which, ironically, *The Nation* itself had fallen prey, as the quoted passage evidences. Additionally, the weekly magazine charged that Villa's greater popularity than Carranza's in press depictions was undeserved and occurred "[p]robably because of superior press facilities."[112] *The Nation* likely assessed the issue of Villa's image promotion correctly, given his energetic propaganda efforts, his being "good copy," and the opportunity the press gave him to promote himself directly through his own voice in media accounts.

The *Los Angeles Times* echoed *The Nation*'s line of thought when, in February 1915, it dismissed Villa's friendship overtures as cynical ruses. Further, the paper opined, "Villa has recognized the fact that the best interests of Mexico would not be advanced by antagonizing the United States."[113] Moreover, the *Times* all but put aggressive words of war in Villa's mouth. It cited him as "having said, in effect, 'War with the United States is inevitable.'"[114]

And so a paradox reemerged. Villa's media image shone as never before after his pro-Wilson stand on Veracruz gained wide attention in late April 1914, and it continued to shine through the winter of 1915; yet elements of Mexicanness dimmed the light. The *New York Times*, probably Villa's most generous media supporter, summed up the negative side of the media position with unusual directness in February 1915. It claimed that Villa "represent[ed] the inherent laziness, savagery, and lack of purpose of the half-breed."[115]

I TOLD YOU SO: VILLA THE LOSER

The two crushing defeats Villa suffered at the hands of the Carrancista general Alvaro Obregón at Celaya in April 1915 signaled the beginning of Villa's military demise. Although United States recognition would not be granted to Carranza until October of that year, by early summer Villa had been all but wiped out as a genuine contender for the Mexican throne. But one would not have known this from the news media accounts.

The favorable press depictions of Villa, which in no small measure had been constructed around his military conquests, stuck with him through defeat after defeat into the early summer of 1915. When by mid-summer it became generally apparent to the American press that Villa's slice of the Revolution was in real jeopardy, the press, rather than recasting him in a pejorative light (which would have followed the military success–favorable framing logic of his approbatory renderings), tended to ignore him. To a lesser extent, Villa also became overshadowed by an improving Carranza image. Newspaper coverage generally adhered to the pattern of presenting Carranza in a more favorable light, whereas magazines, notable in their silence after Celaya, typically followed the pattern of ignoring Villa.

Well into June 1915, the publications I examined continued their favorable casting of Villa. He may have been down but he was definitely not out. A late April cartoon in the *Denver Post* suggested as much (fig. 26). While Villa stands on the other side of a fence—which suggests he has been sidelined, though not necessarily permanently—Carranza, dressed like a dandy and seeking diplomatic recognition, serenades the United States. The United States responds with "AW! GWAN AN' REALLY LICK SOMEBODY," an unsubtle reminder that Villa had been a fighting man while Carranza personally had been reluctant to do battle.

Still, reports about the fighting at Celaya gave the first hints that Carranza's propaganda machine had begun to break through the Villa mystique. Charges and countercharges swirled in reports about who had won and who had not. In fact, Villa had lost stunningly. He claimed to have won, but with the exception of the *Los Angeles Times*, publications proved wary of claims from either camp.

Day-to-day headlines from the *Chicago Tribune*, the *Denver Post*, the *New York Times*, and the *San Francisco Examiner* hinted at the propaganda struggle going on behind the headlines and at Carranza's improving image: " 'I WIN,' SAYS VILLA, AND OBREGON SAYS, 'VICTORY IS MINE'" (April 8),[116] "VILLA MEN ROUTED CARRANZA REPORTS, Washington Still Without News of Big Battle and Villa Agents Silent" (April 9),[117] "CARRANZA VICTORY DENIED BY VILLA, Has Circle Around Obregon, He Says, and Decisive Battle is Yet to be Fought" (April 10),[118] "VILLA TROOPS DRIVE ENEMY IN BIG FIGHT" (April 11),[119] "VILLA THREATENS TO BOMBARD CELAYA . . . Carranza's Army Beaten and Demoralized, [says] Villa's Report on the Recent Engagement" (April 12),[120] "REPORTS VILLA ROUT WITH LOSS OF 14,000

Figure 26. "'aw! GWAN AN' REALLY LICK SOMEBODY!'" Reproduced from the *Denver Post*, April 30, 1915.

. . . VILLA SAYS HE WILL WIN, Is 'Preparing a Decisive Blow'" (April 17),[121] "BIG BATTLE STILL IN DOUBT, Washington Can't Decide Between Conflicting Claims" (April 17),[122] "VILLA'S HOPES ARE SHATTERED" (April 21).[123]

Meanwhile, from late March through the Celaya engagement, the *Los Angeles Times* reported almost gleefully that Villa was losing badly. The story can be read through the daily headlines: "VILLA LOSES HEAVILY . . . VILLA DESERTERS REACH BORDER" (March 29),[124] "CARRANZA DEFEATS VILLA" (April 9),[125] "FIRST ROUT OF VILLA" (April 10),[126] "HEAVY BLOW TO VILLA" (April 14),[127] "Tables Turned. VILLA DEFEATED, OFFICIAL REPORT" (April 20).[128]

In June the *New York Times* queried, "VILLA BEATEN, SEEKING PEACE?"[129] But the same day an editorial discounted the likelihood of Villa's decline. That said, the paper had begun to shift its support perceptibly away from Villa and toward Carranza, although the new support was lukewarm. For example: "If the latest defeat of Villa could be counted a substantial victory for CARRANZA, the Mexican problem would be greatly simplified. But the closest observers of Mexican affairs do not believe that there is any stability in CARRANZA . . . [or that he] would restore order. . . . He lacks the extraordinary personal force of VILLA, who seems, however to be quite immune to civilizing processes."[130] As this passage suggests, Villa's complimentary rendering also endured— in part because the shift toward Carranza came in fits and starts. Despite his active propaganda efforts, Carranza remained hampered by what the press saw as unduly haughty behavior. It seemed, for example, that he "refuses to take advice from anybody, even his own ministers."[131] Villa, at least rhetorically, had always welcomed American advice.

At the same time, the Carranza propaganda machine had become more effective and begun to make inroads against media portrayals of Villa. During the spring it chipped away at Villa's image by successfully placing in the press several damning stories about Villa and Benton, as well as about General Felipe Angeles's alleged Huertista sympathies. As part of its shift toward Carranza, the *New York Times* began to recast the First Chief—with the aid of Carrancista propaganda—in the democratic-American-friend role that Villa had occupied. For example, one mid-July headline read, "CARRANZA BIDS FOR [U.S.] RECOGNITION; Gives Out Statement Telling His Plan for Jeffersonian Rule and Praising Wilson, DESIRES OUR FRIENDSHIP."[132]

Perhaps the most telling image transformation for Villa came with his decline as a news commodity. By the summer of 1915 the papers were full of stories about Carranza's impending recognition. Villa had become, if not quite invisible, then at least more difficult to find in media reports. This was especially apparent in news magazines. Just as the magazines had been slower to pick up the Villa story in late 1913, so, too, after Celaya they proved reluctant to maintain an interest in him.

CONCLUSION

From the fall of 1913 through the battle at Celaya in April 1915, the American press increasingly sketched a picture of Villa as energetic, physically hearty, mentally sharp, emotionally warm (if volatile), and admirably humble. Although Mexicanness, especially the quality of villainy, tarred him now and then, Villa invariably shook it off and moved on to other, favorable castings—in part by playing himself off against Huerta's savagery and Carranza's sneakiness. Meanwhile, the three elements of his foreign policy—appeals to morality, self-interest, and American pragmatism—thrived.

In the Mexican Revolution Villa fought Huerta and then Carranza. In the American news media, the avenue in which he vigorously attempted to market his foreign policy, Villa fought them too, but sometimes secondarily. Foremost he grappled with stereotypes of Mexicanness, over which he generally prevailed, though never completely, from the time of the Tampico incident until the summer of 1915. Indeed, so powerful were the combined effects of his propaganda and his inherently being "good copy" that Villa's image became permeated with thoroughly American traits.

From 1913 through 1915, Villa became increasingly popular in the American press. Although his many positive attributes were tempered in the press by periodic effusions of horror at his villainous behavior, by the beginning of 1915 Villa had become, for the American press on the whole, a warrior-hero. He had been a warrior—a fighting man—from day one; but when he began to act friendly, in the press's estimation, and to effusively proclaim his friendship for the United States, the dynamics of his labeling changed in his favor. His image improved steadily as he pronounced repeatedly for democracy, Woodrow Wilson, improvements in education, land reform, and the virtue of humbleness, as he decried dictatorship while calling for an end to militarism, and as he cast both Carranza and Huerta as his opposites.

But while Villa's image flourished in American press accounts between 1913 and 1915, especially prior to the Benton affair, press judgments also often included analytical postures derived from the long-standing American cultural framing of Mexicans within the categories of backwardness, racial limitations, and moral decrepitude. In such cases, Villa was guilty of Mexicanness, and he was frequently cast indelibly in the shape of a villain.

Given the demonstrated American press practice of negatively stereotyping Mexicans, one might expect that in addressing Villa's most vexing foreign policy problem, the Benton affair, the press would have resorted to the established Mexicanness rubrics. But that did not generally happen. Instead, with the notable exception of the Los Angeles Times, Villa was condemned, to be sure, but not necessarily because of his Mexicanness as such. Instead, the press condemned him largely because he might have been responsible for a cold-blooded killing. This is significant because, while the press roundly condemned Villa, it mostly eschewed employing Mexicanness as a tool of assessment.

Yet even as Villa's warrior-hero image largely prevailed over his Mexican villainy, it continued to be tinged periodically by stereotypes of Mexicanness. Two cartoons—the first from the Los Angeles Times in mid-January 1914 and the second from the Denver Post in early March 1915—illustrate how Villa remained partly diminished by Mexicanness. In the Times sketch (fig. 27), Villa is not singled out but is debased inferentially as a cage full of Lilliputian (read, backward and racially limited) Mexican generals is held at arm's length by a towering Uncle Sam who asks, "What's To Be Done

Figure 27. "What's to be done with 'Em?" Reproduced from the *Los Angeles Times*, January 18, 1914.

With 'Em?" The implication is that if the generals cannot solve their problems peacefully among themselves (suggesting moral decrepitude), Uncle Sam will be disturbed and perhaps forced to take action. The cage itself symbolizes the treatment to be meted out—it is a prison, but one of their own making, which implies backwardness and moral decrepitude. First, Mexicans (that is, "MEXICAN GENERALS," including Villa) are reduced in importance (or are shown as racially limited) by being reduced in size. Second, the Mexicans are confined to their cage, which symbolizes the metaphorical pen (for example, backwardness) from which they cannot escape without the assistance or assent of the United States.

The *Post*'s pictorial (fig. 28) again reduces Villa in importance by reducing him in size relative to Uncle Sam. Carranza gains similar treatment. But here, in March 1915, Villa is near the apogee of his popularity in the press. He no longer bears the countenance of a desperate ruffian or menacing cur (read, backwardness and moral decrepitude). Instead, he is dressed like a blue-collar American—and, like a stereotypically industrious American, he is rolling up his sleeves as a sign that he is ready and willing to go to work. Carranza, by contrast, appears befuddled (signifying backwardness and possibly racial limitations). He also appears to be in need of a good thrashing, as is suggested by his order to Obregón—referring to the population of Mexico City—to "LET 'EM STARVE" (signifying moral decrepitude). Villa is allowed to be powerful, but only over Carranza, as Villa's slightly greater size indicates. Nevertheless, his image here obviously represents an improvement over the dismissive and anonymous treatment of the *Times* cartoon.

The press, then, couched its overall assessment of Villa in contradictory terms. On one hand, he was framed pejoratively because the press identified some of his behavior as exemplifying Mexican villainy. This framing waned over time, but even in its decline, Villa's Mexicanness plagued his image like a parasite,

Figure 28. "LET VILLA DO IT!" Reproduced from the *Denver Post*, March 10, 1915.

feeding off the stereotyped elements of his birthright—backwardness, racial limitations, and moral decrepitude.

On the other hand, Villa was a bona fide Americanized warrior-hero. He had it all—great personal courage, a love of democracy, a marked fondness for Americans (especially the president), and a belief in uplifting the downtrodden. To be sure, he was Mexican, but increasingly after the Tampico incident he was cast incongruously, given his unshedable Mexicanness, as typifying the opposite of what Mexicanness stood for—Americanness.

CHAPTER EIGHT

THE WARRIOR REDUX

Villa in the American Diplomatic Record

In the diplomatic correspondence of the U.S. State Department, Francisco Villa was a warrior all over again. On one hand, Villa emerged, just as he did in the American press, as a valiant, courageous, clever fighting man given at times to capricious behavior, including violence. On the other hand, going even farther than the press in damning Villa, the diplomatic portrayals played up a supposed inordinate viciousness on his part. For some diplomatic correspondents, Villa's behavior reflected stereotyped visions of Mexican savagery, on a par with the press's treatment of Huerta. On the whole, however, in diplomatic correspondence as in the press, approbatory readings of Villa tended to predominate.

In this chapter I examine thematically the general treatment of Mexicans in American diplomatic correspondence in the context of the three frames of Mexicanness discussed in chapter 5—backwardness, racial limitations, and moral decrepitude. Moreover, I explore the ways in which the diplomatic correspondence framed Villa and his foreign policy, again within the context of American perceptions of Mexicanness. Finally, I analyze the decline in Villa's recorded image over the spring and summer of 1915. The examined records include assessments by State Department agents in the field as well as by Wilson's personal emissaries to Mexico.[1]

REMIXING THE MONGREL

The American press's tendency to portray Mexicans along lines that adhered closely to long-held stereotypes—as quarrelsome, excitable, morally weak, untrustworthy, unintelligent, and inclined to commit (and to enjoy committing) violence—surfaced in modified form in United States diplomatic correspondence. Whereas the hackneyed press treatment tended to derive from notions about either bloodline (racial limitations) or cultural influences (backwardness), the diplomatically fashioned Mexican represented an often ambiguous mixture of blood and the conditioning effects of environment. The observed behavior, however—frequently expressed as moral decrepitude—was similar in both cases.

As in the press, so in the diplomatic record backwardness typically reflected being mired in the material trappings and retrograde Weltanschauung of earlier centuries, as well as in violence and immaturity. Racial limitations stemmed from Mexicans' espied genetic inferiority, including mental simplicity and a hedonistic impulse to sate physical cravings in pillage and chaos. Moral decrepitude stressed dishonesty, a love of wanton violence, inherent cruelty, and a predilection for theft, barbarity, and sneakiness. The diplomatic record tended to remix the American press's Mexican mongrel by frequently conflating issues of race, environment, and moral depravity.

TRIAD OF DAMNATION: MEXICANNESS
IN THE U.S. DIPLOMATIC RECORD

For the State Department, perhaps the most serious American strategic concern stemmed from the perceived Mexican inclination for hostility—and potential violence—toward the United States and Americans. Indeed, President Wilson and the two secretaries of state, William Jennings Bryan and Robert Lansing (who replaced

Bryan in June 1915), repeatedly stressed the importance of protecting foreigners, especially Americans, and their interests.[2]

The United States not only expressed concern over hostility and violence directed at clearly defined foreign targets but also seemed to feel that any revolutionary mayhem potentially threatened United States interests. For example, on the subject of the Revolution in Mexico's Pacific states, the commander-in-chief of American naval forces in the Pacific Ocean wrote to Bryan: "These may be taken as the personal opinions or outbursts of fiery individuals, and are not to be unexpected in a country where general excitement prevails and civil war is raging. There is of course some hostility on the part of Mexicans towards Americans, due largely to racial and temperamental differences."[3] Although this report clearly tied Mexican anti-American antagonism to racial limitations ("racial . . . differences"), at the same time it identified some hostile behavior as signifying cultural backwardness ("not to be unexpected . . . where civil war is raging"). In either case, this assessment of a Mexican habit of violence dovetailed neatly with similar press and literary assessments.[4]

Other diplomatic correspondence sketched a similar evaluation of the Mexican character. For example, Marion Letcher, United States consul at Chihuahua, filed a report with Bryan noting the "inherited ideals" of government in Mexico. Such Lamarckian phrasing suggests that Letcher conflated a learned response (that is, stemming from backwardness) with a natural inclination (that is, derived from racial limitations).[5]

Making the case for Mexicans' moral decrepitude, John Lind, former governor of Minnesota and one of President Wilson's personal emissaries to Mexico, identified the Mexican character as essentially greedy. "They are all avaricious," he reported to Bryan, echoing some of Philip Wayne Powell's findings about how Spaniards have been stereotyped in the United States.[6] "They live in the senses," Lind added (read, they are racially limited).[7]

Reporting to Bryan on another occasion, Lind expanded on Mexican identity by bifurcating Mexico's national makeup into two congenitally weak groups—aristocrats, including the Roman Catholic church, and the "toiling Indian masses." He identified both groups as curs who shared the "same blood." He explained: "The vanity and the conceit of the [aristocrats] . . . is mountain high. They call it pride; real pride, they have none. It is probably the outgrowth of four centuries of unconscious comparison with an inferior race. However produced it is a stubborn fact that resists all genuine progress . . . or betterment."[8] Here again, the backwardness–racial limitations–moral decrepitude triad emerges. Mexicans are the products of environmental backwardness ("the outgrowth of four centuries"), racial limitations ("inferior race"), and moral decrepitude ("a stubborn fact that resists all genuine progress . . . or betterment").

According to Duval West, another of Wilson's personal emissaries, one more effect of Mexicans' rapacious appetites was a proclivity for drink: "The uniform use of spiritous liquors by the population, pulque, mescal and distillates from cane and other products of the soil, being had at nominal cost and slight exertion, has been, perhaps, the greatest single factor in holding them at their low level."[9] According to Letcher, an additional factor holding Mexicans in backwardness was an inclination for sexual promiscuity. Mexicans were so sexually debased, Letcher claimed, that syphilis had become the "national disease of Mexico."[10]

Some diplomats identified moral decrepitude as manifesting itself in the way Mexicans behaved toward Americans and the United States. In an example that blends racial limitations and backwardness, the United States consul at Torreón, Theodore Hamm, reported to Bryan that "[h]atred of the American and all things American is instinctive in this race; it is taught the young both at home and at school."[11] Again the roots of the problem are at once innate and learned.

Describing a scene from the Convention of Aguascalientes, State Department agent Leon Canova also combined learned behavior with innate behavior when passing judgment on Mexicans. He wrote to Bryan describing "[m]ore than a thousand hot blooded Latins, practically all of them fresh from scenes of carnage, where the use of weapons was the first instinct and the highest law—men accustomed to live in an atmosphere of death for the past few years."[12] Canova's use of the expression "first instinct" suggests nature, and Spanish nature at that—"hot blooded Latins." But he also links "instinct" to cultural terms—they were "fresh from scenes of carnage" and "men accustomed to live in an atmosphere of death." Again, backwardness and racial limitations collapse into an all-encompassing allegation of moral decrepitude.

Another admixing of racial limitations and backwardness occurred in a State Department report penned by Robert Lansing. He averred that the roots of the Mexican Revolution lay both in the prejudice Mexico's Indians held against whites and in Indian instinct. "There exists and always had existed," he wrote, "since the Spaniards conquered the Indians in Mexico, an instinctive hatred of the white man by the native red man." One result of such a nature-nurture combination, according to Lansing's report, was the possibility that Mexicans might not be capable "of conducting a republican system [of government] in accordance with provisions of their Constitution."[13]

In sum, State Department correspondents used a series of derogatory frames of Mexico and Mexicans, ranging from their supposed coarse hostility and greediness to their haughtiness and moral depravity, to explain the behavior of Mexicans during the Revolution. State Department stereotypes of Mexicans tended to focus more on learned behavior than did press depictions. Diplomatic renderings denounced Mexicans for bad blood, to be sure, but often they also pointed out that much of the Mexicans' reprehensible revolutionary conduct had been learned by force of wartime circumstance. Canova put it this way:

It is very difficult indeed for an American to appreciate the workings of the Latin mind. The functions of conscience, as understood by us, in no way applies to the Latin mind, at least to the Mexican. At first blush, one would be led to believe that these people were suffering from a mental vertigo, but, to one who has had experience with them, this monstrous conduct is but a portrayal of the perfectly logical line of reasoning, from their standpoint. The amazing and horrifying conclusions reached by them, which affronts the normal Anglo-Saxon mind, is for them, the most natural thing in the world.[14]

Canova's report, like many dispatches received at the State Department, tended to conflate and blur learned behavior (backwardness) with instinct (racial limitations). The "Latin" mind, he argues, is different from, and of a lower order than, the "normal" Anglo-Saxon mentality. It is a product of different (in part, revolutionary) influences, which also in part account for its less developed state (and moral decrepitude). Villa was often cast as a typical expression of the State Department's vision of Mexicanness.

VILLA AS DOUBLE

Villa and his foreign policy image were characterized in United States diplomatic correspondence in two basic fashions. First, he was framed as a warrior-savage. This represents a step in ferocity beyond the press's usual characterization of him as warrior-villain. As warrior-savage, Villa was cast in ways similar to the press's portrayals of Huerta—as unnecessarily violent, inherently stupid, avaricious, untrustworthy, vicious, and lustful. But unlike Huerta, he was framed as a successful fighting man.

Second, Villa was cast as a warrior-hero—a valiant and courageous fighting man, struggling for the good of his country. In some cases, the emphasis on Villa's friendship with the United

States significantly reoriented his warrior-hero image; I refer to his image in those instances as that of warrior-friend.

Marion Letcher's bitter denunciations of Villa to Bryan stand as a clear example of Villa's being typecast as a warrior-savage. Letcher portrayed Villa as a Mexican stereotype—a detestably violent, tricky, deceitful, arrogant, unfriendly, duplicitous miscreant.[15] Because Villa was popular both in the American press and in official Washington, Letcher's portrayal was partly a reaction, he acknowledged, to the flattering American press image of Villa "as a devil become saint." This pro-Villa casting, in which the general was fashioned as shrewd, intelligent, and friendly to the United States and Americans, Letcher saw as the work of effective, cynical, untruthful Villista propaganda.[16]

Letcher's appraisal stood in contradistinction to the message of Villa propaganda. Letcher claimed that the real Villa was hostile to America, ignorant (Villa acknowledged as much but couched it in the softer tones of humbleness), and decidedly unintelligent: "The people who know nothing of Villa except through [the press] cannot possibly conceive of the primitiveness of his nature, his terrible moral limitations, his dense ignorance, and his utter guiltlessness of every worthy human emotion." Despite this round condemnation, Villa's battlefield victories impressed Letcher, who found himself compelled at least to acknowledge Villa's military successes. But he did so in decidedly relative terms—Villa was able only when compared with other Mexicans. The passage continues: "That he is energetic, crafty, alert, and the possessor of a certain forceful mother wit and considerable penetration, all to a degree that rather distinguish him from other Mexicans, cannot be denied."[17] In this casting, Letcher plumbs the shallow depths of Mexicanness only to conclude that Villa is cleverer and yet more reprehensible than his typically limited countryman.

Villa was cast as hostile to the United States in other reports as well. Gaston Schmurtz, the United States consul at Aguascalientes, charged Villa with masquerading as a friend to the United States as part of a cynical attempt to further his own political ambitions. Schmurtz called Villa's overtures of friendship to Wilson "positively disgusting . . . contemptible . . . [and] hypocritical."[18] Letcher, meanwhile, described Villa's appearance as a blend of backwardness, especially of an uncivilized, retrograde ancestry, and moral decrepitude, signified in particular by lechery, intemperance, dishonesty, and laziness. Letcher capped this denunciation with an undifferentiated accusation of general mongrelism (that is, racial limitations), referring to

> his loutish, half domineering leer; his bulging eyeballs, with glittering stary [sic] pupils surrounded by half-red white, which give the impression of being blood-shot; his unkempt, erect standing hair; his coarse, thick-lipped mouth, suggesting an admixture of negro blood; his rather delicate hands, giving the lie to the claim some times made that he has ever done an honest day's work; all constitute an ensemble that produces a singularly unpleasant impression upon the mind of a civilized man. . . . [He is a] Frankenstein.

Elsewhere in the same document, Letcher again stressed essential Mexican depravity, noting that Villa's military success could best be explained by the inferior makeup of the federal armies, "one of the most stupid, pig-headed, chicken-hearted organizations on the earth." Not surprisingly, Letcher also viewed Villa as dictatorial in nature and in fact.[19]

In the same document in which he fashioned Mexicans as innately "avaricious," Lind characterized Villa both in flattering terms and in a negative, predetermined way. On one hand: "In Villa they have an intrepid and resourceful general." On the other: "He is the highest type of physical moral and mental efficiency that the conditions and the environment could be reasonably expected to produce." Later in the document, Lind echoed a common complaint: "Like all Mexicans he is avaricious. . . . He is cruel. Life and fate have taught him nothing else. . . . His acts . . . should be judged by Mexican standards. In so far as he allowed any captives to escape death, to that extent he is more humane than the commanders of the federal forces."[20]

In suggesting that Villa "be judged by Mexican standards," Lind makes a distinction that in itself would mark Mexicans merely as different. But in the context of the passage as a whole, the distinction diminishes Villa because it is understood as signifying the inferiority of Mexicanness. Lind stresses Villa's innate weakness ("Like all Mexican he is avaricious") and the effects upon him of a retrograde environment ("Life and fate have taught him nothing else"). In Lind's final judgment, he informed Bryan, "I believe truly that the worst thing that can be said of [Villa] is that he is only a little better than the best of the federal generals."[21]

Although Villa emerged in some diplomatic correspondence as the archetypal Mexican Savage, he also was portrayed as a warrior-friend—a courageous and valiant fighting man struggling for the good of his country, and an American friend. As we saw in chapters 2 and 3, Villa's propaganda operations revolved around his attempts to promote friendship between himself and the United States. And indeed, in the U.S. diplomatic record, favorable depictions of Villa bear close resemblance to the content of his propaganda messages.

The first plank of Villa's warrior-friend construction rested on his status as a commendable fighting man. Canova, who elsewhere stereotyped Mexicans as backward, racially limited, and morally decrepit, somewhat glibly referred to Villa as a "popular chap." He continued, "I have never lost my liking for him. I know him to be a brave, daring fellow who inspires his army."[22]

John Silliman, the United States consul at Saltillo, portrayed Villa as a fighting man who exhibited extreme behavior—for good and ill. On the favorable side, one dispatch to Bryan told how, amid the deplorable war-torn conditions in Mexico City, Villa had informally adopted sixty war orphans to be cared for at his expense in Chihuahua.[23] On other occasions, Silliman identified

Villa's behavior as "discreditable and disgraceful"[24] and "notoriously" corrupt.[25]

A detailed report to Woodrow Wilson from his emissary Paul Fuller sketched Villa heroically as a man who exemplified the characteristics of self-reliance, self-improvement, and self-confidence. Yet Villa remained a work in progress, Fuller's paternalistic tone suggested:

> Villa—still an "incomplete" man, but with elements of such value that two or three years should make him a great man for the good of his country. Without earlier training or opportunities—his sudden rise when the occasion presented itself, and his great success are necessarily somewhat of a peril. His unusual hold upon the loyalty and devotion of his officers and men is only equaled by his fidelity to them and the strong sense of his responsibility to them. . . . Villa has no political aspirations and is not politically ambitious. . . . Villa is an unusually quiet man, gentle in humor, low-voiced, slow of speech, earnest and occasionally emotional in expression, but always subdued, with an undercurrent of sadness. He has no outward manifestation of vanity.[26]

Given the violence of the Revolution (and Villa's role in it), Fuller's report was about as glowing an appraisal of the general as one might be able to expect. Fuller not only avoided Mexicanness stereotypes but framed Villa in a positive way by describing him as a sort of Horatio Alger–type self-made man ("without earlier training or opportunities—his sudden rise when the opportunity presented itself").[27] Fuller's warm assessment stands in marked contrast to Letcher's depiction of Villa. Such divergent assessments must have tormented policymakers in Washington. What was one to believe?

State Department special agent and Villa intimate George Carothers, in a large body of correspondence to the State Department, depicted Villa much as Silliman did—as a person of extremes. On the favorable side, Carothers stressed repeatedly that Villa felt genuine friendship for the United States and for Americans—the centerpiece of Villa's foreign policy and a key concern for Bryan, Lansing, and Wilson. Highlighting pragmatism, on one of many such occasions Carothers reported: "He told me that it was his intention to favor Americans in every way possible, in as much as the United States had never recognized the Huerta government, and that for that reason we deserved more consideration [than other foreign interests]."[28] Indeed, more than on any other issue, Villa's character was assessed by how he dealt with foreign, especially American, interests. Further, although it lacks Villa's hyperbolic flair, this passage echoes the most common theme of Villa's propaganda—friendship.

A mid-December 1913 consular dispatch to Bryan from the American consul at Ciudad Juárez captured the general shape of diplomatic opinion: "General Villa's policy, notwithstanding the seeming harshness and cruelty in some cases, is carrying out the only promising solution for restoring peace. . . . It is my opinion . . . that General Villa wishes to not inflict injury or hardship on none except the enemy of his cause. . . . General Villa left orders with the officials in charge of [Ciudad] Juarez to protect Americans and American property."[29] In this passage, Villa is criticized as being "harsh and cruel," but the charge is tempered by the admission that his actions are also the "only promising solution." And again, the most common Villista propaganda theme stands out: friendship. Villa is presented as intent on providing protection to and for Americans.[30]

In sum, the prevailing diplomatic opinion on Villa into the winter of 1915 was bifurcated between assessments that cast him as a Mexican savage and others that portrayed him as a Mexican warrior-hero and friend. The hero-friend depiction, which also echoed the themes of Villista propaganda, largely prevailed, as is witnessed by American support of Villa until well into 1915.[31] The common denominator shared by the competing diplomatic portrayals of Villa was his undeniable status as a successful fighting man.

VILLA IN DECLINE

Over the winter of 1915 Villa became increasingly strapped for funds as his traditional sources of revenue dried up. Further, beginning in April 1915, he was handed a string of debilitating military losses from which he could not recover. These setbacks ultimately pushed him into a desperate position in which he found it necessary to tax and seize foreign properties and interests hitherto exempted from such treatment. The correspondence of Carothers and of Zach Lamar Cobb, the U.S. customs inspector at El Paso, with the State Department illustrates the decline of Villa's stature in the diplomatic realm throughout this period.

As Villa's behavior toward Americans became less friendly in the face of his failed attempts to secure revenues necessary to continue fighting, his favorable casting faded, too. Carothers had been pro-Villa throughout the Revolution and continued to be into the summer of 1915.[32] Then he changed his tune, and his later portrayals of Villa contributed to a new, ultimately condemnatory framing of the general.

Throughout 1914 and well into 1915, Villa figured as a warrior-friend in Carothers's dispatches. He was stronger and friendlier than Carranza, by Carothers's estimation.[33] The special agent also thought Villa generally provided "excellent order" under difficult conditions.[34] Carothers once even defended Villa from a negative report filed by the Associated Press.[35]

By July of 1915, when it had become clear that Villa's military position was collapsing, Carothers's reports no longer consistently favored the general. Now his dispatches were full of tales of Villa's senseless violence and his all-encompassing hostility toward foreigners, including Americans. On July 22 he wrote to Lansing: "It is told here . . . that Villa executed some thirty railroad men for refusing to work and also a prominent planter for refusing to pay a forced loan. . . . There is growing danger of such occurrences. Since his [military] reverses Villa is becoming harder to deal with. He is sorely pressed for money. I am afraid of conflicts that may arise over forced loans."[36] Matters then became worse almost by the day, according to Carothers's cables.

On July 23 Carothers reported, "You will note the tone of defiance in the several replies from Villa received and forwarded [to you] today."[37] Still, the special agent remained somewhat supportive of Villa and mildly optimistic in tone: "My relations with Villa continue to be very friendly and I firmly believe he thinks he is doing what is necessary to establish peace in his territory but his temper gets the best of him at times and he commits acts which he afterwards regrets."[38]

In early August, Villa's financial condition worsened, and he elicited greater concern from Carothers—and even from members of Villa's government. Carothers wrote:

> Villa is very friendly to me. In the interview in my car he put his hand on my knee and said: "I believe you and I will be friends until death, [I] feel that way towards you and believe you feel the same toward me." At Chihuahua after the incident with the merchants [from whom Villa had demanded money on pain of death] Villa ministers separately called on me at my car and pleaded with me to talk to Villa as they considered I had more influence with him than any other man.[39]

Just two days later Carothers reported: "I wish to place clearly before you my opinion that only the strongest measures will stop the despoiling of American and other foreign property by Villa. . . . It has been impossible for me to obtain from him even the slightest hope of his complying with the wishes of the [United States] Government to release foreign property."[40] This noncompliance represented a clear turn of events from Villa's long-standing primary foreign policy aim of friendship.

By September, Carothers was reporting that Villa "has about lost control of his temper. . . . I fear some severe and regrettable action." The agent had been advised, he said, for his own safety to stay away from Villa "for the present."[41] Finally, by November, weeks after Carranza had received de facto United States recognition, Villa had become a "dangerous menace."[42]

Zach Cobb, the customs inspector, penned telegrams to the State Department that tell a tale similar to Carothers's, with a key difference—his cables reflect a sense of alarm about Villa's capriciously violent and anti-foreign behavior months before Carothers evinced great concern.[43] At the beginning of the tale, however, in 1914, Cobb was still portraying Villa as both physically hearty and actively protective of American interests.[44] "All Americans and foreigners are safe and are receiving every consideration" under Villa's care, he wired to Bryan in a typical dispatch in March 1914.[45]

Later, on the eve of the United States' seizure of Veracruz—after Villa's pro-Wilson stand had helped defuse a war scare—Cobb reported to Bryan that "Villa's attitude ha[s] relieved tension here."[46] Villa's violent behavior remained a source of concern, though. In early June, responding to Bryan's concern about an allegation that Villa had ordered the execution of thirty-two captured federal officers, Cobb noted simply that Villa denied the charges. His source of information was Carothers.[47]

By March 1915, Cobb's depictions of Villa had acquired an ominous tone. Villa was strapped for funds, and his behavior toward foreigners and foreign interests was becoming more demanding and less friendly, by Cobb's accounts. Villa's word was no longer considered trustworthy: "Villa and his authorities do not appreciate the responsibility of making good his assurances. Assurances that are not carried out in good faith are injurious both to our government and to him. It would be better if he made no assurances than for those made not to be lived up to."[48]

Later that month, Cobb's growing concern over Villa's apparent unwillingness to afford full protection to foreign interests led him to charge that Villa and his subordinates "appear . . . to be like indulgent children."[49] Villa's behavior, in Cobb's view, did not improve. Indeed, it got worse.

In early June, Villa was "apparently in defiant humor toward the United States." Further, Cobb opined, "Villa has been losing out fast and there is danger that he will make a grandstand play against the United States intending to boost himself."[50] In mid-July Cobb espied the "probable early elimination of Villa as a major factor."[51] And in late July Cobb expressed concern that Carothers was overestimating Villa's severely reduced capacity to carry on.[52]

By September, Villa's reckless and sometimes violent seizure of foreign assets, Cobb explained simply and contemptuously, "gives Villa the loot."[53] And in November, weeks after Carranza's de facto recognition, when Carothers wired Lansing that he feared Villa was "fully capable of any extreme," he reported that he and Cobb were largely of the same mind.[54]

Like Carothers's reports, Cobb's cables to the State Department were not framed in the triad of Mexicanness attributes. Although Villa's behavior as described in Cobb's reports sometimes bordered on savagery, it was not because Cobb's dispatches were steeped in notions of Mexican backwardness, racial limitations, or moral decrepitude. Instead, Cobb portrayed Villa in the context of how the general's actions related to Cobb's interpretation of U.S. interests. In short, although in 1915 both Cobb and Carothers reported increasingly and sometimes caustically about Villa's descent into wanton and capricious behavior, neither agent portrayed Villa as the archetypal Mexican Savage. Both correspondents, to varying degrees, fashioned him as both friendly and unpredictable.

THE PRESS PRESENCE IN DIPLOMACY:
IMAGE REFLECTIONS OF VILLA

Both United States diplomats and the American press sometimes depicted Villa as a stereotyped Mexican warrior with an inclination for brutishness—either as a villain (in the press, where the best example is the *Los Angeles Times*) or, worse, as a savage (in the diplomatic dispatches, where the best example is Marion Letcher). Other press organs (such as the *San Francisco Examiner*) and different diplomatic agents (such as Leon Canova) stereotyped Mexicans pejoratively but observed in Villa the traits of a warrior-hero.

Yet while the press remained supportive of Villa through 1915, the diplomatic correspondents (for example, Carothers and Cobb) did not. The reasons for this divergence in treatment are twofold. First, Carothers maintained an intimate friendship with Villa and a closeness with the Villa camp's operations that American reporters did not match.[55] Second, unlike the press, which frequently played the game of assessing Villa by comparing him with the unpopular First Chief, Cobb and Carothers largely stuck to the business of assessing Villa by his behavior as it related to official United States interests in Mexico. Third, neither Cobb nor Carothers had any personal stake in Villa's future, whereas the press, having framed him as the likely winner of the Revolution, had its reputation for accuracy and dependability on the line—which may have encouraged the press to resist recognizing the reality of Villa's defeat.

Despite these differences, press and diplomatic portrayals of Villa on the whole resembled each other closely. It seems reasonable to ask, then, in what respects the press influenced the diplomatic assessments of Villa. After all, the State Department files are full of references to the media—and United States diplomatic correspondents utilized press reports in myriad ways.

Sometimes diplomatic documents cited press reports as strictly informational. In a typical instance, Nelson O'Shaughnessy, the United States chargé d'affaires in Mexico, wired to Bryan in mid-October 1913 that he had "seen in the press despatches from the United States the statement that my government is considering recognizing the belligerency of Carranza."[56] On another occasion, Henry Lane Wilson, the United States ambassador to Mexico, noted to Bryan: "Mexican Minister to Russia has given an interview to newspapers in which among other things he says. . . . "[57]

Occasionally news reports were a step ahead of State Department information-gathering. For example, Bryan cabled the United States embassy in London, "Our representatives confirm the newspaper reports to the effect that Lord [Weetman Pearson] Cowdray [a British oil baron] is assisting in the financing of Huerta's government with a view to continuing it."[58] And sometimes press reports were considered more reliable than field information. For example, Wilson's personal emissary John Lind wired Bryan, "This information is based on rumor more or less but I assume the details will be in the Associated Press despatches in the morning."[59]

Other times, the press got it all wrong, according to United States diplomatic correspondents. For example, Bryan wired the United States embassy in Mexico that because news of Lind's mission to Mexico had been "misrepresented" in American press reports, the embassy staff was instructed to "say to the [Huerta] Foreign Office that this [American] Government is not responsible for such [press] misrepresentation."[60] In another case, according to O'Shaughnessy, the press got it wrong "with what seems an absolute negation of patriotism."[61] In some cases, too, the State Department felt compelled to issue press releases to "correct erroneous impressions" made in press reports.[62] The State Department was also sensitive to news leaks that might embarrass or diplomatically undermine the Wilson regime.[63]

Marion Letcher went so far as to claim that the press reports of journalist John Kenneth Turner in 1910–1911 (and the book that came out of them, *Barbarous Mexico*) had helped start the Mexican Revolution.[64] Although Letcher certainly overstated Turner's influence, the underlying premise of his contention—that the press might influence readers in ways prejudicial to Wilson's Mexico policy—was of concern to the State Department. For example, William W. Canada, the United States consul at Veracruz, wired to Bryan about an article "published in Spanish in several Mexican papers and which is of interest because it was actually believed by a large number of Mexicans, not only of the lower class, but even of the middle class."[65]

Bryan's policy was not to respond to inaccurate (read, bad) press, but he made exceptions when "misstatements in regard to international matters may lead to serious consequences."[66] Woodrow Wilson, too, occasionally reacted to news reports. Through his personal secretary, Joseph Patrick Tumulty, he called Lansing's "attention" to a *New York Sun* article of October 27, 1915, titled "VILLISTA FORCES STEADILY DWINDLE."[67] On another occasion, Bryan noted to Cardoso de Oliveira, the Brazilian minister to Mexico and State Department confidante, that Wilson "heartily approves the action taken"—when the information upon which the "action" was assessed came from "press despatches."[68] Wilson also relied on "interesting memoranda prepared"[69] by "our good friend"[70] American journalist David Lawrence, an Associated Press reporter whom Wilson had befriended while Lawrence worked on the staff of the Princeton University undergraduate newspaper and Wilson served as president of the school.[71]

Clearly, then, the press influenced diplomatic agents and policymakers in Washington. The influence reached from agents in the field all the way to the White House. Precisely how news content swayed government officials is unclear (and will likely remain so). Yet the consonance between press and diplomatic framings of Villa and Mexico suggests the prior existence of deeply internalized and widespread American cultural visions of Mexico.

Villa often succeeded in influencing American diplomats to portray him in ways similar to the ways in which he portrayed himself in his propaganda. The fit between these portrayals was close—Villa as warrior-hero, warrior-friend, or both. On the other hand, neither Villa's propaganda nor his personal influence with diplomats met with complete success in framing him in a manner of his own choosing, because of the driving persistence of historically grounded American visions of Mexicanness. These widespread cultural visions promoted the casting of Villa as warrior-villain (in the press) and warrior-savage (in the diplomatic record), and they continually served to undermine the favorable portrayals hard won by Villa's adroit public-relations campaign.

NOTES

A NOTE ON ARCHIVAL SOURCES

Although Francisco Villa left neither an archive nor much in the way of a direct paper trail for the historian to follow, there are numerous sources available to the Villa scholar. I consulted the following five collections. First, the Carranza archive (Manuscritos de Venustiano Carranza, Centro de Estudios de Historia de México, Fundación Cultural de Condumex, Mexico City—hereinafter VC) houses considerable Villa-related foreign policy material in the form of inter-Constitutionalist correspondence, correspondence between Constitutionalists and the United States government and press outlets, and samples of Constitutionalist propaganda materials.

Second, the Foreign Relations archive (Archivo Histórico de la Secretaría de Relaciones Exteriores, Mexico City—hereinafter AHSRE) carries a wealth of Villa-related documents similar to those found in the Carranza archive. Further, the AHSRE collections provide information about Villa from Huertista sources.

Third, the archive of Villa lieutenant Roque González Garza (Archivo de Roque González Garza, Mexico City—hereinafter ARGG), although smaller, offers important documents relating to foreign policy issues throughout 1914–1915. Also, because González Garza promoted Villa's propaganda, his personal papers shed some light on the workings of the Villa propaganda machine.

Fourth, the Records of the Department of State Relating to the Internal Affairs of Mexico, 1910–1929 (hereinafter RDS) are available on microfilm

(National Archives Microfilm Publication, Microcopy no. 274, series 812). These voluminous materials offer an abundance of information about Villa, especially his relationship with the United States government.

Fifth, a more limited source, the Silvestre Terrazas Collection at the Bancroft Library, University of California, Berkeley (hereinafter STC), provides some evidence of Villa's propaganda operations in Mexico. Terrazas alternately served as arms purchaser, propagandist in El Paso, and editor of the Constitutionalist newspaper *El Correo de Chihuahua*.

For a comprehensive guide to revolutionary archival and library holdings in the United States and Mexico, see Lawrence Douglas Taylor, *Revolución mexicana: Guía de archivos y bibliotecas, México–Estados Unidos* (Mexico City: Instituto Naciónal de Estudios Históricos de la Revolución Mexicana, 1987).

CHAPTER ONE. A MAN ON HORSEBACK, A REVOLUTION, AND THE MASS MEDIA

1. *Chicago Tribune*, 31 March 1915, p. 3.
2. *Los Angeles Times*, 6 April 1914, p. 1.
3. *Los Angeles Times*, 6 April 1914, p. 1.
4. *Denver Post*, 16 January 1914, p. 1.
5. *San Francisco Examiner*, 27 May 1914, p. 2.
6. *Chicago Tribune*, 11 March 1915, p. 1.
7. *New York Times*, 25 August 1914, p. 6.
8. For a good discussion of this topic, see Edward Said, *Culture and Imperialism* (New York: Pantheon, 1993).
9. The 1972 benchmark agenda-setting study focused on a political campaign in Chapel Hill, North Carolina. Through extensive public-opinion polling, the authors, Maxwell McCombs and Donald Shaw, tested their theory that the media may determine the salience of respective campaign issues, which the media order hierarchically. By analyzing in-depth interview data in the context of public-opinion polling, they demonstrated the power of the media to influence voters' perceptions—in other words, to set an agenda. In short, they concluded that the media tell their audiences what to think about when thinking politically. See Maxwell E. McCombs and Donald L. Shaw, "The Agenda-Setting Function of the Mass Media," *Public Opinion Quarterly* 36, no. 2 (Summer 1972): 176–187.

More recent studies have leapt from the point to which McCombs and Shaw stepped. The newer scholarship has found that not only do the media tell readers what to think about and how to think about it, but they actually tell readers what to think. That is, the media "frame" issues for their audiences. Erving Goffman's *Frame Analysis: An Essay on the Organization of Experience* (New York: Harper and Row, 1974) now typically serves as the model for agenda-setting research. Goffman defines a "frame" as a "framework or schemata of interpretation" that "allows its user to locate, perceive, identify and label" it by reference to a vast array of constituent elements (p. 21). This reflects the necessary confluence of framing (which, as the metaphorical use of the term implies—is exclusionary by definition) and the research that concludes that the constituent elements of a given frame are socially constructed. Gerald Kosicki observes that "we make interpretations based on abstract conceptual reasoning, and accommodate new information into our existing frames. . . . [Frames] help structure our everyday experience and basically facilitate the process of meaning construction." See Gerald M. Kosicki, "Problems and Opportunities in Agenda-Setting Research," *Journal of Communication* 43, no. 2 (Spring 1993): 115.

Other recent work has added sophistication to agenda-setting "theory" by broadening its parameters. Theoretically, there is no limit. For example, see William A. Gamson and Andre Modigliani, "Media Discourse and the Public Opinion on Nuclear Power: A Constructionist Approach," *American Journal of Sociology* 95, no. 1 (July 1989): 1–37. For more theoretical synopses see Maxwell E. McCombs and Donald L. Shaw, "The Evolution of Agenda-Setting Research: Twenty-Five Years in the Marketplace of Ideas," *Journal of Communication* 43, no. 2. (Spring 1993): 58–67. Also see Everett M. Rogers, James W. Dearing, and Dorine Bregman, "The Anatomy of Agenda-Setting Research," *Journal of Communication* 43, no. 2 (Spring 1993): 68–84. Rogers, Dearing, and Bregman (p. 72) note that the number of scholarly articles that examine agenda-setting tallies more than two hundred.

10. McCombs and Shaw, "Agenda-Setting Function," p. 185. Kosicki (p. 108) cautions against the untoward assumption that agenda-setting has occurred simply because media and public opinion change concurrently, which speaks to the issue of methodological rigor. Audience opinion may change, he stresses, as a result of exposure that gives rise to changes in media presentations. That is, "if real-world problems are driving both audience interest and news coverage, then it is not meaningful to attribute the cause to the media." The overwhelming majority of readers in the media markets examined for this study (Chicago, Denver, Los Angeles, New York, San Francisco, and Washington, D.C.) would not have been responding to "real-world" events in formulating thoughts about Villa in 1913–1915. On the other hand, people

living in the border region where Villa was active would have been more likely to have first-hand knowledge about Villa or, at least, access to information independent of the media. Also see Pamela J. Shoemaker and Stephen D. Reese, *Mediating the Message: Theories and Influences on Mass Media Content* (New York: Longman, 1991), p. 49.

11. See Jill McMillan and Sandra Regan, "The Presidential Press Conference: A Study in Escalating Institutionalization," *Presidential Studies Quarterly* 13, no. 1 (Winter 1983): 239; Richard Lee Strout and Kenneth Crawford, "The Presidents and the Press," in *The Making of the New Deal: The Insiders Speak*, Katie Louchhiem, ed. (Cambridge University Press, 1983), p. 12. Also see Edward James Pollard, *The Presidents and the Press* (New York: Macmillan, 1947), pp. 775–807; Betty H. Winfield, *FDR and the News Media* (Chicago: University of Chicago Press, 1990); Betty H. Winfield, "Franklin D. Roosevelt's Efforts to Influence the News during His First-Term Press Conferences," *Presidential Studies Quarterly* 11, no. 1 (Winter 1981): 189, 191; Halford A. Ryan, *Franklin Roosevelt's Rhetorical Presidency* (New York: Greenwood Press, 1988), p. 2.

12. See Robert D. Crassweller, *Perón and the Enigmas of Argentina* (New York: W. W. Norton, 1987), pp. 200–202. Also see Robert J. Alexander, *The Perón Era* (New York: Columbia University Press, 1951), p. 106; Joseph A. Page, *Perón: A Biography* (New York: Random House, 1983), p. 189; Otelo Borroni and Roberto Vacca, *La vida de Eva Perón* (Buenos Aires: Editorial Galerna, 1970), p. 174; and J. M. Taylor, *Eva Perón: The Myths of a Woman* (Chicago: University of Chicago Press, 1979), pp. 20–22. Also see Americo Ghioldi, *El mito de Eva Duarte* (Montevideo: La Companía Impresora, 1952).

13. See Richard Bourne, *Getulio Vargas of Brazil, 1883–1954: Sphinx of the Pampas* (London: Charles Knight, 1974), p. 86. Also see John W. F. Dulles, *Vargas of Brazil: A Political Biography* (Austin: University of Texas Press, 1967), p. 213; Robert M. Levine, *The Vargas Regime: The Critical Years, 1934–1938* (New York: Columbia University Press, 1970), pp. 25, 56. The DIP, for example, banned Charles Chaplin's film *The Great Dictator* (1940). See Levine, p. 167. Also see Tad Szulc, *Twilight of the Tyrants* (New York: Henry Holt, 1959), p. 82.

CHAPTER TWO. VILLA'S FOREIGN POLICY

1. *Chicago Tribune*, 24 March 1915, p. 1.

2. Friedrich Katz, "From Alliance to Dependency: The Formation and Deformation of an Alliance between Francisco Villa and the United

States," in *Rural Revolt in Mexico and U.S. Intervention*, Daniel Nugent, ed. (San Diego: Center for U.S.–Mexican Studies, University of California, San Diego), p. 233. Also see Manuel Machado, *Centaur of the North: Francisco Villa, the Mexican Revolution, and Northern Mexico* (Austin: Eakin Press, 1988), p. 57; Richard Charles Goerlitz, "Financing Francisco Villa's *División del Norte*" (Master's thesis, University of California, Santa Barbara, 1968), pp. 6–28.

3. Alan Knight has correctly observed that American nonrecognition did not doom Huerta; rather, "events in Mexico did." See Alan Knight, *U.S.–Mexican Relations, 1910–1940: An Interpretation* (San Diego: Center for U.S.–Mexican Studies, University of California, San Diego, 1987), p. 100.

4. See, for example, United States Secretary of State William Jennings Bryan to Frederick Simpich, United States consul at Guaymas: "It is evident the United States is the only first-class power that can be expected to take the initiative in recognizing the new government. It will in effect act as the representative of the others of the world in this matter." Bryan to Simpich, 23 July 1914, in RDS 812/14052a.

5. According to the *El Paso Herald*, Villa planned as early as mid-February to take up arms again. Cited in RDS 812/6528. Even as early as late February, reports from Coahuila indicated that armed insurrection was inevitable: "the government cannot hold." See RDS 812/6096.

6. Henry Lane Wilson, United States ambassador to Mexico, reported the "ex-bandit" Villa's presence in a Mexican prison as late as January 11, 1913. See *Foreign Relations of the United States, 1913* (Washington, D.C.: U.S. Government Printing Office, 1922), p. 693. Throughout the spring and summer of 1913, American consular agents in Mexico occasionally noted Villa's movements. See, for example, RDS 812/6928. Huerta's government also repeatedly sought Villa's extradition from the United States on the grounds that he had committed violent acts of robbery. Bryan initially responded favorably to the requests, but he referred the matter to Arizona authorities. See AHSRE, 9-9-49, nos. 1, 2, 9 (6 February 1913), 13, 15 (7 March 1913), and 18 (8 March 1913). The Huerta government continued its efforts as late as March 1914. See AHSRE 9-9-49, no. 32 (6 March 1914).

7. O'Shaughnessy to Bryan, 18 October 1913, in RDS 812/9275.

8. Bryan to O'Shaughnessy, 23 October 1913, in RDS 812/9275.

9. Reported by Carothers in his "Report on Conditions in Torreón, 25 September–11 October," contained in a letter from Theodore Hamm, American consul in Durango, to Bryan, 11 November 1913, in RDS 812/9658.

10. Carothers, "Report on Conditions."

11. Carothers, "Report on Conditions."

12. Hamm to Bryan, 11 November 1913, in RDS 812/9658.

13. Carothers, "Report on Conditions."

14. Carothers, "Report on Conditions." Also see Hamm to Bryan, 11 November 1913, in RDS 812/9658.

15. Carothers, "Report on Conditions," p. 9. Also see Hamm to Bryan, 11 November 1913, in RDS 812/9658.

16. "Neutrality Matters," 17 November 1913, in RDS 812/10025.

17. Cited in Edwards to Bryan, 21 November 1913, in RDS 812/9852.

18. Letcher to Bryan, 11 December 1913, in RDS 812/10167. Letcher's diplomatic correspondence is steeped in bitterness toward Villa. Also see, for example, a lengthy and detailed attack against the rebel leader in a letter to Bryan, 21 February 1914, in RDS 812/11043.

19. Letcher to Bryan, 21 December 1913, in RDS 812/10301.

20. Moore to Carothers, 27 December 1913, in RDS 812/10301.

21. Hamm to Bryan, 27 December 1913, in RDS 812/10331.

22. Interestingly, on December 18, 1913, only a week after Letcher had launched his fusillade against Villa, Letcher's wife reported to Secretary of War Garrison that "Villa has been the most accommodating and courteous and has not refused any request by Mr. Letcher." Cited in Garrison to Bryan, 18 December 1913, in RDS 812/10247.

23. Edwards to Bryan, 1 December 1913, in RDS 812/9995.

24. Bryan to Carothers, 8 February 1914, in RDS 812/10820.

25. Obregón to the California-Mexico Cattle and Land Company, 10 October 1913, in RDS 812/9898.

26. Bryan to Carothers, 31 January 1914, in RDS 812/10720.

27. Carothers to Bryan, 3 February 1914, in RDS 812/10774.

28. Charles W. Ramsower to Bryan, 12 December 1913, in RDS 812/10336. Also see Berta Ulloa, *La Revolución intervenida: Relaciones diplomáticas entre México y Estados Unidos (1910–1914)* (Mexico: Colegio de Mexico, 1971), p. 74.

29. Carothers to R. L. Bonnet, United States acting consul at Torreón, 10 February 1914, in RDS 812/10903.

30. Carothers complained in a note to Bryan that it was a "thankless job" offering protection to Spanish colonists because "they are the ones who criticize us more than any other nationality, as to the non-recognition of Huerta." See Carothers to Bryan, 24 February 1914, in RDS 812/10995.

31. *New York Times*, 9 February 1914, p. 1.

32. *Chicago Tribune*, 11 February 1914, p. 13.

33. "Neutrality Matters," 6 January 1914, in RDS 812/10545.

34. Edwards to Bryan, 29 January 1914, in RDS 812/10716.

35. Lansing to the governor of Texas, 29 October 1914, in RDS 812/13573.

36. *New York Times*, 31 January 1914, III, p. 1.

37. *New York Times*, 7 February 1914, p. 1.

38. Henry Lane Wilson, *Diplomatic Episodes in Mexico, Belgium, and Chile* (New York: Doubleday, Page, 1927), p. 293.

39. An April 1914 headline in Villa's principle propaganda organ, *Vida Nueva*, noted, "Francisco Villa expels Spaniards from the territory he dominates, BECAUSE HE CONSIDERS THESE PERNICIOUS ALIENS TO BE ENEMIES OF THE NATION" (my translation; the original reads: "Francisco Villa . . . expuls[a] del territorio que domina militarmente a los españoles, PORQUE LOS EXTRANJEROS [SON] PERNICIOSOS ENEMIGOS DEL PUEBLO Y DE LA CAUSA DEL PUEBLO." *Vida Nueva: Diario Político y de Información, Documentos para la Historia de la Revolución Constitucionalista: Periódico Official de Chihuahua*, roll 42, Microfilm 472A, Special Collections, University of Texas, El Paso, (hereinafter *Vida Nueva*), 9 April 1914, p. 1.

40. One accounting tallies 1,477 foreigners killed, of whom 550 were Americans. See Moisés González Navarro, "Xenophobia y xenophilia en la Revolución Mexicana," *Historia Mexicana* 18 (1969): 569–614. Alan Knight claims that this figure is exaggerated because it fails to take into account Americans killed in action during the occupation of Veracruz or during the Punitive Expedition. See Knight, *U.S.–Mexican Relations*, p. 21.

41. Bryan to Wilson's personal emissary, John Lind, 22 February 1914, in RDS 812/10737. Walter Hines Page, American ambassador to Great Britain, to Bryan, 24 February 1914, in RDS 812/10964. Also see Cecil Spring Rice, British ambassador to Mexico, to Bryan, 27 February 1914, in *Foreign Relations of the United States, 1914* (Washington, D.C.: U.S. Government Printing Office, 1922), p. 856; and Spring Rice to Bryan, 16 March 1914, in *Foreign Relations, 1914*, pp. 860–861.

42. Clarence Clendenen, *The United States and Pancho Villa: A Study in Unconventional Diplomacy* (Ithaca: Cornell University Press, 1961), p. 66. Villa was well aware of Benton's "odious" physical abuse of his workers, according to two of Villa's officers. See Luis Aguirre Benavides and Adrián Aguirre Benavides, *Las grandes batallas de la Division del Norte, al mando del general Francisco Villa* (Mexico City: Editorial Diana, 1966).

43. Carothers's statement to the Senate Subcommittee on Mexican Affairs (hereinafter the "Fall Committee"), *Investigation of Mexican Affairs*, 4 vols. (Washington, D.C., 1920), pp. 1784–1785.

44. Clendenen, pp. 66–68; Friedrich Katz, *The Secret War in Mexico: Europe, the United States, and the Mexican Revolution* (Chicago: University of Chicago Press, 1981), pp. 184–185.

45. Clendenen, pp. 66–71.

46. *New York Times*, 23 February 1914, p. 2.

47. See Clendenen, pp. 65–70; Katz, *Secret War*, pp. 184–185, 189–190.

48. Bryan to Lind, 3 March 1914, in RDS 812/11000.

49. Lind to Bryan, 28 February 1914, in RDS 812/11011.

50. Letcher to Bryan, 25 February 1914, in *Foreign Relations, 1914*, pp. 852–853.

51. Letcher to Bryan, 25 February 1914, *Foreign Relations, 1914*, pp. 852–853.

52. Carothers to Bryan, 20 February 1914, *Foreign Relations, 1914*, p. 844. Also see Carothers's statement to the Fall Committee, pp. 1784–1785.

53. Carothers to Bryan, 21 February 1914, in *Foreign Relations, 1914*, p. 845.

54. Carothers to Bryan, 23 February 1914, in RDS 812/11454.

55. Villa to Constitutionalist agent Robert V. Pesqueira, 21 February 1914, AHSRE, L-E-760, no. 216.

56. The *Chicago Tribune* ran two versions of the killing. In the first, after Benton voiced a series of insults—"Damn you Pancho Villa. I am as good a man as you are"—Villa simply drew his pistol and shot Benton in cold blood. In the second, Villa had Benton shot after a sham court-martial. The *Tribune*, citing only an El Paso dateline as its source, ran these stories in the same article on the same day. See *Chicago Tribune*, 21 February 1914, p. 2.

57. *New York Times*, 22 February 1914, p. 1. The *Times* also ran a concurrent Spanish-language statement: "Consejo de guerra sentenció á Benton á muerte con toda justificación, debido á sus crimenes de haber atentado contra mi vida, como lo puedo demonstrar." Also see Villa to *New York Times*, 21 February 1914, p. 1; Villa to *New York Times*, 21 February 1914, AHSRE, L-E-760, no. 216.

58. Constitutionalist agent Sherburne Hopkins to agent Luis Cabrera, 25 February 1914, AHSRE, L-E-760, no. 226. Also see Manuel Urquidi to Constitutionalist foreign minister Isidro Fabela, 3 March 1914, AHSRE, L-E-760, no. 247.

59. *Los Angeles Times*, 23 February 1914, p. 2.

60. From New York, Pesqueira wrote to Carranza: "Benton's shooting has produced a terrible impression in the press, giving rise to public alarm and indignation" (my translation; the original reads: "Fusilamiento

Benton he producido terrible impresion prensa toda publica alarmentes versiones encaminadas levantar indegnación publica"). See Pesqueira to Carranza, 21 February 1914, AHSRE, L-E-760, no. 218. Also see Pesqueira to Villa, 22 February 1914, AHSRE, L-E-760, no. 219; *New York Times*, 23 February 1914, pp. 1–2. Kenneth Grieb notes both American and British press reactions; see his "El caso Benton y la diplomacía de la revolución," *Historia Mexicana* 19, no. 2 (October–December 1969), p. 290. Also see Juan Sánchez Azcona, Constitutionalist agent in London, to Carranza, 21 February 1914, AHSRE, L-E-760, no. 217. The *Literary Digest* synopsized the uniformly anti-Villa positions taken by London's *Sunday Times, Daily Mail, Daily Telegraph, Morning Post*, and *Times*. See *Literary Digest*, 7 March 1914, p. 475.

61. Louis Stevens claims Villa's changing story was a deliberate ploy to befuddle the press, which, Villa felt, had unduly "harassed" him over the incident. See Louis Stevens, *Here Comes Pancho Villa: The Anecdotal History of a Genial Killer* (New York: Frederick A. Stokes Company, 1930), p. 193.

62. Carothers to Bryan, 23 February 1914, in *Foreign Relations*, 1914, p. 849.

63. Interview with Dr. Cleofas Calleros cited in Jessie Peterson and Thelma Cox Knoles, *Pancho Villa: Intimate Recollections by People Who Knew Him* (New York: Hastings House, 1977), p. 33.

64. See Larry D. Hill, *Emissaries to a Revolution: Woodrow Wilson's Executive Agents in Mexico* (Baton Rouge: Louisiana University Press, 1973), pp. 152–153.

65. Carranza's pronouncement raised concern in Washington because of what officials in the State Department saw as the impracticality of U.S. officials being able to adhere to it during wartime conditions. AHSRE, 16-15-62, unnumbered. Also see Grieb, "El Caso Benton," pp. 299–301.

66. Katz, *Secret War*, p. 185.

67. Cabrera to Pesqueira, 4 March 1914, AHSRE L-E-760, no. 253.

68. Bryan to Lind, 25 March 1914, in RDS 812/11265.

69. Hill, pp. 148–154; Machado, p. 62.

70. See William Douglas Lansford, *Pancho Villa* (Brattleboro, Vt.: Book Press, 1965), p. 273.

71. Katz, *Secret War*, pp. 184–185.

72. *Los Angeles Times*, 3 March 1914, p. 1.

73. Zach Lamar Cobb, United States customs inspector at El Paso, to Bryan, 28 March 1914, in RDS 812/11236.

74. Bryan to O'Shaughnessy, 6 April 1914, in RDS 812/11394.

75. Hamm to Bryan, 9 April 1914, in RDS 812/11703. Also see Hamm to Bryan, 13 April 1914, in RDS 812/11706.

76. Alan Knight, *The Mexican Revolution*, vol. 2 (New York: Cambridge University Press, 1986), p. 110.

77. United States Admiral F. F. Fletcher to Secretary of the Navy Josephus Daniels, 9 April 1914, in RDS 812/11497.

78. American troops remained until 23 November 1914. See Robert Quirk, *An Affair of Honor: Woodrow Wilson and the Occupation of Veracruz* (New York: W. W. Norton, 1967), pp. 169–170.

79. Carothers to Bryan, 21 April 1914, in RDS 812/11596.

80. O'Shaughnessy to Bryan, 14 April 1914, in RDS 812/11498.

81. The United States had little reason to be surprised by Carranza's outrage. As early as November 1913, Wilson's personal emissary Bernard Hale had wired to Bryan that Carranza "took occasion solemnly to reiterate and emphasize anew that the Constitutionalists refused to admit the right of any nation on this continent acting alone or in conjunction with European Powers to interfere in the domestic affairs of the Mexican Republic; that they held the idea of armed intervention from outside as inconceivable and inadmissible upon any grounds or upon any pretext. He desired to warn the United States that any attempt in this direction would rekindle old animosities now almost forgotten and be utterly disastrous." See Hale to Bryan, 15 November 1913, in RDS 812/9738.

82. In New York, the Constitutionalist lawyer and publicist Sherburne Hopkins interpreted Carranza's statements as suggesting that the American troops must be withdrawn immediately, and "that if they are not withdrawn the result will be war between the United States and Mexico" (my translation; the original reads: "que si no son retirados el resultado sera la guerra entre Estados Unidos y Mexico"). See Hopkins to Carranza, 24 April 1914, VC, Fondo XXI.

83. A copy of Carranza's note to Wilson is included in Carothers to Bryan, 22 April 1914, in RDS 812/11618. Also see AHSRE, 17-5-17, nos. 110–112, and AHSRE, L-E-1579, nos. 54–55. And see Quirk, *Affair*, pp. 115–119.

84. Edwards to Bryan, 23 April 1914, in RDS 812/11644. Wilson had been advised directly on this very matter by journalist David Lawrence in September 1913. See Lawrence to Wilson, 5 September 1913, in RDS 812/10483.

85. Bryan to Carothers, 21 April 1914, in RDS 812/11608a. Carothers wrote to Carranza: "He [President Wilson] has taken special care to make

a distinction between general Huerta and his followers, on the one hand, and the Mexican people, on the other hand, while reiterating his friendship for the Mexican people and his desire that they achieve the establishment of constitutional government" (my translation; the original reads: "El ha tenido especial cuidado en hacer una distinción entre el general Huerta y sus sostenedores por un lado por el pueblo mexicano por otro, habiendo retirado sus amistades hacia el pueblo mexicano en su mas vivo deseo de que el mismo pueblo logre establecer un gobierno constitucional"). See Carothers to Carranza, 22 April 1914, AHSRE L-E-1579, no. 52.

86. Carranza subsequently toned down his hostile rhetoric, too, which effectively ended the war scare. See Bryan to Marion Letcher, United States consul at Chihuahua, 24 April 1914, in RDS 812/11651.

87. Carothers to Bryan, 23 April 1914, in RDS 812/11654. Also see Villa to Carothers, in Carothers to Bryan, 25 April 1914, in RDS 812/11714.

88. Bryan to Carothers, 24 April 1914, in RDS 812/12282.

89. Cobb to Bryan, 24 April 1914, in RDS 812/11672.

90. *Independent*, 4 May 1914, p. 188.

91. *New York Times*, 8 May 1914, III, p. 3.

92. The makeup of Villa's domestic constituency continues to be debated by scholars. Friedrich Katz, for example, finds Villa more an agrarian populist than does Alan Knight, who considers middle-class support for Villa to have been more crucial. See Katz's and Knight's contributions in Nugent, *Rural Revolt in Mexico*.

93. *Chicago Tribune*, 5 June 1914, p. 2. Also see Carothers to Bryan, 10 May 1914, in RDS 812/11984.

94. Villa to Wilson, 25 April 1914, in RDS 812/11714, 812/12282.

95. Wilson to Scott, 16 April 1914, in *The Woodrow Wilson Papers, vol. 29: 1913–1914*, Arthur S. Link, ed. (Princeton, N.J.: Princeton University Press, 1980), p. 450.

96. *Saturday Evening Post*, 23 May 1914, pp. 1–2.

97. Wilson to Scott, 16 April 1914, in Link, *Wilson Papers*, vol. 29, p. 450.

98. See Robert E. Quirk, *The Mexican Revolution 1914–1915: The Convention at Aguascalientes* (Bloomington: Indiana University Press, 1960).

99. Michael H. Hunt, *Ideology and U.S. Foreign Policy* (New Haven, Conn.: Yale University Press, 1987), p. 110.

100. Bryan to Woodrow Wilson, 23 June 1914, *Wilson Papers*, vol. 30, p. 203.

101. The letter was relayed from Villa through Lázaro de la Garza, Villa's friend, to Felix Sommerfeld, one of Villa's agents in the United States, and then to the American general Hugh Scott and finally to Wilson, 27 June 1914. See *Wilson Papers*, vol. 30, p. 221.

102. Silliman to Bryan, 11 September 1914, in RDS 812/13163.

103. Silliman to Bryan, 12 September 1914, in RDS 812/13171.

104. Villa to Wilson, 17 September 1914, in RDS 812/13258.

105. Wilson to Villa, 19 September 1914, in RDS 812/13258.

106. Cobb to Bryan, 6 October 1914, in RDS 812/13417. Also see Carothers to Bryan, 15 October 1914, in RDS 812/13676.

107. Cobb to Bryan, 6 October 1914, in RDS 812/13417. Also see Carothers to Bryan, 15 October 1914, in RDS 812/13676.

108. Bryan to Monterrey, 11 August 1914, in RDS 812/12804.

109. Simpich to Bryan, 18 August 1914, in RDS 812/12913.

110. Carothers to Bryan, 30 August 1914, in RDS 812/13042.

111. Canova to Bryan, 23 September 1914, in RDS 812/13279.

112. Lansing to Cobb, 16 October 1914, in RDS 812/13547a.

113. Lansing to Cobb, 21 November 1914, in RDS 812/13845.

114. Carothers to Lansing, 21 November 1914, in RDS 812/13856.

115. Bryan to Silliman, 13 December 1914, in RDS 812/14009a.

116. *New York Times,* 11 January 1915, p. 7.

117. Cobb to State Department, 6 February 1915, in RDS 812/14358.

118. Cardoso de Oliveira to State Department, 5 February 1914, in RDS 812/14358.

119. Cobb to State Department, 3 March 1915, in RDS 812/14801.

120. Villa communicated to generals who remained loyal to him: "I declare that in all my acts I am not guided by any other aspiration than the happiness of my country and I solemnly reaffirm that I will not accept the presidency or vice presidency of the Republic either provisional or constitutional." See Cobb to Bryan, 27 September 1914, in RDS 812/13304.

121. Villa's Washington agent, Enrique C. Llorente, to Lansing, 5 February 1915, in RDS 812/14360.

122. *Los Angeles Times,* 11 March 1915, p. 2. Also see *Chicago Tribune,* 11 March 1915, p. 1.

123. The trail of Villa's defeat almost leaps from the pages of American diplomatic accounts, and it lends credence to Obregón's assertion that by early June Villa's forces were fleeing "shamefully." See Silliman to Lansing, 7 June 1915, in RDS 812/15159. Also see Quirk, *Mexican Revolution,* p. 226.

124. See Hill, pp. 309–311.

125. West to Wilson, 4 March 1915, in RDS 812/14622.

126. West to Bryan, 14 March 1915, in RDS 812/16810.

127. Letcher enclosed a copy of the decree in correspondence to Bryan, 27 March 1915, in *Foreign Relations of the United States, 1915*, (Washington, D.C.: U.S. Government Printing Office, 1922), p. 893.

128. Cobb to Bryan, 27 April 1915, in RDS 812/15132.

129. Bryan to Carothers, 7 April 1915, in *Foreign Relations, 1915*, p. 894.

130. Carothers to Bryan, 12 April 1915, in RDS 812/14836. Also see Frederick Sherwin Dunn, *The Diplomatic Protection of Americans in Mexico* (New York: Columbia University Press, 1933), pp. 328–329.

131. Bryan to Carothers, 15 April 1915, in *Foreign Relations, 1915*, p. 899.

132. Carothers to Bryan, 16 April 1915, in *Foreign Relations, 1915*, p. 901. Further, according to Carothers on April 22, Villa "was willing to revoke the whole decree and make a new decree, putting the mining laws on the same basis as the United States laws." Carothers to Bryan, 22 April 1915, in RDS 812/14935.

133. Llorente to Bryan, 19 April 1915, in *Foreign Relations, 1915*, pp. 901–902.

134. See Hanna to Bryan, 15 March 1915, in *Foreign Relations, 1915*, p. 994; Bryan to Hanna, 18 March 1915, in *Foreign Relations, 1915*, p. 994.

135. Hanna to Bryan, 21 March 1915, in *Foreign Relations, 1915*, p. 995.

136. Cobb to Lansing, 7 June 1915, in RDS 812/15155.

137. Cobb to Lansing, 14 July 1915, in RDS 812/15445.

138. Cobb to Lansing, 12 July 1915, in RDS 812/15489.

139. My translation; the original reads: "Todo el día 12 el señor General Villa estuvo muy preocupado pensando . . . No base en él a la vez que una tristeza infinita, una desparación muy grande, porque ansioba encontrar la solución del conflicto que presentiá se aproximaba." Villista agent and convention president Roque González Garza, 12 June 1915, ARGG, Carpeta 14, no. 7.

140. Coen to Lansing, 16 July 1915, in RDS 812/15464.

141. Mark T. Gilderhus, *Diplomacy and Revolution: U.S.–Mexican Relations under Wilson and Carranza* (Tucson: University of Arizona Press, 1977), pp. 15–19.

142. Carothers to Lansing, 19 July 1915, in RDS 812/15490.

143. Cobb to Lansing, 26 July 1915, in RDS 812/15545.

144. Carothers to Lansing, 12 August 1915, in RDS 812/15739.

145. Villa to Llorente and (former Huertista) Manuel Bonilla, 5 August 1915, in RDS 812/15752.

146. In mid-July 1915, State Department official Leon Canova, former special agent to Mexico, noted to Lansing that Villa's political position in

northern Mexico had been set in "great peril" because of ongoing military setbacks. Canova then proposed to the secretary of state a plan to forcibly depose Carranza and replace him with an unnamed party who would be acceptable to "all of the Mexican elements" except Carranza and Carranza's close advisers. See Canova to Lansing, 17 July 1915, in RDS 812/15531–1/2.

147. Lansing to Wilson and Wilson to Lansing, 9 August 1915, in RDS 812/15751–1/2.

148. A. J. McQuatters, representative of the Mine and Smelter Operators Association, to Scott, 13 August 1915, in RDS 812/15963.

149. Carothers to Lansing, 1 September 1915, in RDS 812/16028.

150. Carothers to Lansing, 8 September 1915, in RDS 812/16083. Also see Carothers to Lansing, 10 September 1915, in RDS 812/16100; Letcher to Lansing, 15 September 1915, in RDS 812/16269; and Carothers to Lansing, 17 September 1915, in RDS 812/16219.

151. Carothers dispatched many cables to this effect. See, for example, Carothers to Lansing on 4 October 1915, in RDS 812/16378; 6 October, in RDS 812/16385; 12 October, in RDS 812/16452; and 16 October, in RDS 812/16502.

152. Louis Hostetter, United States consul in Hermosillo, to Lansing, 21 September 1915, in RDS 812/16372.

153. Carothers to Lansing, 9 October 1915, in RDS 812/16441.

154. Jim Tuck, *Pancho Villa and John Reed: Two Faces of Romantic Revolution* (Tucson: University of Arizona Press, 1984), p. 94.

155. Funston to Adjutant General Army, 1 November 1915, in RDS 812/16679.

156. Edwards to Lansing, 25 September 1915, in RDS 812/16381.

157. Cobb to Lansing, 27 October 1915, in RDS 812/16162.

158. Funston to Lansing, 28 October 1915, in RDS 812/16644.

159. Carothers to Lansing, 31 October 1915, in RDS 812/16653.

160. Carothers to Lansing, 5 November 1915, in RDS 812/16717.

161. For examples of the literature on the Columbus raid, see Friedrich Katz, "Pancho Villa and the Attack on Columbus, New Mexico," *American Historical Review* 83 (1978): 101–130; Charles H. Harris and Louis R. Sadler, "Pancho Villa and the Columbus Raid: The Missing Documents," *New Mexico Historical Review* 50, no. 4 (1975): 335–346; Francis Munch, "Villa's Columbus Raid: Practical Politics or German Design?" *New Mexico Historical Review* 44, no. 2 (1969): 189–214; Haldeen Braddy, "Pancho Villa at Columbus: The Raid of 1916," *Southwestern Studies* 3 (Spring 1965): 1–43.

CHAPTER THREE. CUT-AND-PASTE
REVOLUTIONARY

1. John Reed, *Insurgent Mexico* (New York: International Publishers, [1914] 1984), p. 225.

2. On a related topic that has not been explored by Mexicanist scholars, the United States Department of War actively sought to manage the news reported from and about American military actions in Mexico. It published a bulletin containing guidelines and rules to be followed by both news correspondents and military officials—"Regulations Concerning Correspondents with the United States Army in the Field." Among other things, before being allowed into the field, reporters were required to present official accreditation by a recognized publication, agree to eschew reporting falsehoods, dress in provided "olive drab garb," deposit a one-thousand-dollar bond, and pass all reportage through a military censor. The army took the regulations seriously. On at least one occasion, a correspondent for the *New Work World* was "rebuked" for reporting "fake" news. On the other hand, provided a journalist adhered to the regulations, the army would provide full cable privileges. See Lindley M. Garrison, United States secretary of war, to Bryan, 14 May 1914, in RDS 812/11964; American general Frederick Funston to Bryan, 25 May 1914, in RDS 812/12107; Garrison to Funston, 28 July 1914, in RDS 812/12682.

3. This dearth of historical evidence holds true not only for Villa's propaganda but also for his more general role in the Revolution. See Friedrich Katz, "Prologue," in Ruben Osorio, *Pancho Villa, ese desconocido: Entrevistas en Chihuahua a favor y en contra* (Chihuahua: Talleres Graficos, 1991), p. x.

4. Machado, p. 128.

5. Stevens, pp. 116–117. A late 1913 editorial in the *New York Herald*, titled "Is It an Eclipse?" put it this way: "While he may not be dead . . . General Venustiano Carranza has certainly been 'among the missing' ever since the rise of a Villa star." See *New York Herald*, 23 December 1913, n.p., in AHSRE, Legajo 407, Expediente 4 (1).

6. See Machado, p. 46; Clendenen, p. 75.

7. As one sign of U.S. press interest in the Revolution, by mid-May 1914, the American general Frederick Funston noted the presence of twenty American correspondents in occupied Veracruz to cover the occupation story. See Funston to Bryan, 12 May 1914, in RDS 812/11945.

8. For example, two different front-page stories about Villa's first taking of Torreón in the *Los Angeles Times* cited two sources, respectively—

one a *Times* reporter and the other the Associated Press. See *Los Angeles Times,* 9 October, 1913, p. 1. Occasionally, publications cited other publications as sources for a story. For example, the *Chicago Tribune* credited the *New York World* for a story about United States ambassador to Mexico Henry Lane Wilson's alleged meddling in Mexican affairs. See *Chicago Tribune,* 7 March 1913, p. 1.

9. Stevens, pp. 11, 128. Also see Nancy Brandt, "Pancho Villa: The Making of a Modern Legend," *The Americas* (1964–1965): 149.

10. Reed, p. 236.

11. Timothy Turner, *Bullets, Bottles, and Gardenias* (Dallas: South-West Press, 1935), p. 175.

12. Turner, pp. 176–177.

13. See Reed, *passim;* Ernest Otto Schuster, *Pancho Villa's Shadow: The True Story of Mexico's Robin Hood as Told by His Interpreter* (New York: Exposition Press, 1947), Introduction; *New York Times,* 15 February 1914, p. 4; *Los Angeles Times,* 6 April 1914, p. 1.

14. Carothers to Bryan, 10 February 1914, in RDS 812/10903.

15. Stevens, pp. 125–126.

16. Reed, p. 204.

17. Stevens, pp. 125–126.

18. Machado, p. 46.

19. Clendenen, p. 75. Also see Knight, *The Mexican Revolution,* vol. 2, p. 161.

20. *New York Times,* 15 February 1914, III, p. 4.

21. Carlo de Fornaro, *Carranza and Mexico* (New York: Mitchell Kennerly, 1915), pp. 176–177.

22. Fornaro, p. 178.

23. García to Carranza, 5 March 1915, VC, doc. 3182.

24. González to Carranza, 17 March, 1915, VC, doc. 3339.

25. Mende Fierro to Carranza, 26 March 1914, VC, doc. 3489.

26. United States Consul, Monterrey, to Lansing, 1 September 1915, in RDS 812/16132.

27. Elias L. Torres, *Vida y hazañas de Pancho Villa* (Mexico City: Libro Español, 1975), p. 35; Hamilton Fyfe, *The Real Mexico: A Study on the Spot* (London: William Heinemann, 1914), pp. 22–23; Stevens, p. 118.

28. Turner, p. 72.

29. Carrancista Rafael Zubarán Capmany to Carranza, 4 May 1914, VC, Fondo MXV. Other principal arms agents included Lázaro de la Garza, Rodolfo Farías, Rafael Benavides, Darío Silva, and Samuel Dreben—but it is unclear whether they all doubled as press agents. See Goerlitz, p. 9.

30. See Katz, *Secret War*, pp. 135–136 (on Hopkins), 333–337 (on Sommerfeld).

31. Hopkins to Carranza, 13 May 1914, VC, doc. 157. In response to concerns elicited about Hopkins's closeness to Villa, expressed by the United States customs inspector at El Paso, Zach Cobb, Bryan noted: "While it appears that this Department [of State] has not for some years regarded many of the acts of Hopkins as done in the best interests of our country's citizens, and that some of his acts have even been the cause of trouble, the Department would not care to take, officially, any measures to prevent what seems to have been established, namely, a connection between Villa and Hopkins, unless it has clear legal right to do so." See Bryan to Cobb, 28 July 1914, in RDS 812/12741.

32. Michael Smith, "Carrancista Propaganda in the United States, 1913–1917: An Overview of Institutions," unpublished manuscript, Oklahoma State University, 1994, p. 6.

33. Statement of Senator Morris Sheppard, *United States Congressional Record*, 63d Congress, 1st Session, no. 83, 9 August 1913, p. 3600.

34. Statement of Senator William Alden Smith, *United States Congressional Record*, 63d Congress, 1st Session, no. 81, 7 August 1913, p. 3559.

35. 4 March 1914, STC, MB-18, Box 84.

36. Terrazas to Villa, 26 October 1913, STC, "Correspondence with Villa."

37. Malías C. García to Carranza, 17 May 1913, VC, doc. 194.

38. From 1906 to 1911, Llorente had been posted in Chicago and Phoenix, but by the spring of 1913 he was wanted in Mexico on three charges of swindling. AHSRE, 8-26-43, nos. 1, 4; AHSRE, L-E-1289, nos. 7, 56; AHSRE, L-E-1290, no. 335.

39. Roque González Garza to the Associated Press, 24 June 1914, ARGG, Carpeta no. 2, doc. 59; Roque Gonzàlez Garza news release, 25 May 1915, ARGG, Carpeta no. 9, doc. 210; Roque Gonzàlez Garza to Luis de la Garza Cárdenas, 31 May 1915, ARGG, Carpeta no. 9, doc. 197.

40. For examples of Roberts's journalism, see "VILLA RETURNS TO HAVE IT OUT WITH FIRST CHIEF," *San Francisco Examiner*, 30 June 1914, p. 4; "New War Declared by Villa," *San Francisco Examiner*, 26 September 1914, p. 1.

41. State Department agent Leon J. Canova to Bryan, 8 July 1914, in RDS 812/14805.

42. I have been unable to ascertain Muller's fuller identity. See Comadurán (probably former Porfirista *político* Luis J.) to Secretario de Estado del Despacho, 4 April 1914, VC, doc. 871.

43. Samuel Belden, American Carrancista agitator, to Carranza, 2 July 1914, AHSRE, Fondo MVIII.

44. Zubarán to Carranza, 22 October 1914, VC, Fondo XXI-4. Also see Rafael E. Múzquiz to Carranza, 27 July 1914, VC, doc. 1147.

45. Undated, AHSRE, 17-16-145.

46. *New York Times*, 31 October 1913, p. 8.

47. I use the term "Villa" in cases where the source record speaks of no clear distinction between what Villa did and what his subordinates—Villistas—did to promote his image.

48. *Denver Post*, 26 February 1914, p. 1.

49. The *San Francisco Examiner* cited a cable received by a "local" El Paso newspaper, probably the *El Paso Times*—which was known for its Villista sympathies. See *San Francisco Examiner*, 3 August, 1913, p. 2.

50. *New York Times*, 23 November 1913, p. 3.

51. *New York Times*, 28 November 1913, p. 1.

52. *New York Times*, 23 November 1913, p. 3.

53. See, for example, two consecutive articles about Villa in *World's Work:* "'Pancho' Villa at First Hand," by Joseph Rogers Taylor, July 1914: 265–269, and "Villa," by George Marvin, July 1914: 269–284.

54. Katz, "Prologue," p. xiv.

55. *New York Times*, 23 November 1913, p. 2.

56. *Los Angeles Times*, 24 November 1913, p. 1.

57. *San Francisco Examiner*, 24 November 1913, p. 1.

58. *New York Times*, 31 January 1914, p. 3.

59. *Los Angeles Times*, 31 January 1914, p. 2.

60. *New York Times*, 31 January 1914, p. 3.

61. *Chicago Tribune*, 29 January 1914, p. 2.

62. *Los Angeles Times*, 11 February 1914, p. 1.

63. *Chicago Tribune*, 11 February 1914, p. 13.

64. *San Francisco Examiner*, 14 February 1914, p. 2.

65. *New York Times*, 4 February 1914, p. 1.

66. *Literary Digest* cited a similar report in an unnamed New York newspaper: "'The war will soon be over! The war will soon be over!' He then added more quietly: 'I think President Wilson is the most just man in the world. All Mexicans will love him now, and we will look upon the United States as our greatest friend, because it has done us justice.'" *Literary Digest* 48, no. 7 (February 1914).

67. *San Francisco Examiner*, 4 February 1914, p. 1.

68. *Chicago Tribune*, 4 February 1914, p. 2.

69. *New York Times*, 8 January 1914, p. 2.

70. Kevin Brownlow, *The Parade's Gone By* (London: Secker and Warburg, 1968), p. 224.

71. Aurelio de los Reyes, *Medio siglo de cine mexicano (1896–1947)* (Mexico City: Editorial Trillas, 1987), p. 52.

72. *New York Times*, 7 January 1914, pp. 1–2.

73. Aurelio de los Reyes, writing in an untitled report prepared for the Library of Congress, cited in a memorandum from Georgette Dorn to Paul Spehr, 29 March, 1985, p. 5 (hereinafter "Dorn's Memorandum").

74. Reyes, *Con Villa en México: Testimonios sobre camarógrafos norteamericanos en la revolución, 1911–1916* (Mexico City: Universidad Nacional Autónoma de México, 1985), p. 224.

75. According to the *World's Work:* "The advantage of night attacks lay, in Villa's opinion, in the moral effect on the enemy and in the greater protection afforded the attacking side." See *World's Work*, 14 July 1914, p. 267.

76. *New York Times*, 8 January 1914, p. 2.

77. Brandt, p. 158.

78. Reyes, in Dorn's Memorandum, p. 2.

79. Enrique Krauze, *Entre el angel y el fierro: Francisco Villa* (Mexico City: Fondo de Cultura Económico, 1987), p. 27. The *New York Times* reported a slight variation on the title, referring to it as "The Life of General Francisco Villa." *New York Times*, 11 March 1914, p. 2.

80. Krauze, p. 27.

81. *New York Times*, 11 March 1914, p. 2.

82. The other American film companies, some of which had begun operations in revolutionary Mexico in 1911, included Vitagraph Monthly of Current Events, Gaumont Weekly, Animated Weekly of Universal Film Company, Hearst-Selig News Pictorial, Selig-Tribune, and Hearst-Vitagraph News Pictorial, as well as the French concern Pathé's Weekly.

83. Reyes, in Dorn's Memorandum, p. 3.

84. In a letter to Bryan, State Department agent Leon J. Canova referred to the film company as "Hearst's International News Service." However, this rubric appears to be imprecise. Reyes identifies two film concerns with which Hearst was involved—Hearst-Selig News Pictorial (established in 1914) and Hearst-Vitagraph News Pictorial (established in 1916). It was likely the former—Hearst-Selig News Pictorial—to which Canova referred. See Canova to Bryan, 8 July 1914, in RDS 812/14805. Also see Reyes, *Con Villa*, pp. 26–27.

85. Canova to Bryan, 8 July 1914, in RDS 812/14805.

86. Reyes, *Con Villa*, p. 46.

87. *New York Times,* 11 February 1914, p. 2.

88. For the *Times*'s Spanish-language version, see chapter 2, note 57.

89. *San Francisco Examiner,* 22 February 1914, p. 2; *Los Angeles Times,* 22 February 1914, p. 2.

90. *San Francisco Examiner,* 21 February 1914, p. 2.

91. Hill (p. 153) concludes, "The First Chief was motivated solely by a desire to have other nations respect the right of Mexicans to conduct their own investigations." Katz (*Secret War,* p. 185) concurs but opines more subtly that Carranza also wished to force Britain into de facto recognition of the Constitutional movement and that Carranza further aimed to "avoid any, even implicit recognition of the Monroe Doctrine."

92. *New York Times,* 23 February 1914, p. 2.

93. *New York Times,* 23 February 1914, p. 2.

94. *New York Times,* 23 February 1914, p. 2.

95. Cabrera to Pesqueira, 4 March 1914. AHSRE, L-E-813, no. 253.

96. The report was released in June 1914. ARGG, Cuaderno Numero 11, "Asunto Benton."

97. *New York Times,* 24 February 1914, p. 1.

98. *New York Times,* 24 February 1914, p. 1.

99. Hill, p. 163.

100. My translation; the original reads: "Dentro de tres dias habra caido Torreon en nuestro poder y mi siguiente [*sic*] movimiento sera de acuerdo con las circumstancias.") See *San Francisco Examiner,* 20 March 1914, p. 1.

101. Reported in the *Los Angeles Times,* 29 March 1914, p. 1. Also see Bryan to John Lind, Wilson's personal emissary to Mexico, 30 March 1914, in RDS 812/11353b.

102. *San Francisco Examiner,* 6 January 1914, p. 1.

103. *Los Angeles Times,* 26 April 1914, p. 1.

104. *Los Angeles Times,* 28 June 1914, p. 1.

105. Reed, pp. 172–173. Also see *Chicago Tribune,* 30 March 1914, p. 1; *Chicago Tribune,* 31 March 1914, p. 13; Edwards to Bryan, 39 March 1914, in RDS 812/11335; and Cobb to Bryan, 23 March 1914, in RDS 812/11241.

106. See Cobb to Bryan, 23 March 1914, in RDS 812/11241; Edwards to Bryan, 30 March 1914, in RDS 812/11335; and *Chicago Tribune,* 30 March 1914, p. 1. Cables were censored again in June 1914. See *Los Angeles Times,* 28 June 1914, p. 1.

107. See Hill, pp. 162–163.

108. Villa to Carranza, 9 April 1914, VC, Fondo MVIII.

109. Turner, p. 182.

110. Turner, p. 195. Marion Letcher noted that the press car carried ten American reporters and photographers who accompanied Villa south from Chihuahua toward Torreón. Letcher to Bryan, 16 March 1914, in RDS 812/11183.

111. See, for example, Katz, *Secret War*, pp. 298–299; Knight, the *Mexican Revolution*, vol. 2, p. 161; Brandt, p. 151; Clendenen, pp. 84–85.

112. Knight, *The Mexican Revolution*, vol. 2, p. 161.

113. *New York Times*, 19 April 1914, p. 1.

114. *San Francisco Examiner*, 24 April 1914, p. 1.

115. *Chicago Tribune*, 24 April 1914, p. 1. Also see *New York Times*, 24 April 1914, p. 1.

116. Yolanda Argudín, *Historia del periodismo en México: Desde el Virreinato hasta nuestros días* (Mexico: Panorama Editorial, 1987), pp. 129–147; Leopoldo Borrás, *Historia del periodismo mexicano: Al ocaso porfirista al derecho la información* (Mexico: Universidad Autónoma de Mexico, c. 1982), pp. 13–24; Knight, *Mexican Revolution*, vol. 2, p. 181. Also see Fyfe, p. 22; Dolores Butterfield, "The Conspiracy against Madero," *Forum* 50, no. 4 (October 1913): 468; *San Francisco Examiner*, 23 August 1913, p. 2.

117. Terrazas's statement, 12 May 1914, STC, MB-18, Box 84. Also see Friedrich Katz, "Pancho Villa: Reform Governor of Chihuahua," in *Essays on the Mexican Revolution: Revisionist Views of the Leaders*, George Wolfskill and Douglas P. Richmond, eds. (Austin: University of Texas Press, 1979); and Necah S. Furman, "*Vida Nueva*: A Reflection of Villista Diplomacy, 1914–1915," *New Mexico Historical Review* 53, no. 2 (1978): 172.

118. Argudín, pp. 140–141.

119. The place of publication varied for *La Convención*. It began in Aguascalientes but later was issued from centers such as Mexico City, Cuernavaca, and San Luis Potosí. See Diego Arenas Guzmán, *El periodismo en la revolución mexicana (de 1908–1917)*, vol. 2 (Mexico City: Biblioteca del Instituto Nacional de Estudios Históricos de la Revolución Mexicana, 1967), p. 272.

120. See Gaston Schmurtz, United States consul at Aguascalientes, to Bryan, 10 May 1915, in RDS 812/15032; Schmurtz to Bryan, 5 June 1915, in RDS 812/15195.

121. San Antonio Consul to Carranza, 29 March 1915, VC, doc. 3499.

122. Cited in Furman, p. 172. Also see Martín Luis Guzmán, trans. Virginia Taylor, *The Memoirs of Pancho Villa* (Austin: University of Texas Press [1935] 1965), p. 460.

123. My translation; the original reads: "*Vida Nueva* surge a la nueva vida de la Patria, en los momentos transcendentales en que el ejercito del

pueblo conquista uno de sus mas grandes triunfos morales sobre el enemigo." *Vida Nueva,* 1 April 1914, p. 1.

124. Alcalde to Gustavo Espinosa Mireles, 20 May 1914, VC, Fondo MVIII. Alcalde was succeeded by Luis G. Malvaez, who was succeeded in turn by Francisco Lagos Chazaro.

125. The article was headlined, "How Venustiano Carranza provoked them, THE DIVISION OF THE NORTH REMAINS JUSTIFIED BEFORE THE NATION" (my translation; the original reads: "Cómo los provocó Don Venustiano Carranza, LOS DIVISION DEL NORTE QUEDA JUSTIFICADA ANTE LA NACION"). See Canova to Lansing, 30 September 1914, in RDS 812/14041.

126. *Vida Nueva,* 11 June 1915, p. 1. Also see E. W. Jorgesen, secretary of the Batopilas Mining Company, to Lansing, 21 June 1915, in RDS 812/15297.

127. *Vida Nueva* established a mantra of sorts about Carranza's unsuitability for national office, not to mention his scurrilous character more generally. For example, on October 6, 1914, a front-page editorial attacked Carranza for having sold out the revolution in favor of personal political ambitions—whereas Villa had remained true to the revolutionary spirit of President Francisco Madero. These sentiments, frequently embellished by charges that Carranza was inept, capricious, megalomaniacal, politically retrograde, traitorous, and so on continued through 1915. See *Vida Nueva,* 6 October 1914, p. 1.

128. *Vida Nueva,* 28 November 1914, p. 1

129. *Vida Nueva,* 14 November 1914, p. 3; 21 November 1914, p. 3; 22 November 1914, p. 3; 8 December 1914, p. 3; 23 December 1914, p. 1; 2 February 1915, p. 1; 10 February 1915, p. 1.

130. *Vida Nueva,* 26 November 1914, p. 3; 3 January 1915, p. 1.

131. *Vida Nueva,* 9 March 1915, p. 3.

132. Terrazas's statement, 12 May 1914, STC, MB-18, Box 84. Machado (p. 73) cites a much more modest figure of seven thousand dollars.

133. *Vida Nueva* balance sheets can be found in the J. Manuel Muñoz file, STC.

134. *Vida Nueva,* 1 April 1915, p. 1.

135. See, for example, the front-page coverage in early April 1914 of Villa's second taking of Torreón: *Vida Nueva,* 2–5 April 1914, p. 1.

136. *Vida Nueva,* 2 April 1914, p. 1; 7 April 1914, p. 1; 9 April 1914, p. 1; 13 April 1914, p. 1; 27 April 1914, p. 1; 9 May 1914, p. 1. Also see Furman, pp. 173–174.

137. My translation; the original reads: "ES INJUSTICABLE LA INTERVENCION." *Vida Nueva,* 11 May 1914, p. 1.

138. *San Francisco Examiner*, 29 September 1914, p. 4.

139. Press release of E. A. Navarro, 10 December 1914, VC, doc. 2196.

140. Pan-American News Service release, 1915. AHSRE, L-E-811, nos. 55–60.

141. R. E. Múzquiz to Carranza, 5 May 1914, VC, doc. 4150.

142. The source provides no time frame during which the money was to be spent. See Alfredo Breceda to Carranza, 8 August 1914, VC, Fondo MVIII.

143. Carbajal to Carranza, 25 August 1914, VC, doc. 1338.

144. *New York Times*, 25 August 1914, p. 6. Such statements make it relatively easy to read Villa's dissatisfaction with Carranza going back several months. For example, the *Denver Post* quoted Villa: "As I have had occasion to say frequently in the past, the Constitutionalists have not been fighting solely to bring about the elimination of the usurper Huerta. If that were all, his resignation or his removal by force would have brought peace long ago. . . . The land question still remains, as does the abolition of peonage, the prevention of the exploitation of the poor by the rich and powerful." *Denver Post*, 16 July 1914, p. 11.

145. See *Chicago Tribune*, 24 September 1914, p. 2; *Los Angeles Times*, 24 September 1914, p. 1; *San Francisco Examiner*, 24 September 1914, p. 1.

146. Villa statement to the *New York Times*, 27 September 1914, p. 1.

147. Statements to this effect were quoted in the *San Francisco Examiner*, 28 September 1914, p. 1; 15 October 1914, p. 1; and 20 October 1914, p. 1; and to the *Los Angeles Times*, 20 October 1914, sec. 2, p. 4.

148. Statements to this effect were released to the *Chicago Tribune*, 28 September 1914, p. 1; the *Los Angeles Times*, 29 September 1914, p. 1; and the *New York Times*, 29 September 1914, p. 2.

149. Cobb to Bryan, 15 November 1914, in RDS 812/13783; Brazilian ambassador to Mexico (and State Department confidant) Cardoso de Oliveira to Bryan, 28 November 1914, in RDS 812/13940.

150. Schmurtz to Bryan, 11 November 1914, in RDS 812/13914.

151. My translation; the original reads: "Estas declaraciones han causado muy bueno efecto tanto en el ánimo del Gobierno como en el del publico se han publicado en toda la prensa del país." Roque González Garza to José Ortiz Rodriguez, 30 January 1915, ARGG, Carpeta no. 64, docs. 23–24.

152. *New York Times*, 11 January 1915, VII, p. 7.

153. *New York Times*, 4 February 1915, p. 5.

154. *New York Times*, 5 February 1915, p. 1.

155. United States vice-consul Blocker to Bryan, 22 February 1915, in RDS 812/14434.

156. *New York Times,* 5 February 1915, p. 1.

157. *Chicago Tribune,* 6 March 1915, p. 2.

158. *Chicago Tribune,* 11 March 1915, p. 1.

159. *Los Angeles Times,* 11 March 1915, p. 2. Also see *Chicago Tribune,* 11 March 1915, p. 1.

160. *Chicago Tribune,* 30 September 1914, p. 1.

161. *New York Times,* 10 April 1915, III, p. 6.

162. *New York Times,* 12 April 1915, V, p. 6. Also see *Chicago Tribune,* 12 April 1915, p. 5; and *San Francisco Examiner,* 12 April 1915, p. 4.

163. Ramón Puente, *Villa en pie* (Mexico City: Editorial Mexico Nuevo, 1937), p. 123.

164. *San Francisco Examiner,* 3 June 1915, p. 4.

165. Smith, p. 4.

166. *Chicago Tribune,* 10 October 1915, p. 8.

CHAPTER FOUR.
MIXED PROPAGANDA REACTIONS

1. *Mexican Letter,* 30 December 1914, Bulletin no. 32, in VC, unnumbered.

2. My translation; the original reads: "Es falsa caida Torreón y considerarse imposible caiga." See Huerta's minister of foreign relations, José López Portillo y Rojas, to El Paso Consul, 31 March 1914, AHSRE, L-E-791, no. 149.

3. My translation; the original reads: "Torreón sigue en poder Gobierno fuera de todo peligro." López Portillo to Mexican consuls, c. 5 April 1914, AHSRE, L-E-791, no. 111.

4. See, for example, *Denver Post,* 26 February 1914, p. 1.

5. Michael C. Meyer, *Huerta: A Political Portrait* (Lincoln: University of Nebraska Press, 1972), p. 132.

6. A December 23, 1913, issue of *El Diario* alleged that the United States government actively sided with Villa and sought to promote his interests in northern Mexico. See American chargé d'affaires in Mexico City Nelson O'Shaughnessy to Bryan, 23 December 1913, in RDS 812/10418.

7. See O'Shaughnessy to Bryan, 14 February 1914, in RDS 812/10887.

8. O'Shaughnessy to Bryan, 25 December 1913, in RDS 812/10212.

9. Whereas Meyer also identifies as Huertista the publication *El Diario del Hogar,* other scholars cite it as Zapatista. See Argudín, p. 136; and John Womack, *Zapata and the Mexican Revolution* (New York: Alfred A. Knopf, 1968), pp. 19, 202, 395–396.

10. Meyer, *Huerta,* p. 133.

11. See O'Shaughnessy to Bryan, 13 March 1914, in RDS 812/11155.

12. See William W. Canada, United States consul at Veracruz, to Bryan, 5 March 1914, in RDS 812/11154; Edwards to Bryan, 20 November 1913, in RDS 812/9970; and Meyer, p. 133.

13. O'Shaughnessy to Bryan, 25 January 1914, in RDS 812/10684.

14. I want to stress that through September 1914, the term "Constitutionalism" technically included Villa and Villistas as well as partisans of the Carranza camp. Although the Villa and Carranza propaganda machines can be examined discretely, in many instances it is difficult to bifurcate them clearly. I use the "Constitutionalist" rubric to refer to joint Villa-Carranza efforts or to cases in which no clear distinction can readily be made.

15. See Meyer, *Huerta,* p. 133; Borrás, pp. 25–26; Argudín, pp. 136–137. Huerta declined a request from his consul in Los Angeles to establish an anti-revolutionary organ there. See Juán Rarei to Secretaria Relaciones Exteriores, 9 April 1914, AHSRE, 17-5-143, unnumbered.

16. Meyer, *Huerta,* pp. 133–134. Also see "FAVORABLE NEWS ONLY GIVEN OUT AT CAPITAL," *San Francisco Examiner,* 23 August 1914, p. 2.

17. Report of the commander in chief of American Pacific forces, cited in Josephus Daniels, secretary of the navy, to Bryan, 15 October 1913, in RDS 812/9283.

18. Lind to Bryan, 16 January 1914, in RDS 812/106521/2.

19. See, for example, collections of mid-March 1913 clippings from New York, 13 March 1913, AHSRE, 16-10-122, unnumbered, and clippings from late 1913 and early 1914 sent from Washington and New York, 24 December 1913, AHSRE, L-E 407, no. 4. Also see similar reports issued from Douglas, Arizona, Kansas City, Chicago, Virginia–North Carolina, Rio Grande City, and San Francisco, in AHSRE, L-E-813, nos. 169–214.

20. Fornaro, pp. 176–177.

21. Meyer, *Huerta,* p. 134.

22. See "Huerta Asks for Publicity," Huerta to *San Francisco Examiner,* 4 February 1914, p. 1. Also noted in G. Fernández MacGregor to Consul, Havana, 16 March 1914, AHSRE, 16-11-82, no. 18.

23. References to the framing Huerta received in European newspapers—usually negative—are sprinkled throughout the AHSRE files. Newspaper enclosures often accompany the diplomatic dispatches. See,

for example, G. A. Esteva, from Rome (with enclosure), to Relaciones Exteriores, 12 December 1913, AHSRE, 16-11-82, no. 4.

24. *Washington Times,* 28 March 1913, p. 8. Also see *Washington Times,* 20 February 1913, p. 6; 23 February 1913, p. 1; 25 February 1913, p. 6; 3 March 1913, p. 8; 28 March 1913, p. 1; 6 April 1913, p. 10; 10 April 1913, p. 6; 18 April 1913, p. 10; 29 April 1913, p. 6; 21 July 1913, p. 1; 22 July 1913, p. 6; 23 July 1913, p. 6; 26 July 1913, p. 6; 3 August 1913, p. 8; 7 August 1913, p. 6; 21 August 1913, p. 6; 24 August 1913, p. 8; 13 September 1913, p. 6; 17 September 1913, p. 6; 20 September 1913, p. 6.

25. *San Francisco Examiner,* 18 February 1913, p. 1.

26. *Chicago Tribune,* 18 April 1914, p. 1; 30 April 1914, p. 1.

27. *Chicago Tribune,* 21 March 1913, p. 6.

28. *Chicago Tribune,* 24 March 1913, p. 8.

29. *San Francisco Examiner,* 25 February 1913, p. 22.

30. *Denver Post,* 2 March 1913, p. 1.

31. *Denver Post,* 24 February 1913, p. 1. Also see *Chicago Tribune,* 21 February 1913, p. 6; 24 February 1913, p. 8; *Denver Post,* 21 February 1913, p. 1; 2 March 1913, p. 1; *San Francisco Examiner,* 25 February 1913, p. 22. And see Mexican embassy, Washington, to Relaciones Exteriores, 15 August 1913, AHSRE, 16-10-122, unnumbered.

32. See *Chicago Tribune,* 28 January 1914, p. 1; 18 April 1914, p. 1; 30 April 1914, p. 1; *San Francisco Examiner,* 18 February 1914, p. 1; 30 April 1914, p. 24. Also see Meyer, *Huerta,* pp. 196–204.

33. *Los Angeles Times,* 24 March 1913, p. 6; 19 December 1913, II, p. 4.

34. *The Nation,* 25 December 1913, p. 554.

35. See Meyer, *Huerta,* pp. 196–204. There were exceptions, of course. For example, the *Los Angeles Times,* which vociferously supported Huerta, gave Wilson little political credit for the occupation.

36. *San Francisco Examiner,* 16 November 1913, p. 1.

37. My translation; the original reads: "que existen en este Puerto [Veracruz] individuos que se dedican hacer propaganda sediciosa y hacer circular noticias que desdigan el buen nombre de nuestros actuales y legítimos mandatarios y de supuestas victorias de los infames vandidos del Norte." José M. Luján to Secretario de Communicaciones y Obras Publicas, 16 April 1914, VC, doc. 885. Luján later fled to the United States. See Meyer, *Huerta,* p. 214.

38. See Hill, pp. 161–163.

39. From March 25 through April 2, 1914, especially, see the front pages of the *Chicago Tribune,* the *Denver Post,* the *Los Angeles Times,* the *New York Times,* the *San Francisco Examiner,* and the *Washington Times.*

40. *San Francisco Examiner,* 20 February 1914, p. 1.

41. The best example I have seen can be found in the *Chicago Tribune,* 21 March–4 April 1914. Also see the publications listed in note 39 above.

42. El Paso Consul to Relaciones Exteriores, 24 March 1914, AHSRE, L-E-791, no. 150. Also see R. S. Bravo, consul in Laredo, to Relaciones Exteriores, 28 March 1914, AHSRE, L-E-791, no. 87; Bravo to Diebold, 28 March 1914, AHSRE, L-E-795, nos. 93–94; El Paso Consul to Relaciones Exteriores, 31 March 1914, AHSRE, L-E-791, no. 147.

43. My translation; the original reads: "Inexacta noticia. Federales derrotaron Villa." López Portillo to Bravo, 28 March 1914, AHSRE, L-E-791, no. 91. Also see López Portillo to Diebold, 25 March 1914, AHSRE, L-E-795, no. 20; López Portillo to El Paso, 31 March 1914, AHSRE, L-E-791, no. 149.

44. My translation; the original reads: "[R]ebeldes han sufrido serias derrotas en Torreón." Diebold to consuls in New York, San Francisco, St. Louis, Tucson, Brownsville, Los Angeles, San Diego, Kansas City, Galveston, Douglas, and Chicago, 27 March 1914, AHSRE, L-E-795, no. 38.

45. Actually, Diebold's note says two days, but the earliest report he received from López Portillo is dated March 27, one day before the wire. See Diebold to E. T. Simondetti, New York, 28 March 1914, AHSRE, L-E-795, no. 65.

46. Maas to Diebold, 29, 30, 31 March 1914. AHSRE, L-E-795, nos. 82, 87, 101.

47. Diebold to Laredo, 30 March 1914, AHSRE, L-E-795, no. 82; Diebold to J. R. Orci, consul in Los Angeles, 30 March 1914, AHSRE, L-E-795, no. 88; Diebold to San Francisco Consul, 30 March 1914, L-E-795, no. 90; Diebold to consuls in Naco, Douglas, San Francisco, Marfa, Laredo, Los Angeles, and Nogales, 1 April 1914, AHSRE, L-E-795, no. 103.

48. My translation; the original reads: "Unicas noticias podido adquirir aqui respecto situacion Torreon son las publicadas por rebeldes, alarmente y de todo falsas. Desde el 25 Marzo supliquea usted a secretaria guerra y jefes operaciones . . . [que] Gral. Maas de Saltillo telegrafiame varios triunfos nuestra fuerzas." Diebold to Relaciones Exteriores, 31 March 1914, AHSRE, L-E-795, no. 92.

49. See from Los Angeles to Diebold (no. 109), from Laredo (112), and from Nogales (128), 3 April 1914, AHSRE, L-E-795.

50. Berlin embassy to Relaciones Exteriores, 3 April 1914, AHSRE, L-E-791, nos. 100–106.

51. Diebold to St. Louis, San Diego, Brownsville, New York, New Orleans, Galveston, Kansas City, Rio Grande City, Laredo, San Antonio,

San Francisco, Nogales, Los Angeles, and Douglas, 6 April 1914, AHSRE, L-E-795, no. 140.

52. Hill, pp. 162–163. Also see G. Fernández MacGregor to José López Portillo y Rojas, 2 April 1914, AHSRE 17-5-117, no. 90.

53. An internal foreign relations memorandum penned by former Mexican congressman Querido Moheno noted the Huerta regime's "disgust" at Carothers's contrivance and noted his impending expulsion from Mexico. See n.d., AHSRE, 17-5-117, no. 93.

54. Hill, p. 163. Cobb's communication is no more specific than "Constitutionalist." See Cobb to Bryan, 1 April 1914, in RDS 812/11366.

55. Hill, p. 163.

56. Alfredo Margain to Relaciones Exteriores, 1 April 1914, AHSRE, L-E-795, no. 107.

57. My translation; the original reads: "Hace descubierto Carothers pidio Bryan siga propaganda triunfo villistas y caida Torreon. Urge emprenda usted campana prensa para publicar que Torreon no ha caida ni caera; que derrota Villa confirmado plenamente." Fernández MacGregor to López Portillo y Rojas, 2 April 1914, AHSRE, 17-5-117, no. 90.

58. See Relaciones Exteriores dispatches to consuls in Rome, Montevideo, Tokyo, Madrid, Vienna, Guatemala, Buenos Aires, Havana, and Santiago, AHSRE, L-E-791, nos. 69–79.

59. Bravo to Relaciones Exteriores, 3 April 1914, AHSRE, L-E-791, no. 1. In a second dispatch of the same day, he specifically noted the source of the reports—the Associated Press. See Bravo to Relaciones Exteriores, 3 April 1914, AHSRE, L-E-791, no. 2. Also see Juán M. Mateos, Huertista consul in Calexico, to Relaciones Exteriores, 14 April 1914, AHSRE, L-E-791, nos. 18–21; and Huerta Consul, San Antonio, to Relaciones Exteriores, 8 April 1914, AHSRE, L-E-791, no. 31.

60. My translation; the original reads: "que este gobierno sabe han dado instrucciones sus agentes para propalar falsedades los favorezcan." López Portillo to Bravo, 4 April 1914, AHSRE, L-E-791, no. 3.

61. López Portillo circular, 6 April 1914, AHSRE, 17-5-117, no. 91.

62. Diebold to unnamed, c. 4 April 1914, AHSRE, L-E-791, no. 8.

63. Diebold to Relaciones Exteriores, 10 April 1914, AHSRE, L-E-791, no. 38.

64. See Diebold to General Aurelio Blanquet, Secretaria Guerra y Marina, 10 April 1914, AHSRE, L-E-795, no. 165; Diebold to Relaciones Exteriores, 10 April 1914, AHSRE, L-E-795, no. 176; Blanquet to Diebold, 12 April 1914, AHSRE L-E-795, no. 166; El Paso Consul to Relaciones Exteriores, 14 April 1914, AHSRE (R-90-3), no. 1.

65. Subsecretary of foreign relations to Fernández MacGregor, 4 April 1914, AHSRE, L-E-791, no. 110.

66. López Portillo to consuls, c. 5 April 1914, AHSRE, L-E-791, no. 111.

67. From Paris, a consular dispatch read: "In order to destroy the public impression caused in Europe by publication of the great amount of news detailing the rebel taking of Torreón, I will send you ample information to release for publication" (my translation; the original reads: "Para destruir impresion causada opinion publica europa por publicacion gran cantidad detalles toma Torreon por rebeldes, convendria telegrafia luego amplos informes hare publicar"). See 6 April 1914, AHSRE, L-E-791, no. 112. Also see AHSRE, L-E-791, dispatches received from Guatemala (no. 117), Tokyo (120), Honduras (122), Vienna (123), Berlin (124; with enclosures, 125), Rome (126), Madrid (132), and Buenos Aires (134), in AHSRE, L-E-791.

68. Canseco to El Paso, 8 April 1914, AHSRE, L-E-795, nos. 2–4.

69. Jerry Knudson, "The Press and the Mexican Revolution of 1910," *Journalism Quarterly* 46 (Winter 1969): 760–766.

70. Stevens, p. 83.

71. For typical examples of press synopses sent to Carranza, see Manuel Chao and Hermiano Perez Abreu to Carranza, (no day given) April 1914, VC, Fondo MVIII; Perez Abreu to Carranza, 11 April 1914, VC, Fondo MVIII; Arcadio Centella, Jr., to Carranza, August 1914, VC, Fondo MVIII; and Zubarán to Carranza, 7 September, VC, Fondo MVIII. Also see Oficina Información to Carranza, 16 April 1915, VC, Fondo MVIII. Finally, see a seven-page summation of news reports from the *Evening Post* (New York), *New York Herald, New York World,* and *New York Times* in a circular of the Consulado General de Mexico Gobierno Provisional, 5 June 1915, VC, doc. 4479.

72. One reason may have been that Carranza was testing the political waters in the United States. According to Kenneth Grieb, Carranza had planned to revolt against Madero—but then Madero was killed. See Kenneth Grieb, "The Causes of the Carranza Rebellion: A Reinterpretation," *The Americas* 25, no. 1 (July 1968): 25–32.

73. Herbierto Barron to Carranza, 27 January 1913, VC, Fondo MVIII.

74. Many examples of cables to this effect can be found in the Carrancista collection at the Condumex archive (VC). See, for example, Constitutionalist general Pablo González to Carranza, 23 July 1915, VC, Fondo LXVIII-4. Also see Juán Gutiérrez to C. José Z. Garza, consul at Brownsville, 17–21 October 1914, AHSRE, L-E-788, no. 3/1. A series of

headlines in the *San Francisco Examiner* in the spring and summer of 1914 expressed the general media sentiment well: "VILLA REAL MASTER NOW" (18 June 1914, p. 1), "CARRANZA IS COMPLETELY CAST OFF BY GEN. VILLA," (19 June 1914, p. 1), "VILLA RETURNS TO HAVE IT OUT WITH CHIEF" (30 June 1914, p. 4.), "WAR UPON CARRANZA DECLARED BY VILLA" (24 July 1914, p. 1), "NEW WAR [versus Carranza] DECLARED BY VILLA" (26 September 1914, p. 1).

75. *Los Angeles Times*, 24 March 1913, p. 6; 16 December 1913, II, p. 4; 5 February 1914, II, p. 4; 23 February 1914, II, p. 4; *New York Times*, 24 April 1914, p. 12; *San Francisco Examiner*, 28 November 1913, p. 20; 14 December 1913, p. 20; 27 April 1914, p. 16.

76. *Los Angeles Times*, 23 February 1914, II, p. 4.

77. *San Francisco Examiner*, 14 December 1913, p. 20.

78. *Chicago Tribune*, 2 March 1914, p. 1; 3 March 1914, p. 6; 16 March 1914, p. 6; 24 April 1914, p. 6.

79. *New York Times*, 4 January 1915, p. 10.

80. *New York Times*, 30 October 1914, p. 8.

81. *New York Times*, 20 January 1914, p. 8.

82. See *Chicago Tribune*, 10 September 1914, p. 6; *Los Angeles Times*, 4 December 1913, p. 1; 16 December 1913, p. 1; 26 February 1914, II, p. 4; *San Francisco Examiner*, 21 April 1914, p. 24; *New York Times*, 5 October 1914, p. 10.

83. *San Francisco Examiner*, 21 April 1914, p. 24; *Los Angeles Times*, 4 December 1913, p. 1.

84. *Chicago Tribune*, 25 September 1914, p. 6.

85. *New York Times*, 1 February 1914, III, p. 4.

86. *New York Times*, 15 February 1914, III, p. 4.

87. *San Francisco Examiner*, 26 September 1914, p. 17.

88. *New York Times*, 1 February 1913, III, p. 4.

89. *New York Times*, 11 June 1914, p. 14.

90. *Los Angeles Times*, 5 February 1915, II, p. 4.

91. M. Aguirre Berlanga to Carranza, 3 January 1914, VC, doc. 729.

92. Zubarán to Carranza, 20 August 1914, VC, Fondo MVIII.

93. Zubarán to Carranza, 9 September 1914, VC, Fondo MVIII.

94. Villa to Carranza, 9 August 1914, VC, Fondo MVIII.

95. My translation; the original reads "la gente ignorante." Manuel Carbajal to Carranza, 25 August 1914, VC doc. 1338.

96. Zubarán to Carranza, 9 September 1914, VC, Fondo MVIII.

97. García to Timothy Turner, 3 August 1915. AHSRE, L-E-811, no. 26.

98. My translation; the original reads: "Esto muestra una vez cuán exagerados y falsas son las noticias que publica diario de la prensa, danda

cabida en sus columnas a toda noticia sensacional, sin cuidarse de su origen y sin observar que ordinariamente procedan de enemigos del Sr. Carranza o de extranjeros aliados a ellos, y que tiene por único objeto producir escandolo y alarma y extraviar la opinion publica americana. . . . . El Sr Carranza, al contrario de lo que la prensa informa, acaba de telegrafia a esta Agente Confidencial que las manifestaciones . . . que han dado . . . a exageraciones y noticias alarmente y que solo tienden a exitar la opinion publica." Press release issued by Eliseo Arredondo, n.d., AHSRE, L-E-1441, no. 12.

99. Folsom to García, 15 February 1915, AHSRE, L-E-836, no. 5.

100. Carrancista press release issued from New York, n.d., AHSRE, L-E-1441, no. 47.

101. *Mexican Letter*, 30 December 1914, Bulletin no. 32, in VC, unnumbered.

102. Arredondo to Lansing, 26 June 1915, AHSRE, L-E-1441, no. 102.

103. Barron to Carranza, 10 August 1913, VC, doc. 522.

104. C. Mungiat to *La Revolución, El Demócrata* (Mexico City, Piedras Negras, San Luis Potosí, and Monterrey), *El Pueblo* (Veracruz), and the Pan-American News Service, 19 June 1915, VC, Fondo LXVIII-4.

105. J. N. Amador to Carranza, 9 September 1915, VC, Fondo XXI-4.

106. Andrés G. García to Carranza, 25 October 1915, AHSRE, L-E-810 (II).

107. Canova to Bryan, 15 July 1914, in RDS 812/12553.

108. Samuel Belden to Carranza, 16 June 1914, VC, Fondo MVIII.

109. See two cables from Carranza to Andrés G. García, 1 July 1915, VC, XXI-4; Carranza to Arredondo, 2 July 1915, VC, XXI-4; Arredondo to Carranza, 10 July 1915, VC, Fondo XXI-4; Arredondo to Carranza, 7 August 1915, VC, Fondo XXI-4; García to Carranza, 28 August 1915, VC, Fondo XXI-4; Arredondo to Carranza, 4 September 1915, VC, Fondo XXI-4.

110. Arredondo to Lansing, 6 September 1915, in RDS 812/16041.

111. Barron to Wilson, 13 August 1915, VC, doc. 5381.

112. Barron to Carranza, 20 August 1915, VC, doc. 5443.

113. Barron to Carranza, 14 July 1915, VC, Fondo XXI-4.

114. A. Garza González urged Carranza as early as June 1913 to put well-connected Americans on the payroll to influence politicians in Washington. See Garza González to Carranza, 8 June 1913, VC, doc. 411.

115. Weeks received five hundred dollars for unspecified services in the spring of 1915. See Carranza to Arredondo, 14 April 1915, VC, Fondo XXI-4.

116. Weeks to Lane, 19 August 1915, VC, Fondo XXI-4.

117. Lane to Lansing, 26 August 1915, in RDS 812/15961.

118. Unsigned letter to Carranza, 2 January 1915, VC, doc. 2324.

119. My translation; the original reads "enemigo mas encarnizado." Willebaldo Yzaguirre to Zubarán, 14 January 1914, VC, doc. 754.

120. Daniel Palma to Pesqueira, 27 April 1914, VC, doc. 903.

121. See Carranza to Hearst's International News Service, 27 April 1915, VC, XXI-4.

122. E. F. Howe, publisher of the *Imperial Valley Press*, to Bryan, 27 August, in RDS 812/13023.

123. United States assistant attorney general Gerard Warren forwarded a letter, the author of which is unidentified, to Bryan that read: "The *Los Angeles Times* and its owners, Harrison Gray Otis and Harry Chandler, are most bitter enemies of the [Wilson] administration and desire intervention in Mexico for one single reason, namely, to protect their land grab of nearly two million acres" granted them by the Díaz administration. See Warren to Bryan, 22 April 1915, RDS 812.14925. For that matter, one Carrancista referred to the press in Los Angeles as a whole as "totally enemy" (*toda enemigo*). See Miguel Díaz Lombardo to Francisco S. Elias, 24 April 1915, VC, Fondo XXI-4.

124. Antonio Zamacona to Carranza, 19 October 1913, VC, doc. 558. Also see an internal Department of Justice memorandum, 22 April 1915, in RDS/14925.

125. See *New York Times*, 29 October 1914, IV, p. 5.

126. One report noted that Hearst, via the New York press (he owned the *New York American*), was claiming "Villa must be president of Mexico" (my translation; the original reads: "Villa debe ser presidente Mexico"). M. Crolland to Isidro Fabela, 30 July 1914, AHSRE, L-E-854 (I), no. 71.

127. Louis Hostetter, United States consul at Hermosillo, to Bryan, 13 May 1914, in RDS 812/12033.

128. Carrancista colonel Plutarco Elías Calles to Carranza, 11 July 1914, VC, Fondo MVIII.

129. Illegible to Adolfo de la Huerta, 2 July 1914, VC, doc. 987.

130. Hostetter reported to Bryan: "The newspapers have certainly abused him [Maytorena] shamefully and this has caused the trouble. They published shortcomings of the Governor in very insulting language and while the charges were all true and proven the language was unnecessary." See Hostetter to Bryan, 7 June 1914, in RDS 812/12233.

131. Michael Smith identifies six goals giving impetus to Carrancista propaganda: to promote Carranza to Mexican expatriates in the United

States; to "protect Mexican nationalism"; to secure diplomatic recognition from the United States; to generate American public support for Carranza; to "enhance" Carranza's public image; and to defend Carranza and his movement "against criticism and intrigues of his enemies—both Mexican and North American." See Smith, p. 1. Also see Douglas Richmond, *Venustiano Carranza's Nationalist Struggle, 1893–1920* (Lincoln: University of Nebraska Press, 1983), pp. 190–192.

132. By May 1915, Carranza had agents in the United States in Albuquerque, Baltimore, Brownsville, Calexico, Del Rio, Douglas, El Paso, Galveston, Kansas City, Laredo, Los Angeles, Mobile, Naco, New Orleans, New York, Nogales, Philadelphia, Rio Grande City, San Antonio, San Diego, San Francisco, and St. Louis. See Carranza to Carrancista general Francisco Coss, 2 May 1915, VC, Fondo XXI-4. Also see Smith, pp. 10–11.

133. Smith, pp. 5–6.

134. Smith, pp. 1–7.

135. Adrián Aguirre Benavides to Carranza, 20 May 1913, VC, doc. 222.

136. Zubarán to Carranza, 4 July 1914, VC, Fondo MXV.

137. Zubarán to Carranza, 9 July 1914, VC, Fondo MVIII.

138. Douglas boasted of close and highly placed connections in Washington. See Douglas to Veracruz, 20 July 1915, VC, doc. 4990.

139. Douglas received ten thousand dollars for undisclosed purposes in October 1914. See Zubarán to Carranza, 25 October 1914, VC, Fondo XXI-4.

140. Smith, p. 7.

141. Cole's activities centered on Missouri, Kansas, and Texas. See Cole to Carranza, 5 June 1914, VC, Fondo MVIII, and 7 September 1914, VC, Fondo XXI-4. Cole, too, boasted of important Washington connections. See Cole to Carranza, 8 October 1914, VC, doc. 1696, and 11 October 1914, VC, doc. 1714.

142. Belden received twenty-five hundred dollars for "secret press work" (my translation; the original reads "trabajo prensa servicio secreto") in the early spring of 1915. See Arredondo to Carranza, 31 March 1915, VC, Fondo XXI-4.

143. Smith, pp. 7–8.

144. Smith, p. 8.

145. G. H. Velásquez, circular, 31 March 1915, VC, doc. 3596. See also unsigned to Gregorio H. Velásquez, 12 May 1915, VC, doc. 4256.

146. The Carranza archive carries a partial and scattered collection from June 1915 through at least 1916 (I looked no further). See, for example, VC, docs. 4930, 5166, 5213, 5270, 5292, 5304, 5312, 5331, 5645, 5659, 5706,

5766, 7255, and 7274. Synopses and extracts of the contents of Constitutional newspapers were distributed under the title "Summary of the Press" ("Resumen de la Prensa"). See, for example, VC, docs. 3609, 3687.

147. Pesqueira to Carranza, 8 March 1914, AHSRE, L-E-813, no. 265.

148. Branyas to Carranza, 7 October 1914, VC, doc. 1687.

149. Smith, p. 9.

150. Many hundreds of PANS cables to this effect can be found in AHSRE L-E-836 (R-110-6), nos. 1–108.

151. Just what the information was and whether Turner received payment for it remains unclear. See R. E. Múzquiz to Carranza, 22 May 1914, VC, Fondo MVIII.

152. A copy of Turner's prospectus is included in Turner to Andrés G. García, Carrancista consul at El Paso, 21 July 1915, AHSRE, L-E-811, nos. 13–17.

153. Hartland Smith's letter to Bryan, Bryan's response, and the union's letter and enclosure to Smith are located in RDS 812/14422.

154. Alfredo Breceda to Carranza, 22 July 1915, VC, doc. 5009.

155. Pesqueira to García, 18 August 1914, AHSRE, L-E-811, nos. 32–78. See also Smith, pp. 12–13.

156. Unsigned Constitutionalist circulars: 1 December 1913, VC, doc. 600; 4 December 1913, VC, doc. 607. Also see Zubarán to Felipe Riveros, 27 December 1915, VC, Fondo XXI-4.

157. *El Demócrata* did good propaganda work but needed a steady supply of money to do so, Carranza was informed. See Rafael Martínez to Carranza, 7 July 1914, VC, Fondo MVIII. Also see C. M. Samper to Gustavo Espinosa Mireles, 8 July 1914, VC, Fondo MVIII.

158. For sample copies from June 1915, see Edwards to Bryan, 14 June 1915, in RDS 812/15298.

159. Arenas Guzmán, p. 272; Meyer, p. 133.

160. Barron to Carranza, 10 July 1914, VC, doc. 1685.

161. L. Mesa Gutiérrez to Carranza, 3 March 1914, VC, Fondo MVIII.

162. Ramiro Manzanos, circular, 29 (?) February 1914, VC, doc. 2571.

163. C. Mungiat circular to *La Revolución, El Demócrata, El Pueblo,* and the Pan-American News Service, 19 June 1915, VC, Fondo LXVIII-4.

164. Argudín, pp. 138, 142; Borrás, pp. 25–26.

165. Barron to Carranza, 23 May 1914, VC, Fondo MVIII.

166. García to Carranza, 5 March 1915, VC, doc. 3182. García made the request of Carranza again about six weeks later; see García to Carranza, 27 April 1915, VC, doc. 4014. Although short on specifics, an interdepartmental State Department memorandum noted six Constitu-

tionalist papers printed at El Paso, seven at San Antonio, and one at Laredo. See unsigned memorandum to Lansing, 5 December 1914, in RDS 812/14012.

167. See Director, *El Eco de Mexico*, to Carranza, 29 January 1915, VC, doc. 2571.

168. Roque González Garza, c. summer 1913, ARGG, Carpeta 14, unnumbered.

169. Andrés G. García to Carranza, 10 September 1915, VC, doc. 5674.

170. The Constitutionalists purchased paper and ink for *El Progreso* in 1915. See Melquiades T. García to Carranza, 9 February 1915, VC, Fondo XXI-4. See also Gustavo Solano to Andrés G. García, 3 July 1915, AHSRE, L-E-811, no. 4.

171. See Hal Greer to Lansing, 16 August 1915, in RDS 812/15811.

172. Joseph Branyas to Carranza, 7 October 1914, VC, doc. 1687.

173. Arredondo ordered nineteen hundred dollars released to *La Raza* for propaganda in early 1915. See two notes by Mireles, both dated 10 February 1915, VC, docs. 2393, 2394.

174. In 1914 *La Lucha* received one hundred dollars a month. See Juan M. Luján to Elias, 3 April 1914, AHSRE, 17-5-157, nos. 3–14.

175. Smith, pp. 10–11.

176. See H. L. Beach to Carranza, 22 August 1914, VC, Fondo MVIII; Consul, San Antonio, to Carranza, 26 March 1915, VC, doc. 3499; and American Consul, Monterrey, to Lansing, 1 September 1915, in RDS 812/16132.

177. The *Citizen* offered to serve as a Constitutional mouthpiece if it received funds for doing so. See *Tucson Citizen* to Carranza, 25 December 1913, VC, doc. 697.

178. Arredondo to Carranza, 24 March 1915, VC, Fondo XXI-4.

179. My translation; the original reads "para gastos prensa." Carranza to Elias, 30 May 1915, VC, Fondo XXI-4. The Carranza archive frequently notes sums of money being dispatched to consuls and other agents, but it only infrequently notes precisely what the money was earmarked for. Contrast the payment cited here, for example, with an unexplained forty thousand dollars sent to Zubarán by Carranza. It seems fair to assume that at least part of this money contributed to propaganda efforts. See Carranza to Zubarán, 1 October 1914, VC, Fondo MVIII.

180. Carranza also proclaimed the right of his regime to censor outgoing diplomatic reports. He maintained that such reports must be restricted to diplomatic information "without exception" (*sin ninguno excepción*). Under strong protest from the State Department, Carranza

backed off, but he did not retract his assertion about the right to censor. Carranza to Bryan, 11 February 1915, AHSRE, L-E-1441, nos. 5–11. Also see Willilam W. Canada to M. Dávalos, Carrancista official at Veracruz, 7 February 1915, AHSRE, 16-14-22.

181. Canada to Bryan, 25 November 1914, in RDS 812/13897.

182. Oliveira to Lansing, 29 July 1915, in RDS 812/15679. In at least one case an offending newspaper, the *Mexican Herald*, was allowed to continue its operations, albeit censored. Silliman to Bryan, 1 February 1915, in RDS 812/14329. Meanwhile, reports of depredations in the capital circulated until well into the summer months—to Carrancista ire. See Carranza to Arredondo, 1 July 1915, VC, Fondo XXI-4.

183. Silliman to Bryan, 16 January 1915, in RDS 812/14217.

184. Oliveira to Bryan, 9 March 1915, in RDS 812/14537.

185. Oliveira to Bryan, 9 March 1915, in RDS 812/14566. The practice of press intimidation continued to varying degrees in Mexico City for as long as Carranza's forces held the capital. See, for example, United States Consul, Mexico City, to Lansing, 5 October 1915, in RDS 812/16396.

186. Andrés G. García to Arredondo, 1 July 1915, AHSRE, L-E-811, nos. 3, 8. See also San Francisco Carrancista consul R. P. Denegri to Carranza, 31 July 1915, VC, Fondo XXI-4.

187. Heller to Carranza, 15 April 1915, VC, Fondo XXI-4.

188. Inspector General of Police, San Luis Potosí, to Jesus Carranza, 23 July 1914, VC, docs. 1128 and 1135. Also see Carranza to Heller, 15 April 1915, VC, Fondo XXI-4; Andrés G. García to Arredondo, 1 July 1915, AHSRE, L-E-811, no. 3 and (unsigned) no. 8. It may have been Heller's success that prompted the Carrancista consul in San Diego, E. A. González, to suggest the establishment of Constitutional clubs around the United States to promote the Constitutionalist cause. See E. A. González, circular, 21 March 1915, VC, doc. 3517.

189. Reyes, in Dorn's Memorandum. Carranza was fully aware of the propaganda possibilities offered by film. The Compañia Cinematográfica de Propaganda Modernista of Veracruz offered him the opportunity to use films it agreed to shoot for a monthly fee as propaganda weapons. See Luis Meza Herrera to Carranza, 17 May 1915, VC, doc. 4311.

190. Zubarán to Carranza, 13 March 1914, VC, Fondo MVIII.

191. Michael Smith's paper represents the only study to date to examine Carranza's propaganda. It identifies the First Chief's media strategy as having six goals; see note above. Also see Smith, p. 1. I would like to acknowledge the benefit of conversations I held with Professor Smith in Mexico City during the summer of 1994.

192. A note below the masthead of each copy read, "To the Editor: Kindly use the matter in this bulletin as liberally as your space will permit. We supply this service free of charge."

193. Modesto Rolland, *Mexican Letter*, 19 September 1914, Bulletin no. 7, VC, doc. 1558.

194. Pesqueira, *Mexican Letter*, 23 October 1914, Bulletin no. 13, VC, doc. 1827. Also see Oscar K. Goll, *Mexican Letter*, 23 December 1914, VC, doc. 2246.

195. Pesqueira, *Mexican Letter*, 23 October 1914, Bulletin no. 13, VC, doc. 1827.

196. Carranza's Message to the Convention of Aguascalientes, *Mexican Letter*, 13 November 1914, Bulletin no. 18, VC, doc. 2039.

197. *Mexican Letter*, 31 December 1914, Bulletin no. 33, VC, doc. 2295.

198. An unsigned propaganda missive to the United Press Association said it well: "I consider Gutiérrez solely an instrument of General Villa" (my translation; the original reads: "Considero Gutiérrez únicamente instrumento General Villa, quien maneja realmente gobierno Gutiérrez"). See unsigned propaganda missive to the United Press Association of New York, 19 December 1914, VC, doc. 2229. Also see *Mexican Letter*, 25 December 1914, Bulletin no. 31, VC, doc. 2256.

199. *Mexican Letter*, 13 November 1914, Bulletin no. 18, VC, doc. 2039.

200. *Mexican Letter*, 32 December 1914, Bulletin no. 33, VC, doc. 2295.

201. *Mexican Letter*, 23 December 1914, Bulletin no. 30, VC, doc. 2246. Also see *Mexican Letter*, 25 December 1914, Bulletin no. 31, VC, doc. 2256.

202. *Mexican Letter*, 30 December 1914, Bulletin no. 32, VC, unnumbered.

203. *Mexican Letter*, 5 January 1915, Bulletin no. 34, VC, doc. 2347.

204. *New York Times*, 29 October 1914, p. 3.

205. Also see an attack against Villa written by Obregón and printed in the *New York Times*, 7 December 1914, VII, p. 2.

206. *New York Times*, 1 May 1915, p. 12.

207. *New York Times*, 2 May 1915, II, p. 6.

208. *New York Times*, 30 May 1915, II, p. 4.

209. *New York Times*, 15 July 1915, p. 1.

210. *New York Times*, 28 August 1915, p. 6.

211. Pan-American News Service Dispatch, c. August 1915, AHSRE, L-E-811, nos. 55–60.

212. Simpson to Carranza, 22 September 1915, VC, doc. 5788.

213. Barron to Carranza, 22 September 1915, VC doc. 5785.

214. Barron to Wilson, 13 August 1915, VC, doc 5381.

215. Barron to Carranza, 20 August 1915, VC, doc. 5443.

CHAPTER FIVE. THE TROUBLE WITH MEXICANS

1. Arthur G. Petitt argues that popular culture necessarily reflects popular opinion because its success as a commodity depends on its salability. The assumption is that people tend to purchase popular forms of expression—films, novels, newspapers, artworks—that are consonant with their own attitudes, tastes, and opinions. See Arthur G. Petitt, *Images of the Mexican American in Fiction and Film* (College Station: Texas A&M University Press, 1980), pp. xviii–xix. For examples of works that have employed both elements of popular culture and earlier media of expression and considered them to be reflective of popular thinking about Latin America in general and Mexico in particular, see Philip Wayne Powell, *Tree of Hate: Propaganda and Prejudices Affecting United States Relations with the Hispanic World* (New York: Basic Books, 1971); George Black, *The Good Neighbor: How the United States Wrote the History of Central America and the Caribbean* (New York: Pantheon Books, 1988), pp. xix–xx; John J. Johnson, *Latin America in Caricature* (Austin: University of Texas Press, 1980), p. 3; Arnoldo De León, *They Called Them Greasers: Anglo Attitudes toward Mexicans in Texas, 1821–1900* (Austin: University of Texas Press, 1983). Also see Edward Said, *Culture and Imperialism* and *Orientalism* (New York: Pantheon, 1978).

2. The English were in direct imperial competition with Spain and used newly forged printing technologies to propagandize their case. The result, according to Powell, was that Spaniards were the "first to feel the impact of the printing press as a propaganda weapon . . . propaganda which became entrenched as history." Powell dates English and Dutch anti-Spanish bias to the late sixteenth century. He dates other European anti-Spanish feeling even earlier—that of the Germans and Italians to the beginning of the sixteenth century and that of the French "for a thousand years" prior to that. See Powell, pp. 6, 39–40, 47–50, 57–59. Also see Raymund Arthur Paredes, "The Image of the Mexican in American Literature," Ph.D. dissertation, University of Texas, Austin, 1973, pp. 1–29, 318.

3. De León, p. 24. De León also claims that "[b]y projecting onto Mexicans what they [Americans] did not wish to see in themselves, they sought reaffirmation of their righteousness." See De León, p. 36. Also see Fredrick Pike, *The United States and Latin America: Myths and Stereotypes of Civilization and Nature* (Austin: University of Texas Press, 1992), pp. 13–14, 47–49, 99.

4. Cecil Robinson, *With the Ears of Strangers: The Mexican in American Literature* (Tucson: University of Arizona Press, 1963), pp. 78–79.

5. Robinson, pp. vii, 33, 36, 38, 42, 43, 46, 54, 57, 81–82, 94, 264–283; De León, p. 24; Powell, p. vii; J. Johnson, pp. 10–11; Paredes, p. 322.

6. See Robinson, pp. vii–viii, 290–300; De León, p. 23; Paredes, p. 110; Black, pp. xvi, 2–3, 5.

7. Robert W. Johannsen, *To the Halls of the Montezumas: The Mexican War in the American Imagination* (New York: Oxford University Press, 1985), pp. 167–168. And see James A. Clifton, ed., *The Invented Indian: Cultural Fictions and Government Policies* (New Brunswick, N.J.: Transaction Publishers, 1990).

8. Raymond William Stedman, *Shadows of the Indian: Stereotypes in American Culture* (Norman: University of Oklahoma Press, 1982), pp. 134–157.

9. Robert F. Berkhofer, *The White Man's Indian: Images of the American Indian from Columbus to the Present* (New York: Alfred A. Knopf, 1978), p. 27.

10. Berkhofer, pp. 3, 25–26. Also see Pike, p. 99.

11. Stedman, pp. 74–104, 245, 248–249; Berkhofer, p. 28.

12. Stedman, p. 251.

13. Berkhofer, p. 28.

14. De León, p. 23.

15. Paredes, p. 323. Also see Gary D. Keller, *Hispanics and United States Film: An Overview and Handbook* (Tempe, Ariz.: Bilingual Press, 1994), p. 33; J. Johnson, pp. 10, 14–15; Stedman, pp. 193–205; Pike, pp. 144–153; Powell, *passim;* Robinson, *passim.*

16. See Johannsen, *passim;* J. Johnson, p. 14.

17. J. Johnson, pp. 157–159. Also see Albert Boime, *The Art of Exclusion: Representing Blacks in the Nineteenth Century* (Washington, D.C.: Smithsonian Institution Press, 1990), pp. 1–14.

18. Paredes, p. 322.

19. Paredes, p. 322: De León, pp. xi, 24–35, 49–62. Also see Joe S. Bain, "Mexicans in Modern American Fiction," Ph.D. dissertaion, University of California, San Diego, 1983.

20. Robinson, p. viii.

21. Robinson, p. 30. Also see Francisco Armando Ríos, "The Mexican in Fact, Fiction, and Folklore," *El Grito* 2, no. 4 (Summer 1969): 15–16.

22. As an example of the continuity in treatment, in the 1920s a crude environmental determinism was employed to explain Mexicans' apparent lesser intelligence compared with Americans. The concern stemmed in part from low IQ test scores registered by Mexican-Americans in the period 1912–1935. See Nick C. Vaca, "The Mexican-American in the Social

Sciences 1912–1970, Part 2: 1936–1970," *El Grito* 4, no. 1 (Fall 1970): 17–19. On the tendency toward slightly more realistic portrayals of Mexicans in American twentieth-century popular culture, see Allen L. Woll, *The Latin Image in American Film* (Los Angeles: UCLA Latin American Center Publications, 1977), pp. 6–16, 105–116. Also see Keller, pp. 13–36; Black, *passim;* Petitt, pp. 46, 131–139, 155. Thomas Martínez plumbed selected advertisements of the 1960s by large American corporations such as Frito Lay, A. J. Reynolds, Camel Cigarettes, and General Motors and found images similar to those used in the nineteenth century to portray Mexicans. One notable exception, which Martínez does not explain, is that some 1960s advertisements tended to portray Mexicans as overweight. See Thomas Martínez, "Advertising and Racism: The Case of the Mexican-American," *El Grito* 2, no. 4 (Summer 1969): 3–13. Also see Robinson, p. 305; Petitt, pp. x–xviii; Vaca, *passim.*

23. Robinson, pp. 305–307; Petitt, pp. 202–236.

24. See Pike, *passim;* Petitt, pp. 202–236; Keller, *passim;* Robinson, p. 305. Since the turn of the twentieth century, American films have cast Mexicans as racially inferior and culturally retrograde. See Woll, *passim.*

25. For discussions of the stereotype and how it impacted on United States relations with Mexico, see Hunt; De León, *passim;* and John A. Britton, *Revolution and Ideology, Images of the Mexican Revolution in the United States* (Lexington: University of Kentucky Press, 1995).

26. The principle publications include *Collier's, Everybody's,* the *Forum, Harper's,* the *Independent, Literary Digest, McClure's Magazine, The Nation, North American Review,* the *Saturday Evening Post,* and *World's Work.*

27. Although Petitt and others maintain that popular culture reflects general public sentiment, a body of empirically grounded research suggests that the press can in some cases tell its readers what to think. For example, see McCombs and Shaw, "Agenda-Setting Function of the Mass Media"; McCombs and Shaw, "Evolution of Agenda-Setting Research"; Kosicki, p. 115; Rogers, Dearing and Bregman, "Anatomy of Agenda-Setting Research."

28. Donald Paneth, ed., *The Dictionary of American Journalism* (New York: Facts on File, 1983), p. 79.

29. Paneth, p. 116.

30. Paneth, p. 268.

31. Joseph P. McKerns, ed., *Biographical Dictionary of American Journalism* (New York: Greenwood Press, 1989), p. 530. Also see Frank Luther Mott, *A History of American Magazines,* vol. 5 (Cambridge, Mass.: Harvard University Press, 1968).

32. Otis's successor at the *Times*, his son-in-law Harry Chandler, was investigated by the American government for fomenting counterrevolution against Carranza. See William G. Bonelli, *Billion Dollar Blackjack* (Beverly Hills, Calif.: Civic Research Press, 1954), pp. 181–183.

33. Paneth, p. 345.

34. McKerns, p. 499.

35. De León, p. 24. Also see Robinson, p. 284.

36. *Chicago Tribune*, 7 July 1914, p. 2.

37. *Los Angeles Times*, 21 October 1913, II, p. 4.

38. *Los Angeles Times*, 3 January 1914, p. 1.

39. *North American Review* (July 1914): 46. The *Review* was founded in 1815 in Philadelphia to encourage and promote American culture "in the face of European condescension." It moved to New York City in 1877, and by the time of the Mexican Revolution it dealt largely with current events and issues. McKerns, pp. 334–335. Also see Paneth, p. 354.

40. *Saturday Evening Post*, 31 January 1914, p. 22.

41. *Collier's*, 21 March 1914, p. 11.

42. *Everybody's* (June 1914): 820.

43. *Los Angeles Times*, 4 January 1914, II, p. 6.

44. *Los Angeles Times*, 21 October 1913, II, p. 4.

45. Johannsen, p. 22.

46. *The Nation* was founded in 1865 by Edwin Lawrence Godkin. It aimed to serve as a "high-minded, liberal weekly of politics, ideas and literature." See Paneth, p. 289.

47. *The Nation*, 25 December 1914, p. 615.

48. *Chicago Tribune*, 11 January 1914, II, p. 2.

49. *Chicago Tribune*, 28 April 1914, p. 4.

50. *Chicago Tribune*, 4 January 1914, p. 2.

51. *Collier's* magazine was established in 1888 and offered a mixture of current events, poetry, and fiction. In an effort to boost circulation—which edged toward one million during the Revolution—the publication frequently engaged famous fiction writers such as Jack London (who also served as a reporter), H. G. Wells, Henry James, and John Steinbeck. See Alan Nourie and Barbara Nourie, eds., *American Mass-Marketing Magazines* (New York: Greenwood Press, 1990), pp. 56–63. Also see Mott, p. 85.

52. *Collier's*, 13 June 1914, p. 13.

53. *Forum* was established as a journal of "political and social commentary" in 1886 by a group of wealthy New York businessmen, headed by Isaac Leopold Rice. By the time of the Mexican Revolution it had expanded to include fiction and poetry. Its circulation varied from

thirty thousand in 1894 to as low as two thousand in 1923. Mott, pp.
126–127. Also see Paneth, p. 166.

54. *Forum* 51 (January 1914): 46.

55. *Forum* 51 (January 1914): 48.

56. *Forum* 51 (January 1914): 47.

57. *San Francisco Examiner*, 14 June 1913, p. 18.

58. *Chicago Tribune*, 9 June 1913, p. 1.

59. *San Francisco Examiner*, 14 June 1913, p. 18.

60. De León, p. 24.

61. *Forum* 51 (January 1914): 46.

62. The United States press tended not to focus on Mexican sexual
promiscuity and religious corruption, even though both of elements were
common in depictions of Mexicans in other venues of public expression
during the nineteenth and twentieth centuries. See Robinson; De León;
Powell; J. Johnson; and Paredes.

63. I use the term "archetype" to refer to a model of behavior. Peter
Gay writes, "The archetype is a fundamental principle of creativity
anchored in racial endowments, a human potentiality concretely manifested in religious doctrines, fairy tales, myths, dreams, works of art and
literature. Its equivalent in biology is the pattern of behavior." See Peter
Gay, *Freud: A Life for Our Time* (New York: W. W. Norton, 1988), p. 238.

CHAPTER SIX. THE SAVAGE AND THE SNEAK

1. See chapter 5.

2. *Chicago Tribune*, 21 February 1913, p. 6.

3. *Chicago Tribune*, 24 February 1913, p. 8.

4. *San Francisco Examiner*, 25 February 1913, p. 22.

5. *Washington Times*, 26 July 1913, p. 6.

6. *Denver Post*, 2 March 1913, p. 1.

7. *Denver Post*, 1 March 1913, p. 1.

8. *Los Angeles Times*, 20 October 1913, II, p. 2.

9. *Los Angeles Times*, 5 February 1914, II, p. 4.

10. *Los Angeles Times*, 24 March 1913, p. 6.

11. *Los Angeles Times*, 16 December 1913, II, p. 4.

12. *San Francisco Examiner*, 14 December 1913, p. 20.

13. *Los Angeles Times*, 5 February 1914, II, p. 4.

14. *Los Angeles Times*, 23 February 1914, II, p. 4. Also see "No Hope in
Huerta or in Carranza," *San Francisco Examiner*, 28 November 1913, p. 20.

15. *Chicago Tribune*, 16 October 1913, p. 6.

16. *Chicago Tribune*, 9 June 1913, p. 1.

17. *Chicago Tribune*, 2 March 1914, p. 1.

18. *Chicago Tribune*, 3 March 1914, p. 6.

19. *Chicago Tribune*, 16 March 1914, p. 6.

20. *Chicago Tribune*, 24 April 1914, p. 6.

21. *San Francisco Examiner*, 27 April 1914, p. 16.

22. *New York Times*, 20 January 1914, p. 8.

23. *San Francisco Examiner*, 3 March 1914, p. 1.

24. *New York Times*, 24 April 1914, p. 12.

25. *San Francisco Examiner*, 23 April 1914, p. 2.

26. *San Francisco Examiner*, 24 April 1914, p. 24.

27. *Los Angeles Times*, 4 December 1913, p. 1.

28. *Los Angeles Times*, 16 December 1913, p. 1. Also see *San Francisco Examiner*, 21 April 1914, p. 24.

29. *Los Angeles Times*, 26 February 1914, II, p. 4.

30. *New York Times*, 5 October 1914, p. 10.

31. *Chicago Tribune*, 10 September 1914, p. 6.

32. *San Francisco Examiner*, 26 September 1914, p. 17.

33. *San Francisco Examiner*, 29 April 1915, p. 24.

34. *Los Angeles Times*, 25 November 1913, II, p. 4. Also see *Los Angeles Times*, 29 January 1914, II, p. 4.

35. *Los Angeles Times*, 16 July 1914, II, p. 4.

36. *Chicago Tribune*, 17 July 1914, p. 6.

37. The passage reads: "Gen. Villa when asked to express an opinion on Gen. Carranza's note to President Wilson [on the Veracruz occupation] replied: 'It was written with the brain of a Saxon and the soul of a Latin.'" See *Chicago Tribune*, 24 April 1914, p. 1.

38. *New York Times*, 31 October 1913, p. 8.

39. *New York Times*, 23 November 1913, p. 3.

40. *New York Times*, 26 November 1913, p. 1.

41. *New York Times*, 28 November 1913, p. 1.

42. *New York Times*, 29 November 1913, p. 1.

43. *New York Times*, 7 November 1913, p. 2.

44. *New York Times*, 23 November 1913, p. 3.

45. *New York Times*, 28 November 1913, p. 2.

46. *New York Times*, 7 November 1913, p. 2.

47. *New York Times*, 17 November 1913, p. 2.

48. *New York Times*, 23 November 1913, p. 3.

49. *New York Times*, 28 November 1913, p. 1.

50. *New York Times,* 1 February 1913, III, p. 4.
51. *New York Times,* 15 February 1914, III, p. 4.
52. *New York Times,* 30 October 1914, p. 8. Also see *New York Times,* 8 December 1914, p. 10; 4 January 1915, p. 10; and 20 June 1915, II, p. 14.
53. *New York Times,* 7 June 1915, p. 1.
54. *New York Times,* 11 June 1915, p. 14.
55. *Los Angeles Times,* 5 February 1915, II, p. 4.
56. *Chicago Tribune,* 6 April 1915, p. 4.
57. *Los Angeles Times,* 9 April 1915, p. 5.
58. *New York Times,* 9 April 1915, p. 1.
59. *Los Angeles Times,* 10 April 1915, p. 1.
60. *Los Angeles Times,* 14 April 1915, p. 1.
61. *New York Times,* 17 April 1915, p. 4.
62. *Los Angeles Times,* 20 April 1915, p. 5.
63. *Denver Post,* 21 April 1915, p. 4.
64. *Chicago Tribune,* 25 September 1915, p. 8.
65. *New York Times,* 28 August 1915, p. 6.
66. *Chicago Tribune,* 7 September 1915, p. 8.

CHAPTER SEVEN. THE WARRIOR

1. *New York Times,* 21 October 1913, p. 3.
2. *New York Times,* 31 October 1913, p. 8.
3. *New York Times,* 7 November 1913, p. 2.
4. *New York Times,* 23 November 1913, p. 3.
5. *New York Times,* 26 November 1913, p. 1.
6. *New York Times,* 28 November 1913, p. 1.
7. *New York Times,* 28 November 1913, p. 2.
8. *New York Times,* 29 November 1913, p. 1.
9. *New York Times,* 1 December 1913, p. 1.
10. *New York Times,* 3 December 1913, p. 1.
11. *New York Times,* 4 December 1913, p. 1.
12. *Los Angeles Times,* 6 October 1913, p. 1.
13. *Los Angeles Times,* 9 October 1913, p. 1.
14. *Los Angeles Times,* 21 October 1913, p. 1.
15. *Los Angeles Times,* 1 November 1913, p. 2.
16. *Los Angeles Times,* 16 November 1913, p. 1.
17. *Los Angeles Times,* 19 November 1913, p. 1.
18. *Los Angeles Times,* 28 November 1913, p. 1.

19. *Los Angeles Times*, 4 December 1913, p. 1.

20. *Los Angeles Times*, 14 December 1913, p. 1.

21. *San Francisco Examiner*, 26 November 1913, p. 20.

22. *Chicago Tribune*, 11 January 1914, II, p. 2.

23. *Saturday Evening Post*, 9 May 1914, p. 26.

24. *Los Angeles Times*, 24 March 1913, p. 6.

25. *Los Angeles Times*, 16 December 1913, p. II, 4.

26. *Los Angeles Times*, 29 January 1914, p. II, 4.

27. *Los Angeles Times*, 23 February 1914, p. 1.

28. *Los Angeles Times*, 25 February 1914, p. II, 4.

29. *Los Angeles Times*, 12 March 1914, p. 1.

30. *Los Angeles Times*, 20 March 1914, p. 1.

31. *San Francisco Examiner*, 2 March 2 1914, p. 16.

32. *San Francisco Examiner*, 21 February 1914, p. 1.

33. *San Francisco Examiner*, 26 February 1914, p. 20.

34. *San Francisco Examiner*, 10 February 1913, p. 1.

35. *New York Times*, 21 February 1914, p. 1.

36. *New York Times*, 21 February 1914, p. 10.

37. *New York Times*, 23 February 1914, p. 2.

38. Mr. Dooley was created by humorist Finley Porter Dunne. See *New York Times*, 15 March 1914, VI, p. 5.

39. *Everybody's* (June 1914): 819.

40. *New York Times*, 22 February 1914, p. 1.

41. *New York Times*, 23 February 1914, p. 1–2.

42. *New York Times*, 25 February 1914, p. I, 8.

43. *New York Times*, 22 February 1914, p. 1.

44. *Denver Post*, 20 February 1914, p. 1.

45. See *Denver Post*: "General Declares Man Was Executed by Court's Command . . . REBELS SHOOT BRITISH RANCHER FOR THREATS TO KILL GEN. VILLA," 20 February 1914, p. 1; "WORLD POWERS ROUSED BY GEN. VILLA'S EXECUTION OF BRITON AND RIGID INVESTIGATION IS DEMANDED," 21 February 1914, p. 1; "DEMAND FOR BODY OF BRITON IS SPURNED BY REBEL CHIEFTAIN," 23 February 1914, p. 1; "REBELS SAY BENTON WAS A LEGAL CITIZEN OF MEXICO," 24 February 1914, pp. 1–2; "Great Britain Blamed By General Carranza," 28 February 1914, p. 2.

46. *Denver Post*, 21 February 1914, p. 2.

47. *Chicago Tribune*, 21 February 1914, p. 1.

48. *Chicago Tribune*, 13 March 1914, p. 2.

49. *Chicago Tribune*, 20 April 1914, p. 6.

50. *Denver Post*, 24 February 1914, p. 8.

51. Cabrera to Pesqueira, March 4 1914, AHSRE, L-E-760, no. 253.

52. My translation; the original reads: "manifestarle opinion publica estados unidos y Europa continua muy desfavorable." Pesqueira to Carranza, 8 March 1914, AHSRE, L-E-760, no. 265.

53. New York Times, 19 April 1914, III, p. 1.

54. New York Times, 21 April 1914, p. 1.

55. New York Times, 19 April 1914, III, p. 1.

56. New York Times, 24 April 1914, p. 1.

57. New York Times, 26 April 1914, III, p. 1.

58. New York Times, 24 April 1914, XII, p. 1.

59. New York Times, 19 April 1914, III, pp. 1–2; 21 April 1914, pp. 1–2; 24 April 1914, p. 1.

60. New York Times, 24 April 1914, p. 12.

61. New York Times, 26 April 1914, p. III, 1.

62. New York Times, 26 April 1914, p. III, 1.

63. San Francisco Examiner, 20 March 1914, p. 1.

64. San Francisco Examiner, 20 March 1914, p. 2.

65. San Francisco Examiner, 25 March 1914, p. 2.

66. San Francisco Examiner, 28 March 1914, p. 1.

67. San Francisco Examiner, 28 March 1914, p. 2.

68. San Francisco Examiner, 29 March 1914, p. 1.

69. San Francisco Examiner, 21 April 1914, p. 24.

70. See San Francisco Examiner, 21 April 1914, p. 24; 24 April 1914, p. 1; 27 April 1914, p. 16.

71. San Francisco Examiner, 8 May 1914, p. 2.

72. San Francisco Examiner, 17 May 1914, p. 58.

73. San Francisco Examiner, 24 April 1914, p. 24.

74. San Francisco Examiner, 27 March 1914, p. 16.

75. Los Angeles Times, 29 March 1914, p. 1.

76. Los Angeles Times, 1 April 1914, p. 1.

77. Los Angeles Times, 5 April 1914, p. 2.

78. Los Angeles Times, 6 April 1914, p. 1.

79. Los Angeles Times, 7 April 1914, II, p. 4.

80. Los Angeles Times, 6 April 1914, p. 1.

81. Los Angeles Times, 26 April 1914, p. 1.

82. Los Angeles Times, 26 April 1914, II, p. 6.

83. See Chicago Tribune, 22 March 1914, p. 1; 23 March 1914, p. 1; 25 March 1914, p. 2; 28 March 1914, p. 1; 29 March 1914, p. 1; 30 March 1914, pp. 1–2.

84. See Chicago Tribune, 26 March 1914, p. 1; 27 March 1914, p. 1.

85. *Chicago Tribune,* 31 March 1914, p. 1.

86. *Chicago Tribune,* 20 April 1914, p. 6.

87. *Chicago Tribune,* 24 April 1914, p. 1.

88. *Chicago Tribune,* 24 April 1914, p. 6.

89. *Chicago Tribune,* 7 May 1914, p. 6.

90. As originally conceived, the *Literary Digest* offered "condensed rewritings of articles" from a selection of international magazines and newspapers, according to Mott. Established in 1890 by Isaac Kauffman Funk, the magazine's circulation during the Mexican Revolution was between two hundred thousand (the 1909 figure) and four hundred thousand (the 1916 figure). Mott, pp. 217–218. Also see Paneth, p. 265.

91. *Literary Digest,* 18 April 1914, p. 889.

92. For examples of the typically negative framing Carranza received, see *Chicago Tribune* (editorial: "What was wrong with Huerta is not right with Carranza"), 10 September 1914, p. 6; *Chicago Tribune* (headline: "Carranza Must Bow to Villa, U.S. Believes; No Policy Change"), 25 September 1914, p. 1; *Chicago Tribune* (editorial: "Carranza, we suspect, seeks only the continuance of the aristocratic control of Mexico. Villa, we believe, has actually at heart the needs of the land-wanting people of Mexico"), 25 September 1914, p. 6; *Chicago Tribune* (headline: "CARRANZA RUINS PEACE CHANCES"), 23 October 1914, p. 1; *New York Times* (editorial: "That Carranza is well-meaning nobody doubts. But he is weak, vain and opinionated"), 30 October 1914, VIII, p. 4; *New York Times* (editorial: "Carranza, who once seemed to be the coming man, has proved himself to be impossible"), 20 January 1915, p. 8.

93. *Fortnightly Review* (January–June 1914): 1053.

94. *Los Angeles Times,* 8 January 1915, p. 1.

95. *Los Angeles Times,* 5 February 1915, II, p. 4.

96. *San Francisco Examiner,* 27 May 1914, p. 2.

97. *San Francisco Examiner,* 11 June 1914, p. 1.

98. *San Francisco Examiner,* 26 September 1914, p. 17.

99. William Randolph Hearst, *San Francisco Examiner,* 26 September 1914, p. 17.

100. *San Francisco Examiner,* 15 October 1914, p. 1.

101. *San Francisco Examiner,* 16 October 1914, p. 4.

102. *New York Times,* 8 December 1914, p. 10.

103. *New York Times,* 10 January 1915, III, p. 2.

104. *Chicago Tribune,* 7 May 1914, p. 6.

105. *Chicago Tribune,* 17 July 1914, p. 6.

106. *Chicago Tribune,* 21 July 1914, p. 1.

107. See Robinson, pp. viii, 30; De León, p. 36.

108. *New York Times,* 29 September 1914, p. 1.

109. *New York Times,* 15 October 1914, p. 10.

110. *Chicago Tribune,* 7 February 1915.

111. *The Nation,* 17 September 1914, p. 336.

112. *The Nation,* 18 March 1915, p. 293.

113. *Los Angeles Times,* 5 February 1915, II, p. 4.

114. *Los Angeles Times,* 16 January 1915, p. 1.

115. *New York Times,* 5 February 1915, p. 10.

116. *Denver Post,* 8 April 1915, p. 1.

117. *New York Times,* 9 April 1915, p. 1.

118. *New York Times,* 10 April 1915, p. 1.

119. *Chicago Tribune,* 11 April 1915, p. 1.

120. *New York Times,* 12 April 1915, p. 1.

121. *New York Times,* 17 April 1915, p. 1.

122. *New York Times,* 17 April 1915, p. 6.

123. *Denver Post,* 21 April 1915, p. 4.

124. *Los Angeles Times,* 29 March 1915, III, p. 5.

125. *Los Angeles Times,* 9 April 1915, p. 5.

126. *Los Angeles Times,* 10 April 1915, p. 1.

127. *Los Angeles Times,* 14 April 1915, p. 1.

128. *Los Angeles Times,* 20 April 1915, p. 5.

129. *New York Times, 7 June 1915, p. 1.*

130. *New York Times,* 11 June 1915, II, p. 14.

131. *New York Times,* 20 June 1915, II, p. 14.

132. *New York Times,* 15 July 1915, p. 1.

CHAPTER EIGHT. THE WARRIOR REDUX

1. See Hill, *passim.*

2. The State Department files contain many examples. See Bryan to United States Embassy, Mexico City, 23 October 1913, in RDS 812/9275; Bryan to United States Embassy, Mexico City, 24 November 1913, in RDS 812/9873; Bryan to Carothers, 31 January 1914, in RDS 812/10720; Bryan to United States Consul, Monterrey, 13 February 1914, in RDS 812/10870; Bryan to United States Embassy, Mexico City, 6 April 1914, in RDS 812/11394; Bryan to special agent James W. Keys, 7 July 1914, in RDS 812/12414; Lansing to Cobb, 16 October 1914, in RDS 812/13547a; Lansing to United States Consul, Veracruz, 23 November 1914, in RDS

812/13853; Bryan to United States Consul, Veracruz, 27 January 1915, in RDS 812/14304; Bryan to John R. Silliman, United States consul at Saltillo, 27 February 1915, in RDS 812/14475a; Bryan to Cardoso de Oliveira, Brazilian minister to Mexico, 5 March 1915, in RDS 812/14488; Bryan to Woodrow Wilson, 5 March 1915, in RDS 812/14496a; Wilson to Bryan, 6 March 1915, in RDS 812/14504-1/2; Wilson to Carranza, 11 March 1915, in RDS 812/14573; Bryan to United States Consul, Nuevo Laredo, 7 April 1915, in RDS 812/14799; Lansing to Villa's agent Enrique Llorente, 21 April 1915, in RDS 812/14823; Lansing to Silliman, 19 June 1915, in RDS 812/15253; Lansing to Oliveira, 16 July 1915, in RDS 812/15454.

3. Cited in Josephus Daniels to Bryan, 15 October 1919, in RDS 812/9283.

4. See chapters 4 and 5.

5. Letcher to Bryan, 17 October 1913, in RDS 812/9484.

6. See Powell, *passim.*

7. Lind to Bryan, 5 December 1913, in RDS 812/10077.

8. Lind went on to suggest to Bryan that the aristocrats' "pride must be humbled. . . . This can only be done by their own people, their own blood, the people of the North. They can do it to perfection if given a fair chance. To make a dog feel that he really is a cur he must be whipped by another dog and preferably by a cur." See Lind to Bryan, 15 November 1913, in RDS 812/10077.

9. West to Bryan, 10 February 1915, in RDS 812/14622.

10. Letcher to Bryan, 25 August 1914, in RDS 812/13232.

11. Hamm to Bryan, 23 May 1914, in RDS 812/11998.

12. Canova to Bryan, 1 November 1914, in RDS 812/13702.

13. Private memorandum of Robert Lansing, 4 May 1914, in RDS 812/13976.

14. Canova to Bryan, 16 December 1914, in RDS 812/14097.

15. In February 1914, Letcher wrote to Bryan: "Villa's record is unlovely, viewed from any angle whatever. Butcher by trade . . . his peculiar life bred in him daring, cunning, animal craftiness and alertness . . . [yet] he is today the same brutal, overbearing and untamed savage that he was when he first took up the trade of highwayman." Letcher to Bryan, 21 February 1914, in RDS 812/11043.

16. Letcher to Bryan, 25 August 1914, in RDS 812/13232.

17. Letcher to Bryan, 25 August 1914, in RDS 812/13232. Also see Letcher to Bryan, 21 February 1914, in RDS 812/11043.

18. Schmurtz to Bryan, 15 June 1915, in RDS 812/15284. Also see Schmurtz to Bryan, 27 April 1915, in RDS 812/14698; Schmurtz to Bryan,

3 May 1915, in RDS 812/14997; Schmurtz to Bryan, 24 June 1915, in RDS 812/15346.

19. Letcher to Bryan, 25 August 1914, in RDS 812/13232. Also see Letcher to Bryan, 21 February 1914, in RDS 812/11043.

20. Lind to Bryan, 5 December 1913, in RDS 812/10077. Also see Lind to Bryan, 19 January 1914, in RDS 812/10600.

21. Lind to Bryan, 5 December 1913, in RDS 812/10077.

22. Canova to Bryan, 10 September 1914, in RDS 812/13220. Also see Hill, p. 275.

23. Silliman to Bryan, 11 December 1914, in RDS 812/13995.

24. Silliman to Bryan, 8 January 1915, in RDS 812/14168.

25. Silliman to Bryan, 13 January 1915, in RDS 812/14195.

26. Fuller to Wilson, 20 August 1914, in RDS 812/15103.

27. Also see Fuller to Bryan, 17 August 1914, in RDS 812/14204.

28. Cited in Hamm to Bryan, 15 November 1913, in RDS 812/9658.

29. United States Consul, Ciudad Júarez, to Bryan, 15 December 1913, in RDS 812/10336.

30. For a sampling of similar reports, see "Neutrality Matters," 17 November 1913, in RDS 812/10025; Letcher to Bryan, 30 November 1913, in RDS 812/10054; Thomas Edwards, United States consul at Ciudad Júarez, to Bryan, 1 December 1913, in RDS 812/9995; Lindley M. Garrison, secretary of war, to Bryan, 4 December 1913, in RDS 812/10047; Zach Lamar Cobb, U.S. customs inspector at El Paso, to Bryan, 22 March 1914, in RDS 812/11236; Cobb to Bryan, 28 March 1914, in RDS 812/11323; Hamm to Bryan, 13 April 1914, in RDS 812/11706; Canova to Bryan, 23 September 1914, in RDS 812/13279; Phillip Hanna, U.S. consul at Monterrey, to Bryan, 14 March 1915, in RDS 812/14593; Hanna to Bryan, 27 March 1915, in RDS 812/14719.

31. See Knight, *Mexican Revolution*, vol. 2, p. 343. Also see Clendenen, p. 176.

32. Carothers had nearly been fired by the State Department in 1912 because his gambling habit frequently left him unable to meet financial obligations and thus could have compromised his diplomatic position. Yet when the Orozco rebellion erupted in 1912, Carothers's "tireless" efforts to protect Americans and American property were rewarded when his pending dismissal was dropped. He got into hot water two more times when charges of corruption were leveled at him. In the first case, in the spring of 1914, Secretary Bryan chose to overlook the charges, in part because Carothers was forthcoming about the business arrangement in question and even offered to resign if Bryan deemed it necessary. A

second, more serious allegation was leveled at Carothers by Lind in July 1914. Lind informed Bryan that Carothers not only had an unsavory reputation in Mexico but was viewed as being in cahoots with Villa. In short, Carothers "is a crook," Lind wrote to Lansing. (Canova, on the other hand, had reported to Bryan that he had been "deeply impressed" with Carothers's work and "his evident desire to serve the department in an efficient manner.") Yet again Carothers was absolved of wrongdoing after meeting with Secretary Bryan to discuss the allegations. See Hill, pp. 132–134, 197–198, 228–229; Lind to Lansing, 23 July 1914, in RDS 812/17050; Carothers to Boaz Long, chief of the Division of Latin American Affairs at the State Department, 27 May 1914, in RDS 812; and Canova to Bryan, 28 June 1914, in RDS 812/12386.

33. The files are full of examples of this. For example, see Carothers to Bryan, 9 April 1914, in RDS 812/11461; Carothers to Bryan, 21 April 1914, in RDS 812/11587; Carothers to Bryan, 25 April 1914, in RDS 812/11704; Carothers to Secretary of State, 19 July 1915, in RDS 812/15493.

34. Carothers to Bryan, 6 April 1914, in RDS 812/11419.

35. Carothers to Bryan, 10 February 1914, in RDS 812/10903.

36. Carothers to Lansing, 22 July 1915, in RDS 812/15518.

37. Carothers to Lansing, 23 July 1914, in RDS 812/15530.

38. Carothers to Lansing, 23 July 1915, in RDS 812/16530.

39. Carothers to Lansing, 3 August 1915, in RDS 812/15626.

40. Carothers to Lansing, 5 August 1915, in RDS 812/15658.

41. Carothers to Lansing, 1 September 1915, in RDS 812/15997.

42. Carothers to Lansing, 8 November 1915, in RDS 812/16739.

43. Carothers frequently used Cobb as a go-between in his communications with the State Department. Cobb apparently thought highly of Carothers, too, and came to his defense when Carothers was accused of corruption during the spring of 1914. See Hill, pp. 157, 198. Hill cites Cobb for portraying Villa more realistically than did Carothers over the spring and summer of 1915. "Slowly," though, writes Hill, "Carothers overcame his feelings of loyalty and admiration for Villa and saw things as they really were." Clendenen, on the other hand, argues that Cobb became nearly obsessive—"a one-man consular and diplomatic force"—in his desire to see Villa vanquished. See Hill, p. 343; Clendenen, p. 215.

44. Cobb wrote to Bryan, "Villa is advancing toward Mexico while others talk." Cobb to Bryan, 17 November 1914, in RDS 812/13803.

45. Cobb to Bryan, 28 March 1914, in RDS 812/11323. Also see Cobb to Bryan, 23 March 1914, in RDS 812/11236.

46. Cobb to Bryan, 24 April 1914, in RDS 812/11672.

47. Cobb to Bryan, 2 June 1914, in RDS 812/12134.

48. Cobb to Bryan, 2 March 1915, in RDS 812/14473. Also see Cobb to Bryan, 27 April 1915, in RDS 812/14938; Cobb to Bryan, 27 April 1915, in RDS 812/15132.

49. Cobb to Bryan, 22 March 1915, in RDS 812/14694.

50. Cobb to Bryan, 1 June 1915, in RDS 812/15099. On June 7, 1915, Cobb wrote Bryan, "With the indications of Villa's economic distress the counter-revolutionists are very active again." See Cobb to Bryan, 7 June 1915, in RDS in 812/15155. Also see Cobb to Lansing, 30 June 1915, in RDS 812/15339.

51. Cobb to Lansing, 19 July 1915, in RDS 812/15489. Also see Cobb to Lansing, 14 July 1915, in RDS 812/15445; Cobb to Lansing, 15 July 1915, in RDS 812/15457; Homer C. Coen, United States vice-consul at Durango, to Lansing, in RDS 812/15464; Cobb to Lansing, 26 July 1915, in RDS 812/15546.

52. Cobb to Lansing, 30 July 1915, in RDS 812/15590. Also see United States vice-consul Blocker to Lansing, 6 August 1915, in RDS 812/15683; United States Consul at Nuevo Laredo to Lansing, 21 August 1915, in RDS 812/15926.

53. Cobb to Lansing, 13 September 1915, in RDS 812/16141. Also see Cobb to Lansing, 3 September 1915, in RDS 812/16029; Cobb to Lansing, 7 September 1915, in RDS 812/16071.

54. Carothers to Lansing, 8 November 1915, in RDS 812/16739.

55. Although the American journalist John Reed, by his own account (*Insurgent Mexico*), became intimate with Villa, he stayed only a few months in Mexico. Carothers, on the other hand, was close to Villa throughout Villa's rise and fall.

56. O'Shaughnessy to Bryan, 17 October 1913, in RDS 812/9249.

57. Henry Lane Wilson to Bryan, 25 October 1913, in RDS 812/9378.

58. Bryan to United States embassy, London, 9 November 1913, in RDS 812/10437.

59. Lind to Bryan, 11 January 1914, in RDS 812/10514.

60. Bryan to American embassy, Mexico City, 8 August 1914, in RDS 812/10637.

61. O'Shaughnessy to Bryan, 15 March 1914, in RDS 11177.

62. See Lansing to Cobb, 24 August 1915, in RDS 812/15869.

63. American general Frederick Funston to Bryan, 28 July 1914, in RDS 812/12670. Another time, O'Shaughnessy wired Bryan in concern about "two scurrilous and personally insulting editorials" directed at

President Wilson by the Mexico City daily *El Imparcial*—which raises the issue of the perceived ability of the press to sway public opinion. See O'Shaughnessy to Bryan, 14 February 1914, in RDS 812/10887.

64. Letcher to Bryan, 17 October 1913, in RDS 812/9484. Also see John Kenneth Turner, *Barbarous Mexico* (Austin: University of Texas Press, [1910] 1969).

65. Canada to Bryan, 6 December 1913, in RDS 812/10271.

66. Bryan to American Consul, Laredo, 5 November 1913, in RDS 812/9540.

67. Tumulty to Lansing, 27 October 1915, in RDS 812/17086.

68. Bryan to Oliveira, 26 December 1914, in RDS 812/14084a.

69. Wilson to Bryan, 26 August 1913, in RDS 812/10483. Also see Wilson to Bryan, 10 September 1913, in RDS 812/10484.

70. Tumulty to Bryan, 13 May 1914, in RDS 812/12108.

71. Hill, p. 334.

BIBLIOGRAPHY

PRIMARY MATERIALS

Archives

Archivo de Isidro Fabela. Mexico City.
Archivo de la Palabra, Biblioteca Nacional de Antropología e Historia Eusebio Dávalos Hurtado. Mexico City.
Archivo de Roque González Garza. Mexico City.
Archivo Historico Genaro Estrada, Secretaria de Relaciones Exteriores. Mexico City.
Archivo Municipal del Estado de Chihuahua. Chihuahua City, Mexico.
Manuscritos de Venustiano Carranza, Centro de Estudios de Historia de Mexico, Fundación Cultural de Condumex, Mexico City.
The Silvestre Terrazas Collection, Bancroft Library, University of California, Berkeley.

United States Government Sources

Foreign Relations of the Unites States, 1913. Washington, D.C., United States Government Printing Office, 1922.
Foreign Relations of the Unites States, 1914. Washington, D.C., United States Government Printing Office, 1922.
Foreign Relations of the Unites States, 1915. Washington, D.C., United States Government Printing Office, 1922.
The Lansing Papers. 2 vols. Foreign Relations of the United States. Washington, D.C., United States Government Printing Office, 1939.

Link, Arthur S., ed. *The Woodrow Wilson Papers*, vols. 28–35. Princeton, N.J.: Princeton University Press, 1980.

Records of the Department of State Relating to the Internal Affairs of Mexico, 1910–1929. Record Group 59, M-274, Series 812.

Senate Subcommittee on Mexican Affairs (the "Fall Committee"). *Investigation of Mexican Affairs*. 4 vols. Washington, D.C., 1920.

United States Congressional Record, 63d Congress, 1st Session.

Media Sources

American Review of Reviews
Chicago Tribune
Collier's
Denver Post
Everybody's
Fortnightly Review
Forum
Harper's
Literary Digest
Los Angeles Times
McClure's
The Nation
New York Herald
New York Times
North American Review
San Francisco Examiner
Saturday Evening Post
Vida Nueva: Diario Político y de Información, Documentos para la Historia de la Revolución Constitucionalista: Periódico Official de Chihuahua
Washington Times
World's Work

SECONDARY MATERIALS

Aguirre Benavides, Luis. *De Francisco I. Madero a Francisco Villa (memorias de un revolucionario)*. Mexico City: n.p., 1966.

Aguirre Benavides, Luis, and Adrián Aguirre Benavides. *Las grandes batallas de la Division del Norte, al mando del general Francisco Villa*. Mexico City: Editorial Diana, 1966.

Alducín, Rafael. *La Revolucion Constitucionalista, los Estados Unidos y el A.B.C.* Mexico City: Talleres Linotipográficos de "Revista de Revistas," 1916.

Alexander, Robert J. *The Perón Era.* New York: Columbia University Press, 1951.

Arenas Guzmán, Diego. *El periodismo en la revolución mexicana (de 1908–1917),* vol. 2. Mexico City: Biblioteca del Instituto Nacional de Estudios Historicos de la Revolución Mexicana, 1967.

Argudín, Yolanda. *Historia del periodismo en Mexico: Desde el Virreinato hasta nuestro dìas.* Mexico City: Panorama Editorial, 1987.

Arnold, Oren. *The Mexican Centaur: An Intimate Biography of Pancho Villa.* Tuscaloosa, Ala.: Portals Press, 1979.

Arreola, Antonio. *Francisco Villa: Biografía illustrada.* Mexico City: n.p., 1979.

Atkin, Ronald. *Revolution! Mexico, 1910–1920.* Bristol, England: Western Printing Services, 1969.

Bain, Joe S. "Mexican Americans in Modern American Fiction," Ph.D. diss., University of California, San Diego, 1983.

Baker, Ray Stannard. *Woodrow Wilson, Life and Letters: President, 1913–1914,* vol. 4. New York: Doubleday, Doan and Company, 1931.

Beltrán, Enrique. "Fantasía y realidad de Pancho Villa." *Historia Mexicana* 16 (1966–1967): 71–84.

Berkhofer, Robert F. *The White Man's Indian: Images of the American Indian from Columbus to the Present.* New York: Alfred A. Knopf, 1978.

Berry, Nicholas O. *An Analysis of the* New York Times' *Coverage of U.S. Foreign Policy.* New York: Greenwood Press, 1990.

Black, George. *The Good Neighbor: How the United States Wrote the History of Central America and the Caribbean.* New York: Pantheon Books, 1988.

Boime, Albert. *The Art of Exclusion: Representing Blacks in the Nineteenth Century.* Washington, D.C.: Smithsonian Institution Press, 1990.

Bonelli, William G. *Billion Dollar Blackjack.* Beverly Hills, Calif.: Civic Research Press, 1954.

Borrás, Leopoldo. *Historia del periodismo mexicano: Del ocaso porfirista al derecho a la información.* Mexico: Universidad Nacional Autónoma de Mexico, c. 1982.

Borroni, Otelo, and Roberto Vacca. *La vida de Eva Perón.* Buenos Aires: Editorial Galerna, 1970.

Bourne, Richard. *Getulio Vargas of Brazil, 1883–1954: Sphinx of the Pampas.* London: Charles Knight, 1974.

Braddy, Haldeen. "The Faces of Pancho Villa." *Western Folklore* 11, no. 2 (April 1952): 93–99.

———. *Cock of the Walk, Qui-qui-ri-qui! The Legend of Pancho Villa.* Albuquerque: University of New Mexico Press, 1955.

———. "Pancho Villa at Columbus: The Raid of 1916." *Southwestern Studies* 3 (Spring 1965): 1–43.

Brandt, Nancy. "Pancho Villa: The Making of a Modern Legend." *The Americas* (1964–1965): 146–162.

Britton, John A. *Revolution and Ideology: Images of the Mexican Revolution in the United States.* Lexington: University of Kentucky Press, 1995.

Brownlow, Kevin. *The Parade's Gone By.* London: Secker and Warburg, 1968.

Bullock, Marion Dorothy. "Pancho Villa and Emiliano Zapata in the Literature of the Mexican Revolution." Ph.D. diss., University of Georgia, 1982.

Bulnes, Francisco. *The Whole Truth about Mexico: President Wilson's Responsibility.* Trans. Dora Scott. New York: M. Bulnes Book Company, 1916.

Butterfield, Dolores. "The Conspiracy against Madero." *Forum* 50, no. 4 (October 1913): 468.

Carranza, Venustiano. "Reply of don Venustiano Carranza to the Chief of the Northern Division: Refutation of the Manifesto of General Francisco Villa." n.p., c. 1915.

Cervantes, Federico. *Francisco Villa y la revolución.* Mexico City: Instituto Nacional de Estudios Historicas, 1985.

Cigarroa, Miguel Lozoya. *Francisco Villa: El Grande.* Durango: Impresiones Gráficas México, 1988.

Clendenen, Clarence. *The United States and Pancho Villa: A Study in Unconventional Diplomacy.* Ithaca, N.Y.: Cornell University Press, 1961.

Clifton, James A., ed. *The Invented Indian: Cultural Fictions and Government Policies.* New Brunswick, N.J.: Transaction Publishers, 1990.

Coerver, Donald M., and Linda B. Hall. *Texas and the Mexican Revolution.* San Antonio, Tex.: Trinity University Press, 1984.

Crassweller, Robert D. *Peron and the Enigmas of Argentina.* New York: W. W. Norton, 1987.

Dakin, Fred H. "Some Notes on Pancho Villa." University of California, Berkeley. Microfilm roll, 1933.

De León, Arnoldo. *They Called Them Greasers: Anglo Attitudes toward Mexicans in Texas, 1821–1900.* Austin: University of Texas Press, 1983.

Dulles, John W. F. *Vargas of Brazil: A Political Biography.* Austin: University of Texas Press, 1967.

Dunn, Frederick Sherwin. *The Diplomatic Protection of Americans in Mexico.* New York: Columbia University Press, 1933.

Eisenhower, John S. *Intervention: The United States and the Mexican Revolution, 1913–1917.* New York: W. W. Norton, 1993.

Estol, Horacio. *Realidad y leyenda de Pancho Villa.* Mexico City: Editorial Divulgación, 1956.

Fabela, Isidro. *La Victoria de Carranza.* Mexico City: Editorial Jus, 1978.

Ferrer de M., Gabriel, ed. *Documentos de la revolución mexicana.* Mexico City: Secretaria de Educación Publica, 1945.

Fornaro, Carlo de. *Carranza and Mexico.* New York: Mitchell Kennerly, 1915.

Furman, Necah S. "Vida Nueva: A Reflection of Villista Diplomacy, 1914–1915." *New Mexico Historical Review* 53, no. 2 (April 1978): 171–192.

Fyfe, Hamilton. *The Real Mexico: A Study on the Spot.* London: William Henemann, 1914.

Gamson, William A., and Andre Modigliani. "Media Discourse and Public Opinion on Nuclear Power: A Constructionist Approach." *American Journal of Sociology* 95, no. 1 (July 1989): 1–37.

Gay, Peter. *Freud: A Life for Our Time.* New York: W. W. Norton, 1988.

Gerome, Frank. "United States–Mexican Relations during the Initial Years of the Mexican Revolution." Ph.D. diss., Kent State University, 1968.

Gilderhus, Mark T. *Diplomacy and Revolution: U.S.–Mexican Relations Under Wilson and Carranza.* Tucson: University of Arizona Press, 1977.

Gilly, Adolfo. *The Mexican Revolution.* Trans. Patrick Camiller. Norfolk, England: Thetford Press, [1971] 1983.

Goerlitz, Richard Charles. "Financing Francisco Villa's Division del Norte." Master's thesis, University of California, Santa Barbara, 1968.

Goffman, Erving. *Frame Analysis: An Essay on the Organization of Experience.* New York: Harper and Row, 1974.

González Navarro, Moisés. "Xenophobia y xenophilia en la Revolución Mexicana." *Historia Mexicana* 18 (1969): 569–614.

Grassman, Curtis Edwin. "Woodrow Wilson, John Lind, and Mexico." Master's thesis, University of California, Los Angeles, 1966.

Grieb, Kenneth J. "The Causes of the Carranza Rebellion: A Reinterpretation." *The Americas* 25, no. 1 (July 1968): 25–32.

———. "El caso Benton y la diplomacía de la revolución." *Historia Mexicana* 19, no. 2 (October–December 1969): 282–301.

———. *The United States and Huerta.* Lincoln: University of Nebraska Press, 1969.

Guzmán, Martín Luis. *The Eagle and the Serpent*. Trans. Harriet de Onís. Gloucester, Mass.: n.p., [1928] 1969.

———. *The Memoirs of Pancho Villa*. Trans. Virginia Taylor. Austin: University of Texas Press, [1935] 1965.

Haley, P. Edward. *Revolution and Intervention: The Diplomacy of Taft and Wilson with Mexico, 1910–1917*. Cambridge, Mass.: MIT Press, 1970.

Hall, Linda, and Donald M. Coerver. *Revolution on the Border: The United States and Mexico, 1910–1920*. Albuquerque: University of New Mexico Press, 1988.

Harris, Charles H., and Louis R. Sadler. "Pancho Villa and the Columbus Raid: The Missing Documents." *New Mexico Historical Review* 50, no. 4 (October 1975): 335–346.

Harris, Larry A. *Pancho Villa and the Columbus Raid*. El Paso, Tex.: McMath, 1949.

Herrera, Celia. *Francisco Villa: Ante la historia*. Mexico City: Editorial Libros de Mexico, 1964.

Hill, Larry D. *Emissaries to a Revolution: Woodrow Wilson's Executive Agents in Mexico*. Baton Rouge: Louisiana State University Press, 1973.

Hunt, Michael H. *Ideology and U.S. Foreign Policy*. New Haven, Conn.: Yale University Press, 1987.

Johannsen, Robert W. *To the Halls of the Montezumas: The Mexican War in the American Imagination*. New York: Oxford University Press, 1985.

Johnson, John J. *Latin America in Caricature*. Austin: University of Texas Press, 1980.

Johnson, William Weber. *Heroic Mexico: The Narrative History of a Twentieth-Century Revolution*. Garden City, N.Y.: Doubleday, 1968.

Katz, Friedrich. "Alemania y Francisco Villa." *Historia Mexicana* 12 (1962–1963): 88–102.

———. "Pancho Villa and the Attack on Columbus, New Mexico." *American Historical Review* 83 (1978): 101–130.

———. "Pancho Villa: Reform Governor of Chihuahua." In *Essays on the Mexican Revolution: Revisionist Views of the Leaders*, George Wolfskill and Douglas P. Richmond, eds. Austin: University of Texas Press, 1979.

———. *The Secret War in Mexico: Europe, the United States, and the Mexican Revolution*. Chicago: University of Chicago Press, 1981.

———. "From Alliance to Dependency: The Formation and Deformation of an Alliance between Francisco Villa and the United States." In *Rural Revolt in Mexico and U.S. Intervention*, Daniel Nugent, ed., 229–249. San Diego: Center for U.S.–Mexican Studies, University of California, San Diego, 1988.

————. "Prólogo." In *La mirada circular: El cine norteamericano de la revolución mexicana, 1911–1917,* by Margarita de Orellana. Mexico City: Editorial Joaquín Mortiz, 1991.

————. "Prologue." In *Pancho Villa, ese desconocido: Entrevistas en Chihuahua a favor y en contra,* by Ruben Osorio. Chihuahua: Talleres Gráficos, 1991.

Keller, Gary D. *Hispanics and United States Film: An Overview and Handbook.* Tempe, Ariz.: Bilingual Press, 1994.

Kennedy, Captain. *The Life and History of Pancho Villa, the Mexican Bandit: A True and Authentic History of the Most Noted Bandit Who Has Ever Lived.* Baltimore: I. and M. Oltenheimer, 1916.

Knight, Alan. *The Mexican Revolution.* 2 vols. New York: Cambridge University Press, 1986.

————. *U.S.–Mexican Relations, 1910–1940: An Interpretation.* San Diego: Center for U.S.–Mexican Studies, University of California, San Diego, 1987.

Knudson, Jerry W. "The Press and the Mexican Revolution of 1910." *Journalism Quarterly* 46 (Winter 1969): 760–766.

Kosicki, Gerald M. "Problems and Opportunities in Agenda-Setting Research." *Journal of Communication* 43, no. 2 (Spring 1993): 100–127.

Krauze, Enrique. *Entre el ángel y el fierro: Francisco Villa.* Mexico City: Fondo de Cultura Economica, 1987.

Langley, Lester D. *Mexico and the United States: The Fragile Relationship.* Boston: Twayne Publishers, 1991.

Lansford, William Douglas. *Pancho Villa.* Brattleboro, Vt.: Book Press, 1965.

Levine, Robert M. *The Vargas Regime: The Critical Years, 1934–1938.* New York: Columbia University Press, 1970.

Llorente, Enrique. *General Francisco Villa: His Policy in Dealing with Certain of the Clergy and Reactionary Element in Mexico—Its Justification.* Washington, D.C.: Confidential Agency of the Provisional Government of Mexico, 1913.

MacCorkle, Stuart Alexander. *American Policy of Recognition towards Mexico.* Baltimore: Johns Hopkins University Press, 1933.

Machado, Manuel A. *Centaur of the North: Francisco Villa, the Mexican Revolution, and Northern Mexico.* Austin: Eakin Press, 1988.

Margo, Dr. A. *Who, Where, and Why Is Villa?* New York: Latin-American News Association, 1916.

Martínez, Thomas. "Advertising and Racism: The Case of the Mexican-American." *El Grito* 2, no. 4 (Summer 1969): 3–13.

Marvin, George. "Villa." *World's Work* (July 1914): 269–284.

McCombs, Maxwell, and Donald M. Shaw. "The Agenda-Setting Function of the Mass Media." *Public Opinion Quarterly* 36, no. 2 (Summer 1972): 176–187.

————. "The Evolution of Agenda-Setting Research: Twenty-Five Years in the Marketplace of Ideas." *Journal of Communication* 43, no. 2 (Spring 1993): 58–67.

McKerns, Joseph P., ed. *Biographical Dictionary of American Journalism.* New York: Greenwood Press, 1989.

McMillan, Jill, and Sandra Regan. "The Presidential Press Conference: A Study in Escalating Institutionalization." *Presidential Studies Quarterly* 13, no. 1 (Winter 1983): 231–141.

Meyer, Michael C. "The Militarization of Mexico, 1913–1914." *The Americas* 27, no. 3 (January 1971): 293–306.

————. *Huerta: A Political Portrait.* Lincoln: University of Nebraska Press, 1972.

Mexican Foreign Office. *Diplomatic Dealings of the Constitutionalist Revolution of Mexico.* Mexico City: Imprenta Nacional, n.d.

Miranda, Pindaro Uriostegui, ed. *Testimonios del proceso revolucionario de Mexico.* Mexico City: Impreso en los Talleres de AGRIN, 1970.

Mott, Frank Luther. *A History of American Magazines,* vol. 5. Cambridge, Mass.: Harvard University Press, 1968.

Munch, Francis. "Villa's Columbus Raid: Practical Politics or German Design?" *New Mexico Historical Review* 44, no. 2 (April 1969): 189–214.

Nourie, Alan, and Barbara Nourie, eds. *American Mass-Marketing Magazines.* New York: Greenwood Press, 1990.

Nugent, Daniel, ed. *Rural Revolt in Mexico and U.S. Intervention.* San Diego: Center for U.S.–Mexican Studies, University of California, San Diego, 1988.

Orellana, Margarita de. *La mirada circular: El cine norteamericano de la revolución mexicana, 1911–1917.* Mexico City: Grupo Editorial Paneta, 1991.

Osorio, Ruben. *Pancho Villa, ese desconocido: Entrevistas en Chihuahua a favor y en contra.* Chihuahua: Talleres Gráficos, 1991.

————, ed. *La correspondencia de Francisco Villa, y cartas telegramas de 1912 a 1913.* Mexico City: Talleres Graficos, 1986.

Paneth, Donald, ed. *The Dictionary of American Journalism.* New York: Facts on File, 1983.

Paredes, Raymund Arthur. "The Image of the Mexican in American Literature." Ph.D. diss., University of Texas, Austin, 1973.

Peterson, Jessie, and Thelma Cox Knoles. *Pancho Villa: Intimate Recollections by People Who Knew Him.* New York: Hastings House, 1977.

Pettit, Arthur G. *Images of the Mexican American in Fiction and Film.* College Station: Texas A&M University Press, 1980.

Pike, Fredrick B. *The United States and Latin America: Myths and Stereotypes of Civilization and Nature.* Austin: University of Texas Press, 1992.

Poncelot, Victor. Gen. *Francisco Villa, Candidate for the Nobel Peace Prize: A Little Biography of a Great Man.* N.p., 1914.

Powell, Philip Wayne. *Tree of Hate: Propaganda and Prejudices Affecting United States Relations with the Hispanic World.* New York: Basic Books, 1971.

Puente, Ramón. *Hombres de la revolución: Villa (sus memorias auténticas).* Los Angeles: Spanish-American Printing Company, 1931.

———. *Villa en pie.* Mexico City: Editorial Mexico Nuevo, 1937.

Quirk, Robert E. *The Mexican Revolution, 1914–1915: The Convention at Aguascalientes.* Bloomington: Indiana University Press, 1960.

———. *An Affair of Honor: Woodrow Wilson and the Occupation of Veracruz.* New York: W. W. Norton, 1967.

Reed, John. *Insurgent Mexico.* New York: International Publishers, [1914] 1965.

Reyes, Aurelio de los. *Con Villa en Mexico: Testimonios sobre camarógrafos norteamericanos en la revolución, 1911–1916.* Mexico City: Universidad Nacional Autónoma de México, 1985.

———. Untitled report prepared for the Library of Congress, cited in a memorandum from Georgette Dorn to Paul Spehr, 29 March 1985.

———. *Media siglo de cine mexicano (1896–1947).* Mexico City: Editorial Trillas, 1987.

Richmond, Douglas W. *Venustiano Carranza's Nationalist Struggle, 1883–1920.* Lincoln: University of Nebraska Press, 1983.

Ríos, Francisco Armando. "The Mexican in Fact, Fiction, and Folklore." *El Grito* 2, no. 4 (Summer 1969): 14–28.

Robinson, Cecil. *With the Ears of Strangers: The Mexican in American Literature.* Tucson: University of Arizona Press, 1963.

Robledo, Federico P. *El constitucionalismo y Francisco Villa: A luz de la verdad.* Matamoros, Mexico: Edición de "El Democrática," 1985.

Rogers, Everett M., James W. Dearing, and Dorine Bregman. "The Anatomy of Agenda-Setting Research." *Journal of Communication* 43, no. 2 (Spring 1993): 68–84.

Ryan, Halford. *Franklin D. Roosevelt's Rhetorical Presidency.* New York: Greenwood Press, 1988.

Said, Edward. *Orientalism.* New York: Pantheon, 1978.

———. *Culture and Imperialism.* New York: Pantheon, 1993.

Sandos, James A. "Pancho Villa and American Security: Woodrow Wilson's Mexican Diplomacy Reconsidered." *Journal of Latin American Studies* 13, no. 2 (1981): 293–311.

Schuster, Ernest Otto. *Pancho Villa's Shadow: The True Story of Mexico's Robin Hood as Told by His Interpreter.* New York: Exposition Press, 1947.

Shaw, Donald M., and Shannon E. Martin. "The Function of Mass Media Agenda Setting." *Journalism Quarterly* 69, no. 4 (Winter 1992): 902–920.

Shoemaker, Pamela J., and Stephen D. Reese. *Mediating the Message: Theories of Influences on Mass Media Content.* New York: Longman Publishing Group, 1991.

Smith, Michael M. "Carrancista Propaganda in the United States, 1913–1917: An Overview of Institutions." Unpublished manuscript, Oklahoma State University, July 1994.

Stedman, Raymond William. *Shadows of the Indian: Stereotypes in American Culture.* Norman: University of Oklahoma Press, 1982.

Stein, Max. *Francisco "Pancho" Villa, Peon Chief, Terror of Mexico: An Unbiased, Complete, Illustrated History and Description of the Mexican Situation.* Chicago: n.p., c. 1916.

Stevens, Louis. *Here Comes Pancho Villa: The Anecdotal History of a Genial Killer.* New York: Frederick A. Stokes, 1930.

Strout, Richard Lee, and Kenneth Crawford. "The Presidents and the Press." In *The Making of the New Deal: The Insiders Speak,* Katie Louchhiem, ed., 12–19. Cambridge, Mass.: Harvard University Press, 1983.

Szulc, Tad. *Twilight of the Tyrants.* New York: Henry Holt, 1959.

Taylor, J. M. *Eva Peron: The Myths of a Woman.* Chicago: University of Chicago Press, 1979.

Taylor, Joseph Rogers. "'Pancho' Villa at First Hand." *World's Work* (July 1914): 265–269.

Taylor, Lawrence Douglas. *Revolución mexicana: Guía de archivos y bibliotecas, México–Estados Unidos.* Mexico City: Instituto Naciónal de Estudios Históricos de la Revolución Mexicana, 1987.

Terrazas, Silvestre. *El verdadero Pancho Villa: El centauro del norte . . . sus heroicas y acciones revolucionarias.* Chihuahua: Gobierno del Estado de Chihuahua, 1984.

Torres, Elias L. *Vida y hazañas de Pancho Villa.* Mexico City: El Libro Español, 1975.

Tuck, Jim. *Pancho Villa and John Reed: Two Faces of Romantic Revolution.* Tucson: University of Arizona Press, 1984.

Turner, John Kenneth. *Barbarous Mexico.* Austin: University of Texas Press, [1910] 1969.

Turner, Timothy. *Bullets, Bottles, and Gardenias.* Dallas: South-West Press, 1935.

Ulloa, Berta. *Archivo histórico diplomático mexicano. Guías para la historia diplomática de Mexico, no. 3: Revolución mexicana, 1910–1920.* Mexico City: Secretaría de Relaciones Exteriores, 1963.

———. *La Revolución intervenida: Relaciones diplomáticas entre México y Estados Unidos (1910–1914).* Mexico City: El Colegio de Mexico, 1971.

Vaca, Nick C. "The Mexican-American in the Social Sciences, 1912–1970, Part 2: 1936–1970." *El Grito* 4, no. 1 (Fall 1970): 17–51.

Velasco, Herlinda, María Dolores Aréchiga, and Guillermo González Cedillo. *Con Villa y Zapata: Tres relatos testimoniales.* Mexico City: Instituto Nacional de Estudios Historicos, 1991.

Weeks, George F. *Seen in a Mexican Plaza: A Summer's Idyll of an Idle Summer.* New York: Fleming H. Revell, 1918.

Wilson, Henry Lane. *Diplomatic Episodes in Mexico, Belgium and Chile.* New York: Doubleday, Page, 1927.

Winfield, Betty H. "Franklin Delano Roosevelt's Efforts to Influence the News during His First-Term Press Conferences." *Presidential Studies Quarterly* 11, no. 1 (Winter 1981): 189–199.

———. *FDR and the News Media.* Chicago: University of Illinois Press, 1990.

Wolfskill, George, and Douglas P. Richmond, eds. *Essays on the Mexican Revolution: Revisionist Views of the Leaders.* Austin: University of Texas Press, 1979.

Woll, Allen. *The Latin Image in American Film.* Los Angeles: UCLA Latin American Center Publications, 1977.

Womack, John. *Zapata and the Mexican Revolution.* New York: Alfred A. Knopf, 1968.

INDEX